DAILY LIFE IN

STUART ENGLAND

Recent titles in
The Greenwood Press "Daily Life Through History" Series

DAILY LIFE IN

STUART ENGLAND

JEFFREY FORGENG

The Greenwood Press "Daily Life Through History" Series

GREENWOOD PRESS
Westport, Connecticut • London

Library of Congress Cataloging-in-Publication Data

Forgeng, Jeffrey L.
　Daily life in Stuart England / Jeffrey Forgeng.
　　p. cm. — (Greenwood Press "Daily life through history" series,
　ISSN 1080–4749)
　Includes bibliographical references and index.
　ISBN-13: 978–0–313–32450–5 (alk. paper)
　ISBN-10: 0–313–32450–6 (alk. paper)
　1. England—Social life and customs—17th century.　I. Title.
　DA380.F66　2007
　942.06—dc22　　　2006039687

British Library Cataloguing in Publication Data is available.

Library of Congress Catalog Card Number: 2006039687
ISBN-13: 978–0–313–32450–5
ISBN-10: 0–313–32450–6
ISSN: 1080–4749

First published in 2007

Greenwood Press, 88 Post Road West, Westport, CT 06881
An imprint of Greenwood Publishing Group, Inc.
www.greenwood.com

Printed in the United States of America

The paper used in this book complies with the
Permanent Paper Standard issued by the National
Information Standards Organization (Z39.48–1984).

10　9　8　7　6　5　4　3　2　1

The publisher has done its best to make sure the instructions and/or recipes in
this book are correct. However, users should apply judgment and experience
when preparing recipes, especially parents and teachers working with young
people. The publisher accepts no responsibility for the outcome of any recipe
included in this volume.

CONTENTS

ACKNOWLEDGMENTS

Any work of substance owes something to more people than just its author. I would like to thank Michael Tovey for sharing with me his work on archival materials relating to Chedworth; Kathryn Sherwin for sharing some of her interpretations of seventeenth-century recipes; Jim Johnson of Greenfield Village for facilitating research on the Rose Cottage; and Laura Robinson Hanlan of Worcester Polytechnic Institute for her tireless patience. Above all, I would particularly like to give thanks for the contributions of Margaret Taylor, of the Collège du Léman, who sowed the seed; the old stalwarts of the Tabard Inn Society and Tower Hamlets Trained Bands, who nourished it; and Christine Drew of Worcester Polytechnic Institute, who helped bring it to fruition.

Introduction

The seventeenth century is among the most dramatic and significant in the history of the English-speaking world; alien to modern eyes at first, on closer inspection we increasingly find in it the reflection of many of the structures and forces that shape our lives today. Under the Stuarts were fired the first shots in the ongoing cultural wars between tradition and reform; this century saw the plantation and flourishing of the English-speaking settlements in the New World that would eventually become the superpower of today; it also witnessed the establishment of the first modern political parties, as well as such mundane but ubiquitous cultural phenomena as tea, coffee, and the three-piece suit.

Yet to write of English daily life in the seventeenth century is a complex task. The degree of change, at both the macroscopic and microscopic levels, was prodigious, and the effect on daily life was profound. The life of an Englishman in 1700 was in many ways closer to the lives of his descendants in 2000 than to those of his predecessors in 1500.

At the opening of the 1600s, England was a country divided between a theoretically medieval social order and increasingly modern social realities. The country was under the sovereignty of a monarch whose authority was widely regarded as a divine appointment; feudal and manorial custom provided the language of an elaborate social hierarchy; the armored and mounted horseman was regarded as the pinnacle of military technology; and participation in the state church was mandated under sanction of heavy legal penalties. Yet the material realities did not support these inherited constructs. Already for centuries, the actual power of the traditional authorities was being undermined by new social, economic, and military developments. During the 1600s, the conflict between old and new was dramatically played out. Over the course of the century, England executed its king for treason against the nation; entrepreneurialism definitively replaced tradition as the dominant principle of agrarian life; armor essentially vanished from the battlefield, while the cavalry were displaced by musket-armed footsoldiers as the backbone of the army; and religious pluralism was accepted as a permanent fact of English life. Social change is always incremental and continuous, but this century stands as a significant turning point in the transition from a medieval to a modern world.

In 1648 the Presbyterian commentator Clement Walker complained of radicals in the New Model Army:

They have cast all the mysteries and secrets of government . . . before the vulgar (like pearls before swine), and have taught both the soldiery and people to look so far into them as to ravel back all governments to the first principles of nature . . . They have made the people thereby so curious and so arrogant that they will never find humility enough to submit to a civil rule.[1]

In many ways, this is precisely what seventeenth-century England has to offer the student of history. Not only did the political and social struggles of the century "ravel back all governments to the first principles of nature," but there also was a qualitative increase in the level of documentation relating to the details of daily life, casting the mysteries and secrets of the past before the curious present. Diaries and memoirs, quite rare in England before 1600, are numerous from the 1600s. Samuel Pepys is deservedly the most famous example: his record of daily events gives us a surprisingly candid and detailed account that chronicles the diarist's day-to-day experiences, emotional state, and digestive fluctuations. Material culture is also documented to a degree far beyond that available for any prior period: Randle Holme's *Academy of Armory* in particular offers an ambitiously comprehensive account of the details of seventeenth-century technology and material culture, under the guise of a treatise on heraldry. Didactic works such as the translation of Comenius's illustrated *Orbis Sensualium Pictus* offer the kind of valuable beginner's orientation to various topics that can only be had from a children's book. Over the course of the century emerged a growing body of treatises on a wide range of quotidian activities, including household management, education, and games, especially after 1650. Meanwhile, an increasing number of regional and local antiquarians were documenting the details about specific localities and regions within the country: among the most famous is William Gough's *History of Myddle,* which offers an in-depth look at the life and history of this Shropshire village.

Although information on the period is abundant, approaching the material can be challenging. This book is heavily shaped by my own experiences and frustrations in trying to learn about and teach this period of history. There is a vast body of specialized scholarship on the seventeenth century, but surprisingly little for the adult reader who is interested in the period but lacks a grounding in the fundamentals that shaped Stuart society. Many of the defining features of seventeenth-century life, such as the systems of landholding and legal administration, are bewilderingly opaque to the modern observer; I suspect that even many scholars involved in seventeenth-century studies have only an impressionistic understanding of some of the basic features of Stuart society. Writing this book has certainly been an excellent opportunity for me to identify and clarify the gray areas in my own understanding, and I hope it will similarly benefit others.

This book represents the fruits of a decade and a half of focused research since the early 1990s; years of experience as an interpreter of seventeenth-century living history at Greenfield Village, Plimoth Plantation, and various other sites in North America and Great Britain; and ongoing experience teaching early modern history to engineering undergraduates, as well as interpreting the collections of a museum heavily weighted toward the seventeenth century. As with my other books in this series, it is heavily influenced by my past experience as a practitioner of living history: the imaginative and practical demands of placing oneself in the shoes of a seventeenth-century person can be a great help in focusing one's attention on the crucial factors that most shaped people's day-to-day existence. It is the trivial yet fundamental aspects of the day that dominate the actual experience of daily life—food, water, excretion, light, heat. Such mundanities are easily overlooked by the armchair historian (though this is much less true of historians today than it was half a century ago), but they are brought vividly into focus by the effort of trying to reconstruct the actual experience of an ordinary person's daily existence—and to deal with one's own quotidian needs in a seventeenth-century framework. The issue is all the more challenging in a twenty-first-century world where most of us are in many ways isolated from the physical realities of our own existence—the sources of our food and drink, the material realities of birth and death, or the technology that supports our daily activities.

Living history can also widen our experiences and enrich our lives by exposing us to different modes of living, not unlike the enriching experience of travel to foreign cultures. To enhance this creative and imaginative aspect of the book, I have also included hands-on samples of aspects of daily living in the form of recipes, games, songs, and dances.

TECHNICAL NOTES

Because this book is intended for the general reader, I have tried to streamline the apparatus, while including enough documentation to allow it to be used as a launching point for further research. Core bibliographies for the book as a whole and for each individual chapter are given at the end of the book, as well as classified bibliographies for a few additional major topics. Smaller lists of sources are included in the footnotes to the passages relevant to their topic. In citing seventeenth-century sources, I have modernized the spelling and punctuation of the original texts to conform to modern American practice. The glossary at the end is intended as a convenient reference for potentially unfamiliar terms and technical information. Uncredited illustrations are my own.

NOTE

1. Clement Walker, *History of Independency* (London: n.p., 1648), 1.140.

1

A History of England in the Seventeenth Century

At the opening of the 1600s, Elizabeth I, last monarch of the Tudor line, was 67 years old. She had ruled England for nearly half a century, a lengthy reign that few of her predecessors had ever matched. Her long years on the throne allowed her to build on the efforts of her father, Henry VIII, and her grandfather, Henry VII: over the course of the 1500s, the Tudors had transformed England from a land of feudal civil war into a largely stable and centralized monarchy.

Henry VII had come to the throne in 1485 as the first Tudor king, after defeating Richard III at Bosworth Field, the final battle of the Wars of the Roses. These civil wars, which had involved intermittent fighting since 1455, pitted two rival branches of the royal family against one another, each backed by shifting alliances of mighty aristocratic families. Henry VII devoted much of his reign to curtailing the power of his aristocratic subjects, and he found willing allies in England's Parliament. The House of Commons, the lower of the two parliamentary houses, was a semi-representative body dominated by the interests of the upper tiers of urban and rural society, just below the aristocracy. The classes they represented shared Henry's interest in limiting the powers of the feudal nobility and were happy to support Henry's efforts to strengthen the crown at the cost of the great aristocrats.

Henry VII's policy of collaboration with Parliament was continued by his son Henry VIII. In the 1530s, when the Pope refused to grant Henry a divorce from Catherine of Aragon, he arranged for Parliament to declare the English church independent of the Catholic hierarchy.

Map of England.

The break with Rome was welcomed by those who hoped to see the country embrace the Protestant Reformation that was beginning to take hold in many parts of Europe. Henry, now in charge of England's national church, had little interest in Protestantism, but his divorce and subsequent marriage to Anne Boleyn inevitably brought England into Europe's Protestant camp.

Henry's six wives yielded him only one son, the sickly Edward VI, whose rule lasted only from 1547 to 1553. After Edward's death, the throne passed to Catherine of Aragon's daughter Mary, whose attempt to bring England back into the Catholic church did not outlast her five-year reign. Henry's last remaining child, Anne Boleyn's daughter Elizabeth, came to the throne in 1558. She continued her father's policy of moderate Protestantism and collaboration with Parliament to enhance royal power, and her success in stabilizing English political institutions was demonstrated by the peaceful transfer of power at her death in 1603 to James Stuart.

JAMES I (1603–1625)

James, a great-great-grandson of Henry VII, already ruled Scotland as James VI; now he acquired a second realm as James I of England. He was enthusiastically welcomed by his new subjects, and his popularity was enhanced by the Gunpowder Plot of 1605, when government agents foiled an attempt by Guy Fawkes and a band of Catholic conspirators to blow up the houses of Parliament while the king was present. The day of the plot's interruption, November 5, was made a national holiday, and the event contributed to a growing anti-Catholic spirit in English culture.

James was equally enthusiastic about his newly acquired realm, especially after two decades of governing western Europe's poorest and most unruly kingdom. Unfortunately, the apparent power and wealth of the English crown had been largely a result of astute management by his predecessor. James would prove much less adept than Elizabeth at navigating the turbulent waters of English politics—and the shallows of English royal finances. Three issues above all plagued James's reign: religion, money, and the shape of England's government.

Elizabeth had attempted to steer a course of moderate Protestant reform, but a vocal and influential minority of Englishmen were discontent with the persistence of "Catholic" practices in the English church. Reformist Protestants sought to restore what they saw as the pure Christian practices authorized by Christ and the apostles, as documented in the Bible. Known to their opponents as Puritans, they called for the reform or elimination of institutions that lacked scriptural authority, including the hierarchy of bishops, observation of saints' days, and elaborate religious rituals. By the end of Elizabeth's reign, a small number of reformists had rejected the English church altogether, forming illegal "separatist" congregations outside of the church's authority.

James was doctrinally sympathetic to the Puritans, but hostile to their interference with his authority over the church. The bishops in particular were royal appointees who could be extremely useful in maintaining royal authority: as James famously expressed it, "No bishop, no king." James clashed repeatedly with the Puritans over the matter of church reform, and the conflict soured James's relationship with Parliament, where Puritan thinking was influential. However, James did respond to reformist calls for an improved translation of the Bible, sponsoring a translation project that produced the 1611 "Authorized Version," still known today as the "King James Bible."

Money had also been a chronic problem for English monarchs, and only Elizabeth's careful management of funds had kept her from bankruptcy—even so, she had passed on to James a monarchy that was £400,000 in debt. The crown's ordinary revenues, derived from royal landholdings and various traditional taxes, were barely enough to support the normal expenses of maintaining the government and royal household. Incautious spending would force the crown into debt, and the massive cost of waging war was impossible without supplementary taxes known as subsidies, which could only be granted by Parliament. James lacked Elizabeth's capacity for fiscal restraint: he spent lavishly on himself and on his favorite courtiers, driving the crown deeper and deeper into debt. Efforts by James's ministers to enhance meager royal revenues by better exploiting existing royal prerogatives again aroused the hostility of Parliament. A revision of customs duties in 1608, while long overdue (the last one had been in the 1550s), marked a transformation of customs from a form of economic control to a strategem for enhancing crown revenues, and such maneuvers would prove a major source of contention between crown and Parliament during the upcoming years.

Parliament's power of the purse was just one facet of the complex power relationship between the monarch and Parliament. It was generally agreed that a statute passed by the houses of Lords and Commons, and signed into law by the king, was the highest authority in the land. But there were strongly divergent opinions as to the relative powers and privileges of king and Parliament independent of each other. England had (and has) no constitutional document laying out the structure of its government: the roles of the various bodies were defined by tradition, which was open to multiple interpretations. James believed that kings were ordained by the grace of God and that the privileges of Parliament were ultimately ordained by the grace of the king. The parliamentarian leaders agreed that kings were divinely constituted, but felt that the privileges and powers of Parliament were sanctioned by ancient custom and were not dependent on the royal will. James, opinionated by nature, was less tactful than Elizabeth in articulating his views on government, and he delighted in lecturing Parliament on the royal prerogative:

The state of monarchy is the supremest thing upon earth, for kings are not only God's lieutenants upon earth, and sit upon God's throne, but even by God himself they are called gods . . . for that they exercise a manner or resemblance of divine power upon earth. . . . to judge all and to be judged not accountable to none.[1]

Such pronouncements, though consistent with traditional political thinking at the time, were hardly diplomatic. James clashed repeatedly with Parliament over issues of royal prerogative, and in his later years he warned ominously that his son "would live to have his bellyful of Parliaments."

James's reign also saw some important developments overseas that would have major long-term consequences both in England and around the world. Ireland was nominally conquered by the Norman kings of England as early as the 1100s, but it long remained largely unchanged by the English presence. As of the early 1500s, English settlement was mostly limited to the coastal area around Dublin, known as "the Pale." Elizabeth's reign had seen a number of rebellions against English rule, and the crown had initiated a policy of "plantation" by which lands were confiscated from Irish subjects to be granted to Englishmen. The new landlords would settle their domains with English colonists, yielding economic profits for themselves and increased political control for the English crown. This process accelerated significantly under James, who undertook a vigorous campaign of plantation that relocated large numbers of Scottish Presbyterians to Ulster, traditionally the heart of Irish rebelliousness.

Colonialism in Ireland provided a model for more ambitious ventures that would take English plantations across the Atlantic. The privately chartered Virginia Company established the first lasting English settlement at Jamestown in 1607, and in 1620 a small community of Separatists established a village of their own at Plymouth. These ventures to a distant and unfamiliar land were risky: many of the first Virginian settlers succumbed to fever, while their Plymouth counterparts fell victims to the New England cold. But for an overcrowded and land-hungry nation, the prospect of estates in the New World was a powerful incentive to emigration, especially during the tumultuous political events of the following reign.

CHARLES I (1625–1649)

James died in 1625, leaving the combined English and Scottish throne to his son Charles. Very soon, the strained relations between king and Parliament took a dramatic turn for the worse. Within the first few years of his reign, Charles allowed himself to be dragged into fruitless wars with both of Europe's chief powers, France and Spain. Charles's ministers, wishing to circumvent Parliament, tried to cover the costs of these enterprises through questionable measures, including a mandatory "loan" from taxpayers and forced billeting of troops, summarily imprisoning some of those who resisted. Yet these strategems were still insufficient to cover the costs of war, and Parliament was summoned in 1628 to make up the shortfall with

subsidies. Parliamentary leaders took the opportunity to air their grievances, particularly in the matters of church reform, unapproved taxation,
and imprisonment without trial. Positions hardened on both sides, until
Charles dissolved Parliament in 1629 and for the next decade attempted to
rule without it.

During Charles's 11 years of personal rule, his administrators continued their highly unpopular policy of enhancing limited royal revenues
through measures of dubious legality. At the same time, his Archbishop
of Canterbury, William Laud, angered reformist Protestants through
religious policies that increased the church's emphasis on ritual. In
Laud's view,

Unity cannot long continue in the Church when uniformity is shut out at the church
door. No external action in the world can be uniform without some ceremonies . . .
Ceremonies are the hedge that fences the substance of religion from all the indigni-
ties which profaneness and sacrilege too commonly put upon it.[2]

The implementation of Charles's policies provoked deep hostility
among many Englishmen, though the policies were still generally blamed
on the king's ministers rather than on the king himself.

Military conflicts proved the catalyst that unraveled Charles's precarious autocracy. When Laud attempted to impose his church policies on
Scotland in 1636, Scots of all classes signed the "National Covenant,"
vowing to defend their presbyterian form of worship. Charles mustered
an army for the "First Bishops' War," but the ragtag English militia that
marched north in 1639 was forced to halt in the face of the far superior
Covenanter army. Desperate for money to raise a viable military force,
Charles summoned Parliament, hoping that the prospect of war with the
Scots would win him support from his English subjects. He was soon
disillusioned, for 10 years of autocratic rule had deeply antagonized the
parliamentary classes. The House of Commons expressed its grievances
with renewed zeal, and Charles dissolved the "Short Parliament" within
a month. In 1640, the Covenanters crossed into northern England, and
Charles was forced to convene a new Parliament to raise money to buy
off the invaders. This assembly would ultimately be known as the "Long
Parliament," for in various permutations it would meet as late as 1660.
During 1641, the legislators forced the king to sign a series of measures
that condemned his chief officials to execution as well as forcing him
to agree to statutes restricting royal power: these statutes abolished the
"prerogative courts" that could be used to enforce royal will, outlawed
the taxation measures that had supported Charles's personal rule, and
established a three-year cap on the time that could pass between sit-
tings of Parliament, with provisions to ensure that a Parliament would
be assembled even if the king did not summon it.

Late in 1641, another uprising broke out, this time among Charles's Catholic subjects in Ireland. An army had to be raised, but opinion in Parliament was now divided. Some felt that Parliament's goals had been met, but many feared that once the king had an army at his disposal, he would reverse the recent reforms. The king, having agreed to Parliament's demands, had regained much of the goodwill lost during the 1630s and was determined to act while his hand was relatively strong. On January 4, 1642, he violated ancient custom by entering the House of Commons in person with an armed following, fruitlessly seeking to arrest the opposition leaders. This display of force catalyzed Parliamentary resistance. Parliament took action to secure military control over London, and the king left the city to make military preparations of his own. Negotiations finally broke down in June, and in August the king raised his war-banner in Nottingham against his Parliamentary opponents.

After a brief season of inconclusive fighting, Charles established his headquarters in Oxford, about 50 miles from the English capital. There followed two more years of warfare in which Parliament's military commanders repeatedly failed to make effective use of their substantial strategic advantages. In 1644, Parliament's forces were augmented by an allied Covenanter army from Scotland, and at the end of the year, Parliament passed legislation mandating a complete reformation of their own military. The New Model Army came into being in 1645, crushing the king's army that summer at Naseby, and in 1646 Charles surrendered himself to the Scots, who eventually handed him over to Parliament.

Parliament now had the delicate job of negotiating a peace with a captive king whom they did not trust, but to whom they still professed loyalty. The situation was aggravated by divisions within the Parliamentarian cause, a patchwork coalition that had united in war, but that was becoming increasingly fragmented in victory. Many of the Parliamentarian leaders had a deeply vested interest in the status quo and wanted only to ensure that the reforms of the Long Parliament endured. At the far end of the spectrum were those who wanted to see substantial political reforms, such as extension of voting rights and freedom of worship for independent Protestant congregations. Such ideas had become influential in the New Model Army, which increasingly saw itself as a force for political reform: the "Declaration of the Army" emphasized that this was no "mere mercenary army hired to serve any arbitrary power of a state, but called forth and conjured by the several declarations of Parliament, to the defence of our own and the people's just rights and liberties."[3] This political radicalism in the army was seen as a serious threat by the social elites who dominated Parliament: in their view, control of Parliament and control of religion were essential for maintaining the traditional social and economic order.

Conservative Parliamentarians tried to demobilize the army, but pay was hopelessly in arrears, and the army, under the somewhat ambivalent leadership of the generals Oliver Cromwell and Henry Ireton, occupied London. Political divisions within the army, reflecting divisions in the country at large, came to the fore as officers debated the shape of England's political future:

[Leveller Colonel Thomas] Rainborough: . . . The poorest he that is in England hath a life to live as the greatest he; and therefore . . . every man that is to live under a government ought first by his own consent to put himself under that government; . . . the poorest man in England is not at all bound in a strict sense to that government that he hath not had a voice to put himself under. . . .

    Ireton: . . . No person hath a right to an interest or share in the disposing of the affairs of the kingdom, and in determining or choosing those that shall determine what laws we shall be ruled by here . . . that hath not a permanent fixed interest in this kingdom.[4]

Charles saw such divisions as an opportunity, and he escaped to rally support among the Scots and Parliamentarian conservatives. The military crisis gave Ireton and Cromwell the opportunity to crush radicalism in the ranks, as a second civil war took place in 1648, culminating in a swift victory for Cromwell and the New Model Army. Charles was recaptured by the army, and his machinations had strengthened the hand of his opponents, who purged Parliament of those who were sympathetic to the king. The remaining "Rump" Parliament tried Charles for treason, and he was beheaded in London on January 29, 1649.

Figure 1.1 A satire on the conflict between "Cavaliers" and "Roundheads" (Jackson 1885).

THE COMMONWEALTH AND PROTECTORATE
(1649–1660)

For the next 11 years, England would be without a king. The Rump abolished the monarchy and House of Lords, declaring England a Commonwealth and putting executive government in the hands of a Council of State, with Cromwell at its head. The Scots, appalled by Charles's execution, proclaimed his son as Charles II, but the ensuing Third Civil War ended in the young king's flight to France in 1651.

Now that the military situation was stabilized, Cromwell expected the Rump Parliament to dissolve itself to make way for fresh elections, but the Parliamentary leaders were fearful of both royalist sentiment and army-based radicalism and refused to release their hold on power; they also engaged in a costly war with the Netherlands and refused to deliver the religious liberties desired by the army. In 1653 Cromwell intervened, bringing soldiers to Westminster to forcibly disband Parliament.

Cromwell became the de facto military ruler of England, taking the title "Lord Protector." A new Parliament was assembled, chosen by the government on the basis of nominations solicited from the local Independent churches, but this so-called "Barebones" Parliament (named for one of its members) lacked the political skills and credibility of the elected Parliament. When a new elected Parliament was summoned in 1654, the old issues resurfaced. The classes who dominated Parliament still opposed the liberty of conscience favored by Cromwell and the army, and Cromwell found himself constantly obliged to resort to force and authoritarianism in trying to implement reform. By the time Cromwell died in 1658, he was king in all but name and reverence. Before his death, he named his son Richard to succeed him as Lord Protector, but the generals of the New Model Army forced Richard to resign in 1659. Effective rule was now in the hands of the generals, but by this point, the Commonwealth government was both morally and fiscally bankrupt. To avert anarchy, General George Monck recalled the Long Parliament, who invited Charles II to return to England in May 1660 (Monck's regiment, retained by the restored king, would eventually become the modern Coldstream Guards).

The Commonwealth ultimately failed, yet in many ways it was a highly successful experiment. Not only did Cromwell's military consolidate its hold on the British Isles, but in wars with the Netherlands and Spain, the English military also gained a reputation in Continental Europe that it had not known since the Middle Ages. Parliament established systems of operation by committee so successful that they were perpetuated by the restored royal government after 1660.

Above all, the 1650s were a period of outstanding cultural effervescence. The presses poured forth an unprecedented level of literature that included treatises on education, games, and courtly life. The government also extended a degree of religious toleration unprecedented in England's history. The poet John Milton, for a time an important spokesman for the Commonwealth, was among the most articulate advocates for both freedom of worship and freedom of the press: "Give me the liberty to know, to utter, and to argue freely according to conscience, above all liberties."[5] In this environment, spiritual life was enriched by the flourishing of long-suppressed religious sects and the emergence of new ones, of whom the most enduring would be the Quakers. The Commonwealth's comparatively tolerant attitude facilitated the return of Jews to England after 350 years of exclusion, and even Catholics were more leniently treated than under previous governments. Meanwhile, the political arena saw the emergence of new ideas of social organization, largely suppressed, but advocating such forward-looking causes as equal rights for women and universal education.

CHARLES II (1660–1685)

This period of experimentation came to an abrupt end with the royal Restoration of 1660. Charles II would prove the most politically adept of England's Stuart monarchs, but his success was in part due to his cynicism: he was prepared to sacrifice almost anyone and anything in order to secure his own hold on power. Among the first parliamentary statutes of the Restoration was the Act of Indemnity and Oblivion (1660), which granted a general pardon to all but a handful of individuals involved in the wars against him and his father. Charles went on to forge an alliance with the conservative elites who dominated Parliament—many of whom had been opponents of the monarch in the previous decades. King and Parliament essentially restored the status quo of 1642, addressing but not actually solving the issues of finance, religion, and constitution that had plagued the Stuart monarchy.

In the area of royal finances, the king renounced the powers of extraparliamentary taxation, and a parliamentary committee calculated the normal expenditures of the royal government and granted customs and excise taxes to supplement the crown's meager revenue from land. The grant fell far short of the expected income at first, but it vastly expanded with the growth of English trade during the remainder of the century, so that ultimately, Charles and his successor James were much less dependent financially on Parliament than their father and grandfather had been.

The distribution of power in the Restoration government was based on the reforms instituted by the Long Parliament. The three-year cap on the period between Parliaments was retained, but the mechanism for enforcement was removed, and Charles actually ignored the act toward the end of his reign, summoning no Parliament after 1681. He retained the authority to issue proclamations, but the prerogative courts were not restored, so he was dependent on the common law courts for enforcement, though he still retained the power of appointing and dismissing judges. The king also retained the executive power to override the law in particular cases where he deemed it necessary, a privilege that would prove a major point of contention.

Perhaps the most striking feature of the Restoration was the redrawing of the religious map. Charles, himself of Catholic leanings, preferred a policy of religious toleration, but the events of the Civil Wars and Interregnum had left the conservative elites hostile to religious diversity and determined to promote conformity to the national church. Independent congregations were forbidden, and measures were enacted to ensure that all officers in the government and military were participants in the national church, taking an oath to uphold it in its existing form. These measures did not eradicate religious dissent, but they did largely exclude the "Nonconformists"—those taking part in alternative Protestant congregations—from involvement in the state, and reformist Puritanism was deprived of any role in the national church. Partly as a result, the Restoration saw an increasing redirection of the former Puritan and Separatist segments of society into the fields of commerce, science, and technology.

The redirection of reformist energies contributed to a flowering of both science and commerce during the Restoration period. The Royal Society was founded, under Charles's nominal patronage, as an organization to promote scientific and technological study in England; this community of scientists would nourish the work of such figures as Robert Boyle (1627–1691) and Sir Isaac Newton (1642–1727). England's overseas commerce was also expanding significantly, as the English began to overtake the Dutch as the world's leading merchant power. Commercial conflict with the Netherlands led to war in 1665–1667, and although this war ended poorly for England, the treaty granted England the New World territories between New England and Virginia, which would become the colonies of New York, New Jersey, Delaware, and Pennsylvania. England's colonial holdings also expanded southward with the establishment of Carolina in 1663, and its global presence was further increased by the acquisition of trading and military bases in the eastern hemisphere: Bombay (Mumbai) was acquired in 1668, and Calcutta would come into English hands in 1690.

Even the two great catastrophes of Charles's reign were heralds of improvement. London's great Plague of 1665, which may have claimed as many as 100,000 lives, was to be the last major English outbreak of this disease, which had been endemic since the mid-1300s. The Great Fire of 1666, which destroyed most of the City of London, became an opportunity for the rebuilding of the capital; Christopher Wren's rebuilt version of St. Paul's Cathedral remains one of the most important landmarks in the London skyline. It is characteristic of anti-Catholic prejudice in Stuart England that both disasters were seen by many Englishmen as the fruits of Catholic conspiracies.

The final years of Charles's reign were dominated by the interrelated issues of religion and the royal succession. Protestants across Europe were alarmed at the increasing power of England's age-old rival, France. Under Louis XIV,

France was pursuing an aggressively expansionist and Catholicizing policy, but Charles chose to align himself with the king who had harbored him during his exile. In 1670, he and Louis concluded the Treaty of Dover, which committed Charles to join Louis in a war against the Protestant Dutch and which included secret provisions by which Charles received a stipend from the French king and undertook to restore Catholicism in England. Although the secret provisions were not revealed even to some of Charles's ministers, anti-Catholic sentiment in England was outraged when Charles followed up on his treaty obligations by issuing the Declaration of Indulgence in 1672, suspending penal laws against both Catholics and Nonconformists.

Many in the governing classes were willing to tolerate the Nonconformists, but Catholicism was another matter entirely. When Charles summoned Parliament in 1673 to obtain funds for the Dutch war, Parliament forced him to cancel the declaration and then passed the Test Act, which required all officeholders to take an oath that effectively declared their adherence to the Church of England. Charles's brother and heir apparent, James, had secretly converted to Catholicism a few years earlier and therefore resigned his office as Lord Admiral, making his conversion public knowledge. Charles sought to offset James's unpopularity as a Catholic through a marriage alliance with the Protestant Dutch: James's daughter Mary was wedded in 1677 to William of Orange, Stadhouder of the Netherlands—effectively the king of the Dutch Republic and a grandson of Charles I on his mother's side.

Charles's efforts did little to allay fears of a Catholic conspiracy, which came to a head in 1678 with the uncovering of the "Popish Plot," an alleged plan among English Catholics to assassinate the king and leading Protestant figures, place James on the throne, and restore Catholicism as the national religion. Much of the supposed plot was a fabrication, although there was some kernel of reality, but the story confirmed popular fears and prejudices. There were rumors that a French and Spanish army had landed and that Catholics were arming themselves, placing bombs under churches, and plotting to burn London again (among those arrested was Samuel Pepys, whose uniquely detailed diaries of his daily life are cited extensively in this book). A bill was proposed in Parliament to exclude James from the throne, and it was during this crisis that the pro-exclusion and anti-exclusion parties coalesced under the names "Whig" and "Tory"—these parties would maintain political continuity (eventually renamed "liberal" and "conservative") into the twentieth century.

James's due succession was the one principle on which Charles would never compromise. The bill was defeated, but when Charles died in 1685, his brother inherited a country whose people were profoundly suspicious of his intentions.

JAMES II (1685–1688)

Almost immediately upon his accession, James began to confirm those suspicions through measures intended to strengthen the position of

Catholics in England. He suspended penal laws against non-Anglicans, appointed Catholics into the army, and dismissed established officials at all levels of government in favor of Catholics and Catholic sympathizers. Such measures were illegal by the provisions of the Restoration statutes, but James invoked his executive authority to override laws in cases where he felt it was in the national interest, and the courts upheld his argument. James's pro-Catholic policies raised suspicion and hostility across English society, but fears of a Catholic restoration were eased by the knowledge that James and his Catholic wife Catherine of Gonzaga had no child.

The situation changed with the birth of James's son James Edward in June 1688. Opponents of a Catholic succession spread the rumor that the child was not the king's and had been smuggled into the queen's bedchamber in a bedpan. Several leading lords took the initiative of sending an embassy to William of Orange, who had indeed encouraged the English to approach him in this matter. William's wife Mary was James's daughter by his first wife, and the couple were invited to come to England with a military force, theoretically to protect England's Protestant church against the ill-defined Catholic threat—although in reality both sides recognized that the real goal was to evict James from the throne. William was more than willing to accept such an opportunity, for as a Protestant neighbor to France, he was on the front line, facing the ambitions of Louis XIV.

William landed in southwestern England with a substantial military force on November 5, 1688. As William organized his army, the English elites contemplated the situation. They were supposedly loyal subjects of their legitimate king and should have flocked to his support, but they had no interest in seeing a Catholic James III on the throne. A few actually initiated military risings in William's support, but the majority acted by not acting: there was no expression of widespread support for the king in the face of this foreign invasion, a deafening silence that called into question James's ability to rule his own kingdom. As William moved his army toward London, more civilian and military leaders entered into negotiations with the invader, and before William reached the capital, James lost his nerve, fleeing to France on December 23. The events were later described by the diarist Elizabeth Freke in terms that many contemporaries would have echoed:

1688, November 15. The good prince of Orange, King William the Third, came over out of Holland to be our deliverer from popery and slavery. God sent him when we were just past all hopes to be our helper, and relieved us when we were past all hopes. He landed near Exeter, in the west of Dorsetshire, with about 12 sail of ships of his own, and about 12 thousand men in them. Against whom King James went with near 60,000 to oppose him, but want of courage carried him back to London, when he with his queen and pretended prince of Wales run for France.[6]

James's flight provided a pretext for resolving the constitutional crisis. It was now possible for the country's leaders to maintain that he had abandoned his throne, allowing them to offer it to William and Mary, who

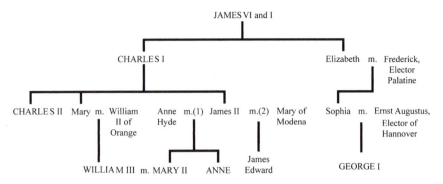

Figure 1.2 Family tree of the Stuarts.

were crowned as joint monarchs in April 1689. Nonetheless, this transfer of power was highly questionable according to the customs of royal succession. In the eyes of many, James remained the legitimate king. He attempted to regain the crown by landing with French support in Ireland, where he mustered an army of Catholic supporters, but his Franco-Irish army was defeated by William's royal troops and Protestant Ulstermen at the Battle of the Boyne in 1690. Nonetheless, defeat at the Boyne did not kill Jacobitism—the movement in support of the exiled James III and later his son James Edward and grandson Charles Edward (best remembered as "Bonnie Prince Charlie"). The Jacobite cause would remain an important presence in English politics until its final military defeat at the battle of Culloden in 1746.

WILLIAM AND MARY (1689–1702)

The establishment of William and Mary on the throne, known as the "Glorious Revolution" for its lack of bloodshed, established a line of royal succession and a political settlement that has remained unbroken to the present day. To consolidate and define the terms of the transfer of power, Parliament passed a series of measures. The Triennial Act provided for a new Parliament to be assembled every three years. The Toleration Act allowed freedom of religious worship for most Protestants (Quakers and Unitarians were among those still officially excluded from toleration), although the Church of England retained its privileged position as the established church—not until 1871 would Oxford and Cambridge be opened to Nonconformists. Perhaps most important, the "Bill of Rights" outlined grievances against James and required the new monarchs to assent to certain constitutional principles:

That the pretended power of dispensing with laws or the execution of laws by regal authority, as it hath been assumed and exercised of late, is illegal . . .

That levying money for or to the use of the Crown by pretence of prerogative, without grant of Parliament, for longer time or in other manner than the same is or shall be granted, is illegal;

That it is the right of the subjects to petition the king, and all commitments and prosecutions for such petitioning are illegal; . . .

That the subjects which are Protestants may have arms for their defence suitable to their conditions and as allowed by law; . . .

That the freedom of speech and debates or proceedings in Parliament ought not to be impeached or questioned in any court or place out of Parliament;

That excessive bail ought not to be required, nor excessive fines imposed, nor cruel and unusual punishments inflicted.

William, though hardly a personable man, was an able administrator, and he managed to work effectively through the parliamentary system to achieve his goals—the chief priority being his war to contain the ambitions of Louis XIV. By this time, the Whig and Tory parties were well established as the dominant groupings in parliamentary politics, and William chose his ministers of state based both on their amenability to his own political agenda and on their ability to deliver votes on the floor of Parliament. This practice would ultimately give rise to the modern parliamentary system in which governmental leadership is placed in the hands of the party that can deliver a majority of votes. William was constantly frustrated by the complex political maneuvering required in dealing with Parliament and even gave serious thought to abdicating the English throne. Yet the parliamentary system forced him to build support for his policies, enabling him to conduct a prolonged and expensive, yet ultimately successful war with a far larger kingdom. William's reign saw the emergence of Britain as a force to be reckoned with at the global level, a development that owed much to the dynamism of the parliamentary system.

William ruled jointly with Mary until her death in 1694 and then alone until his own death in 1702, when the throne passed to Mary's sister Anne, who reigned until 1714, the last monarch of the Stuart line.[7]

NOTES

1. Cited Barry Coward, *The Stuart Age: A History of England 1603–1714* (London and New York: Longman, 1980), 91.

2. Cited Roger Lockyer, *Tudor and Stuart Britain 1471–1714* (London: Longman, 1964), 255.

3. Cited Godfrey Davies, *The Early Stuarts 1603–1660* (Oxford: Clarendon Press, 1959), 146–47.

4. A.S.P. Woodhouse, *Puritanism and Liberty, Being the Army Debates (1647–9) from the Clarke Manuscripts with Supplementary Documents* (Chicago: University of Chicago Press, 1951), 53–54.

5. John Milton, *Areopagitica: A Speech of Mr. John Milton for the Liberty of Unlicenc'd Printing to the Parlement of England* (London: n.p., 1644), 35.

6. Elizabeth Freke, *The Remembrances of Elizabeth Freke 1671–1714*, ed. Raymond A. Anselment (London: Cambridge University Press for the Royal Historical Society, 2001), 227.

7. For narrative histories of the period, see Further Reading and Bibliography.

2

SOCIETY AND GOVERNMENT

England began the 1600s with a population around 4 million; by 1650 the figure had topped 5 million, declining slightly in the second half of the century. These figures include the populations of Cornwall and Wales, by this time largely integrated into the English political and economic system, although significant numbers of people in both regions were culturally not English, speaking Cornish or Welsh as their native language. The figure does not include Scotland, still governed as a separate kingdom even though the accession of James I in 1603 brought Scotland and England under the same monarch. Various measures, such as shared citizenship, were instituted during the century to begin a process of integration, but full consolidation of the United Kingdom did not take place until 1707.[1]

There were also small but important communities of foreigners within England. Some of these were merchants, ambassadors, travelers, and other temporary residents. However, some areas had significant communities of permanent foreign residents: London in particular was home to many Protestant immigrants from France and the Netherlands, and their numbers grew after Louis XIV's revocation of the Edict of Nantes in 1685 made Protestantism illegal in France.

Somewhere between native and foreign were the gypsies. The Romany, as they called themselves, had actually originated in India centuries earlier and had spread across Europe during the late Middle Ages. By the 1500s, they had begun to appear in England, where they were erroneously believed to have come from Egypt. By the Stuart age, they were a familiar sight in the English countryside, generally living in itinerant communities apart from settled English society. Their wandering way of life was antithetical to contemporary English ideas of order, and they were subject to intermittent repression, even to the point of execution as felons, although such extreme severity had fallen out of use by the latter half of the century.[2]

Among the native English there was considerable regional diversity. Population, wealth, and urbanization were weighted toward the south and east, whereas the less fertile west and north were generally poorer, less densely populated, and culturally more conservative. These broad patterns overlay a complex patchwork of local variation. England's diverse geography fostered a variety of local microcultures, which thrived in an environment where a significant part of the population had little experience of their own country beyond the closest market town. Although travel was a common experience for many, there was always a core of sedentary residents in any locality to maintain its distinctive cultural identity.

CLASS STRUCTURES

Probably the defining feature of seventeenth-century English society was its hierarchical class structure. The pioneering statistician Gregory King assembled estimates of the numbers and income of the various classes in England in 1688, and although his figures are not necessarily accurate, they do provide an impression of how the classes were perceived by contemporaries and a rough profile of households at various levels.

These classes were not merely a reflection of contemporary differences in wealth or prestige. The seventeenth-century class structure was a holdover from the feudal hierarchy of the Middle Ages, in which every person was theoretically incorporated into a pyramidal "chain of command," personally subordinated to the authority of their immediate superior, as well as exercising authority over the individuals directly below them; these relationships were passed on from parent to child, providing social stability from generation to generation. Stability was enhanced by the system's economic foundation on agricultural landholdings. Throughout the Middle Ages, agriculture had been the most important generator of income, and an individual's feudal status was anchored in a relationship to an agricultural landholding: at each level of the hierarchy, a landholding was granted by the feudal superior to his subordinate in exchange for service.

King and Aristocracy The realities of seventeenth-century life were actually quite far from this medieval theory, but the feudal hierarchy nonetheless remained essential to seventeenth-century Englishmen's understanding of their own society. At the apex of the hierarchy was the king, who held sovereign authority over all the land in his kingdom, parceling out extensive landholdings to his

Table 2.1
Gregory King's Estimates of English Socioeconomic Classes in 1688

Social rank	Number of families	Heads per family	Number of persons	Yearly family income
Temporal lords	160	40	6,400	£3,200
Spiritual lords	26	20	520	£1,300
Baronets	800	16	12,800	£800
Knights	600	13	7,800	£650
Esquires	3,000	10	30,000	£450
Gentlemen	12,000	8	96,000	£280
Persons in greater offices and places	5,000	8	40,000	£240
Persons in lesser offices and places	5,000	6	30,000	£120
Eminent merchants and traders by sea	2,000	8	64,000	£400
Lesser merchants and traders by sea	8,000	6	64,000	£198
Persons in the law	10,000	7	12,000	£154
Eminent clergymen	2,000	6	40,000	£72
Lesser clergymen	8,000	5	52,000	£50
Freeholders of the better sort	40,000	7	280,000	£91
Freeholders of the lesser sort	120,000	5 ½	660,000	£55
Farmers [i.e., tenant farmers]	150,000	5	750,000	£42
Persons in liberal arts and sciences	15,000	5	75,000	£60
Shopkeepers and tradesmen	50,000	4 ½	225,000	£45
Artisans and handicrafters	60,000	4	240,000	£38
Naval officers	5,000	4	20,000	£80
Military officers	4,000	4	16,000	£60
Common seamen	50,000	3	150,000	£20
Laboring people and outservants	264,000	3 ½	1,275,000	£15
Cottagers and paupers	400,000	3 ¼	1,300,000	£7

(continued)

Table 2.1
(Continued)

Social rank	Number of families	Heads per family	Number of persons	Yearly family income
Common soldiers	35,000	2	70,000	£14
Vagrants (e.g., gypsies, thieves, and beggars)	30,000	[n/a]	30,000	£2

Source: Adapted from Peter Laslett, *The World We Have Lost* (London: Methuen, 1971), 32–33, 245 fn. 27.

"tenants-in-chief." Probably the most important function of medieval kings was their leadership in war, and seventeenth-century monarchs retained their prerogative of control over the military, as well as over foreign affairs in general. The monarch was also responsible for the administration of law. For this purpose, England was divided into 40 counties or shires, with another 12 in Wales. In each shire, the crown appointed the judicial and administrative officials who administered national laws and policies at the local and regional level.

The king also had the power to grant titles of nobility, although most titles were inherited rather than bestowed. The highest-ranking members of the aristocracy were the peerage, who in theory held their extensive estates directly from the king, bearing titles of rank that were passed from generation to generation and having the right to sit in the House of Lords. In descending order, these titles were duke, marquess, earl, viscount, and baron. The title itself was not the sole marker of status. The value of a family's estates contributed to their prestige, and the age of the title was considered especially important. Newly granted titles never counted as much as those of long inheritance, although over a span of generations, a few ambitious families were able to find acceptance in aristocratic circles.

In the Middle Ages, the upper nobility had been military leaders who could be called on in times of war to bring substantial contingents of knights to serve the king. By the end of the Middle Ages, feudal armies had been replaced by professional ones. Many leading positions in the Stuart military still went to the nobility, but they no longer enjoyed a monopoly on military leadership. The nobles also continued to enjoy privileges in government, particularly as the House of Lords in Parliament, as well as exercising a certain amount of influence in the church, often having a right to appoint local clergy. Above all, the nobility were seen as the gold standard of cultural status in English society. They were expected to live opulent lives that reflected their social importance, maintaining multiple stately residences in town and country and supporting large households of relatives and employees. They set the fashions, and socially ambitious Englishmen imitated them or even attempted to join their ranks by acquiring landed estates and royally granted titles.

Below the peers were the baronets, whose title was newly granted by definition. In 1611, James I needed cash for a military expedition to Ireland, and he created this title as a means of raising funds: baronetcies were initially sold for £1,100, though the price soon plummeted. Originally intended as a temporary stopgap measure, the baronetcy became an enduring feature of the English aristocracy. The title was inherited and allowed the holder to add the title "Sir" to his name, but not to sit in the House of Lords.

Below the nobles were the gentry—knights, squires, and gentlemen. These were essentially the heirs of medieval land-   **Gentry** holders whose estates were more or less sufficient to support an individual knight and his small military entourage. This basic estate was called a manor, and the more wealthy in this class might own multiple manors. The military significance of the manor had long since vanished, but a gentleman still needed to have lands whose revenues were sufficient to support him in an appropriately gentlemanly style without needing to labor—he was expected to live in a fine house, maintaining a household of servants and enjoying the clothing, food, and lifestyle of a gentleman. Like the aristocracy, the status of a gentry family reflected their title, their wealth, and the antiquity of their status. The title of knight, the highest in this class, was granted only to the recipient himself and was not heritable. The status of squire was heritable, but less clearly defined. A squire was typically a gentleman whose family had enjoyed gentlemanly status for multiple generations, so that a well-established gentry family would eventually be considered squires.

The definition of the gentry as a leisured class does not mean that they never worked. In the transforming economy of the 1600s, hands-off landowners could easily find their fortunes diminished, so many of the gentry devoted substantial energy and effort to the management of their estates. Certain professions were also considered to confer gentlemanly status, among them the priesthood, law, university teaching, and commissioned rank in the military. Many younger sons of the gentry went into these fields as an appropriately gentlemanly way of earning a living.

Below the rank of the gentry there was a theoretically sharp divide, reflecting the medieval distinction between   **Commoners** the warrior class—the knights—and those who were not professional warriors. In reality, the decline of feudal armies had made the distinction much less meaningful, and the lower end of the gentry was not always easy to distinguish from the upper end of the yeomanry. A yeoman was the holder of a substantial rural "freeholding." He had a perpetual right to his land that he could pass on to his heirs, and his estates might actually be larger than those of the poorest gentlemen, but in theory, he might be seen handling a plow in person.

Below the yeoman in status was the husbandman, who worked his own landholding but had enough land to sustain his family, typically a few dozen acres. The lowest level of landholders were the cottagers, whose holdings were not enough to sustain them, perhaps little more than the cottage they lived in, so that they needed to sell their labor to make ends meet. Husbandmen and cottagers were essentially the heirs of medieval serfs—the landholdings had been passed on to the seventeenth-century descendents, but the status of serfdom had died out. Serfs had paid for their holdings chiefly through labor service, but by the seventeenth century, labor service had largely been transformed into cash rents. The legal status of these landholdings were highly variable: some might be equivalent to freeholds, whereas others might be held for only the term of a lease—from a few years to a few generations—and some inhabited a gray area in between.

Hierarchy and Change   This hierarchical system extended from the public sphere of society into the domestic sphere of the household, as will be explored more fully in the following chapter. Indeed, the home was one of the few domains in which the hierarchy still retained the concept of feudal-style allegiance. Women and servants were essentially regarded as the feudal subordinates of the male head of household: to murder one's husband or master was regarded by law as "petty treason," a crime second only to treason against the monarch in the severity of punishment.

Outside of the home, the network of personal loyalties that had integrated the feudal hierarchy was largely defunct, yet the hierarchy of degrees persisted. The principle of hierarchy was firmly ingrained into the etiquette of everyday life. People were expected to show respect when in the presence of their social superiors, in particular by removing their hats and using a properly respectful form of address. In any encounter between two people, their respective statuses were instantly manifested by who doffed their hat. Among the recurring complaints about the Quakers was their refusal to remove their hats in this manner, as well as their insistence on using the familiar "thou" in place of the more formal "you."

By the latter part of the century, defense of the traditional hierarchy had become one of the political cornerstones of the Tories, for whom tradition, stability, and social organization rooted in inherited landholdings were the preeminent needs of a well-ordered society. Nonetheless, the feudal model had never been entirely adequate for understanding English society even in the heyday of feudalism, and by the 1600s, the areas in which England was growing most quickly were precisely the ones that fit least comfortably into this feudal framework.

One of these sectors was urban society. Towns still accounted for a minority of the population, but they exercised social and economic influence disproportionate to their size, and they were growing quickly. In principle, the towns imitated the hierarchical structure of feudalism. They were under the authority of the king; below him were the wealthy urban elite who controlled the systems of civic and economic governance; below them were the independent tradesmen and craftsmen; and at the base were the hired workers. Yet status and interpersonal relationships in the towns lacked the stability of the feudal hierarchy. Urban wealth and power were based on access to capital and information (in such forms as skills, technologies, and market opportunities), and these commodities were much less static than land. Status and interpersonal relationships were also more heavily mediated by money than in the traditional feudal environment, which made them much more fluid. Families with wealth found it easier to break into the upper echelons of urban society than into the landowning elite, and the wage-based bonds between employer and employee were far less rigid than the land-based bonds of feudalism. The elastic economic structures required by capitalistic enterprise were fundamentally at odds with the stable hierarchy of feudalism. Already by the end of the Middle Ages, the myth of the "self-made man" was familiar in the story of Richard Whittington: in popular versions of this tale printed in the 1600s, Dick Whittington rises from poverty, through apprenticeship, to become Lord Mayor of London (with some assistance from his legendary cat).

Entrepreneurialism had traditionally been associated with towns, but by the 1600s, it was shaping rural society as well. Successful merchants bought their way into the landowning class, and established landholders were increasingly taking a mercantile approach to land management. Already in the late Middle Ages, economic growth was offering opportunities to landholders who were able to take advantage of them through talent, good luck, or lack of scruples. Accelerating inflation after 1500 offered further incentive to take an entrepreneurial approach to land. In an inflationary environment, the stable revenues generated by land would effectively shrink over time, so landholders sought ways to squeeze more revenues out of their holdings. Raising tenants' rents was one of the simplest, though it inevitably undermined feudal stability and antagonized tenants in a society that had no concept of inflation. Improving agricultural efficiency was another possibility. The seventeenth century was a period of active experimentation with new agricultural technologies, and there existed an avid readership for a burgeoning literature of self-help books aimed at the innovative rural landholder. But these improvements also came at a social cost. Agricultural innovation worked best on large, consolidated landholdings that were not subject to intrusion by villagers claiming traditional rights of communal land use, and economies were often achieved by hiring fewer laborers who could work more efficiently, leaving a growing portion of the rural community without work. The resulting trend toward enclosure and displacement of the rural poor was a source of acute social friction that repeatedly boiled over into violence.

The Underclass These developments in the countryside contributed to a growing underclass in both town and country who fit poorly into the hierarchical model of society. The offspring of poor rural families had limited economic prospects: there were always more laborers available for day-work in the countryside than there were jobs available. Many of them traveled from village to village over the course of the year to seek temporary employment wherever they could find it. Others immigrated to the towns to join the growing numbers of the urban poor and laborers. High rates of mortality in the towns meant there was always some demand for new laborers, although here, as in the countryside, supply of labor always exceeded demand. For people in this class, life was a precarious economic balancing act, and at any time they might slide in one direction or the other, taking work when it was available or resorting to begging or crime when it was not.[3]

The unemployed and underemployed poor were a source of acute anxiety to the settled classes. They were often referred to as "masterless men" (although they included women as well): without oversight by a superior, or even a fixed place of residence, they were difficult to control and were seen as threat to the social order. The governmental response had been defined by the Elizabethan Poor Laws of the late 1500s, which tried to create a system of support and control to handle this growing class. Under these laws, those genuinely unable to labor—orphans, the elderly, the infirm—were to be supported by the parish in which they lived, based on a tax levied on the more substantial parishioners. Those who were able-bodied but had no employer might be sent to compelled labor in a workhouse or else be whipped and expelled from the parish, theoretically to return to their home parish. The system did provide some benefits to some of the needy, but it had serious shortcomings. It took limited account of the scarcity of work for many of these people, and there was strong incentive for parishes to expel the poor to avoid taking responsibility for them. These problems would persist through the following century, until the "masterless men" were absorbed into the factories of the Industrial Revolution—creating an entirely new set of social problems.[4]

The Whig Model The increasing fragmentation of the medieval hierarchy called for a different social model from the feudalistic worldview associated with the Tories. Entrepreneurialism required freedom to pursue individual profit, but also protection against the potential threat of the growing underclass. The ideology that emerged during the century to meet this need was ultimately championed by the Whigs, and its watchwords were "liberty" and "property." In this model, the state was seen as a compact between the sovereign and the people. The people owed obedience and loyalty to their sovereign, and in turn, the sovereign was bound to preserve the liberties and property of his subjects. Those who lacked property, however, were not necessarily part of this equation. Most of the propertied classes insisted that they should be subject to the rule of their social superiors because it was believed that they could not be trusted with liberty—if they were given political power, it was feared, they would appropriate the property of others. Exactly whom one included in "the people" was a matter of contention, depending on whom one was willing to trust. Only a very few suggested that women should take part in public decision-making. Not many more openly advocated universal suffrage for men, either: the *Agreement of the People*, proposed by army radicals in 1647, excluded servants and paupers from the vote, and Cromwell's comparatively progressive regime enfranchised only those who held property worth £200 or more a year. By the end of the century, the franchise in parliamentary elections, although greatly expanded over that of 1600, still represented only about 5 percent of the population.

This "Whig" model of society began to take shape during the conflict between Parliament and king in the first half of the century; elements of it can even be seen in the monarchist political theory of Thomas Hobbes, whose political treatise *Leviathan* appeared in 1651. Its most influential expression was by John Locke in his *Two Treatises upon Government* (1689): "Man being born . . . with a title to perfect freedom, and an uncontrolled enjoyment of all the rights and privileges of the law of nature, equally with any other man, or number of men in the world, hath by nature a power . . . to preserve his property, that is, his life, liberty and estate, against the injuries and attempts of other men."[5] Although this view of society contrasted with the hierarchical ideology of the Tories, the difference was more of emphasis than substance, and both models played a role for most people in the ruling elites.

Although these "Whig" and "Tory" models predominated among the ruling classes, there were other political perspec- **Radicalism** tives at the margins that are less well documented than those of the ruling elites. The events of the 1640s and 1650s brought to the fore currents of thought that challenged both of the dominant models and that also challenge our own assumptions about political thinking among the classes whose voices are rarely heard in this period of history. Both within the army and in civilian circles, the Civil War gave rise to expressions of alternative visions of society. The Levellers, particularly active within the New Model Army, argued for a republican society without divisions of status. The Diggers, who called themselves the "True Levellers" and who briefly took over common lands in the village of Walton-on-Thames, not far from London, advocated the abolition of private property. Some called for universal manhood suffrage, some even for equality for women. Female petitioners to Parliament in 1649 declared that "we have an equal share and interest with men in the Commonwealth," and the Quakers removed the woman's promise to obey from their marriage ceremony.[6] Such currents of thought were vigorously suppressed by the authorities, but they remind us that the ideologies of the elites were not always uncritically accepted by the disenfranchised, even if the currents of resistance usually remained under the surface in response to governmental suppression.[7]

THE CHURCH

The inherited hierarchical structures of medieval feudalism were paralleled by a church hierarchy that had also taken shape during the Middle Ages. England was divided into two archbishoprics (Canterbury and York), 26 bishoprics (four of them in Wales), 60 archdeaconries, and something over 9,000 parishes, each home to anywhere from several hundred to several thousand souls (the average number was around 500, but urban parishes tended to have more people and rural ones fewer). The English church had been placed under royal authority by Henry VIII, but in practice, the Stuart monarchs rarely intervened directly in church affairs, exercising authority chiefly through their power to appoint the bishops, who were the chief governing authorities of the church.

At the local level, administration of parish affairs was usually in the hands of local elites, in the form of a vestry council. The vestry was drawn from leading men in the community, and they appointed churchwardens to act as executive officers for the parish. The actual powers and structure of the vestry varied according to the parish traditions: some vestries had inherited the right to appoint their own parish clergy, whereas in other parishes that right lay with the local manor lord. With the decline of feudalism, the parish had assumed an increasingly important function as a unit of social organization: even those who lacked a "master" could still theoretically be assigned to a parish. Many of the functions of government were therefore exercised through the parish, including taxes, the militia, and the poor laws.

The national church enjoyed a privileged position in Stuart society. All Englishmen were required by law to attend services under pain of a shilling fine and to receive communion three times a year, although these laws were rarely enforced except as a means of intimidating Catholics and Nonconformists, and freedom of worship for most Protestants was definitively established by the Glorious Revolution in 1688 (Catholics, Quakers, and non-Christians were among those not included). The church was in principle supported by mandatory tithes, amounting to a tenth of every parishioner's annual income in cash or in kind, although in many parishes these tithes actually went to the manor lord or some other third party, who paid out a part of the money to support the parish priest. The church also wielded significant legal power, since matters such as marriage, wills, and sexual conduct were under the jurisdiction of ecclesiastical courts, although these courts began to fall into disuse from the time of the Glorious Revolution. Not least of all, the pulpit was viewed as one of the most important vehicles for the state's propaganda.

The status of the national church was one of the central political issues of the century. Stuart England had inherited the medieval concept of a Christian kingdom in which the church and state were closely interconnected: to be a member of society was to be a member of the church. England's Protestant Reformation had initially strengthened this relationship by incorporating the national church into the national state. Yet it had also opened the door to calls for further religious reformation and ultimately for the establishment of religious institutions independent of the national church. Reformists within the English church during the first half of the century were known as Puritans to their opponents. Their beliefs were diverse, but many of them wanted to see reform or even abolition of the episcopacy; some advocated government of the church by councils of clergymen, or "presbyteries," in the Scottish style.

Other reformists saw the English church as an obstacle to true Christian worship and formed independent "separatist" congregations. The Separatist sects were generally organized as individual congregations of like-minded worshippers, without much organizational structure coordinating the congregations. Many in the mainstream regarded the Separatists as disloyal, even treasonous, because they rejected royal control over the nation's religion, and their very presence bred faction and division within the body politic. Thomas Edwards, himself a Presbyterian, expressed a common fear that freedom of worship would prove the thin edge of the wedge: "If a toleration were granted, men should never have peace in their families more, or ever after have command of wives, children, servants."[8]

During the Civil Wars and Interregnum, Presbyterianism and Separatism enjoyed a brief period of political ascendancy, with the English church temporarily being reorganized along Presbyterian lines, and religious toleration for Independent Protestant congregations implemented under Cromwell's Protectorate. Indeed, the political and intellectual tumult of the period fostered the growth of a variety of new Separatist sects, of whom the most enduring would be the Quakers.[9]

When the Restoration reestablished the traditional episcopal structure of the English church, Separatists, now generally referred to as Nonconformists or Dissenters, were actively suppressed, though this persecution never succeeded in eradicating their congregations. Presbyterian reformism was deliberately excluded from the national church, so that former Puritans were forced either to conform or to establish their own Presbyterian congregations, joining the ranks of the Nonconformists. Only with the provisions of the Glorious Revolution in 1689 were the Nonconformists granted lasting freedom of worship. Overall, Dissenters in the latter half of the 1600s may have constituted around a twentieth of the population, mostly consisting (in descending order of numbers) of Presbyterians, Independents, Baptists, and Quakers.[10]

At the other end of the religious spectrum, some English families had never accepted Protestantism, particularly in northern England, where there were still significant numbers of Catholics. Catholicism was widely considered treasonous in the eyes of English Protestants, for it not only denied royal supremacy over the church, but also actively promoted foreign influence within England. A variety of measures had been enacted to control or suppress Catholicism: Catholics were forbidden to hold office in the government or military, their freedom of travel was subject to strict controls, they could be fined for failure to attend services at the parish church, and Catholic priests and Catholic Mass were prohibited, except in the private residences of foreign ambassadors. The zeal with which these laws were enforced varied by time and place over the course of the century, but even when enforcement was lax, anti-Catholic sentiment was widespread, and Catholics were not included in the religious toleration granted in 1689. In the latter half of the century, Catholics may have accounted for about 1 percent of the population.[11]

A very small minority in England were not even Christian at all. Officially, Jews had been banned from the country in 1290, though a small number, generally foreign-born, could be found living in England as of the early 1600s. Officially, they were categorized as Spanish Catholics, who as foreigners resident in the country were permitted to practice their religion privately. During the 1650s, Oliver Cromwell began negotiations with Jewish residents of the Netherlands, and in 1656 the Jews were quietly readmitted, although they remained legally equivalent to foreigners, and anti-Semitic feeling in England remained strong. Foreign residents in England were similarly permitted to conduct their own religious services. Atheism was also present in Stuart society, but because it was subject to punishment under the law, nonbelievers generally kept their ideas to themselves and outwardly conformed to the predominant religious norms.

GOVERNMENT AND LAW

The government of England had evolved by accretion over the course of the Middle Ages, and by the 1600s, it operated as a complex patchwork of legal authorities and jurisdictions, sometimes overlapping one another, sometimes leaving gaps where cases might fall between the cracks. The most powerful governmental body was the combination of monarch and Parliament. Parliament was divided into the House of Lords, consisting of about two hundred noblemen and bishops, and the House of Commons, made up of about five hundred members, two from each shire and two from each borough (town). A bill passed by both houses and signed by the monarch was the most powerful instrument available to government.

The actual implementation of parliamentary will was heavily dependent on the king. The king summoned and dissolved parliaments, held the ultimate authority in appointing officeholders, and in general exercised the executive functions necessary to the day-to-day functioning of the state. The failure of the Protectorate made it clear how much the government of England relied on the sense of legitimate rule provided by the inherited crown. On the other hand, the failure of the Stuart kings also made clear how much the crown's power depended on the goodwill of the privileged classes. The rural gentry and substantial urban citizenry staffed the royal civil service, collected taxes, administered the laws, and commanded the militia, and they were accustomed to considerable freedom in running the affairs of their own localities. James II's attempts to oust the traditional local leadership from power left him without supporters in the face of William of Orange's invasion in 1688, leading to the collapse of his own government.

Administration of the laws involved a complex network of courts and other legal officials; in many respects there was no **Courts** clear distinction between administrative, legislative, and juridical authority. The most important courts were based at the governmental seat in Westminster, at the western edge of London. The Court of King's Bench was essentially the highest court in the juridical hierarchy, with a broad mandate to handle criminal and civil cases. The Court of Common Pleas dealt purely in civil matters. Both courts administered "common law"—the unwritten legal customs established by long tradition—and "statute law," the laws established by act of Parliament. Edward Chamberlayne in 1674 summarized how these two forms of law were understood:

> The common law of England is the common customs of the kingdom, which have by length of time obtained the force of laws . . . and of all laws must be the best for the English, for the written laws made in England by kings . . . or by parliaments . . . are imposed upon the subject before any probation or trial whether they are beneficial to the nation or agreeable to the nature of the people; but customs bind not the people till they have been tried and approved time out of mind . . . . Where the common law is silent, there we have excellent statute laws, made by the several kings of England by and with the advice and consent of all the lords spiritual and temporal, and with the consent of all the commons of England, by their representatives in parliament.[12]

Common and statute law also governed the operations of the Court of the Exchequer, which in principle presided over civil cases in which the crown had a financial interest. For cases that were not soluble through common or statute law, litigants could petition the Court of Chancery, which functioned as a kind of proxy for the monarch, administering "natural" justice as a court of equity. Maritime cases were under the jurisdiction of the Admiralty Court, one of the few legal institutions governed by the traditions of Roman civil law. Civil law also applied in the ecclesiastical courts, which had jurisdiction over such areas as marriage law, enforcement of wills, and morals. Prior to 1641, there were a few "prerogative courts" directly under royal authority, most notoriously the Court of Star Chamber, which operated as a function of the Privy Council. The prerogative courts were abolished in the reforms of the Long Parliament and not reestablished at the Restoration.

At the local level, there were still remnants of the old manorial courts, convened by the authority of the manor lord and known either as a "court baron" or "leet court." These courts served both juridical and legislative functions, administering the common interests of the manor's residents. Similar local courts were held in the towns. However, the most important local official responsible for administration of the law was the justice of the peace, who was generally recruited from the gentry and who worked on a volunteer basis. A justice of the peace heard minor local cases and could administer punishments up to the level of whipping. If the case was more serious, he would carry out the preliminary investigations and then send the case up to a jury court. The quarter sessions courts were organized by the county justices of the peace four times a year at the county seat, and they dealt with minor crimes and misdemeanors such as rioting, trespassing, and stealing, as well as administrative matters such as fixing prices and wages, maintenance of roads and bridges, and relief of the poor. By the 1630s, local justices were also meeting monthly in "petty sessions" to provide timely handling of these sorts of cases. Felonies such as homicide, rape, grand larceny, arson, and witchcraft were tried by the courts of assize, staffed by Westminster justices who traveled circuits of the county seats twice a year.

Figure 2.1 Bringing a case before a magistrate (Furnivall 1877).

Lady Anne Clifford in 1616 recorded an incident in which her employees clashed with those of her uncle over their employers' respective rights in a hay meadow, illustrating both the legal and extralegal processes that were often involved in property conflicts of the day:

I sent my folks into the park to make hay, where they being interrupted by my uncle Cumberland's people, 2 of my uncle's people were hurt by Mr. Kidd—the one in the leg, the other in the foot; whereupon complaint was made to the judges at Carlisle, and a warrant sent forth for the apprehending of all my folks that were in the field at that time, to put in surety to appear at Kendal at the Assizes.[13]

Law enforcement was relatively weak. There was no professional police force, and the job of enforcement largely fell to citizens working on an unpaid, part-time basis. The most important local law-enforcement official was the parish constable, typically a volunteer of yeoman status or the equivalent. Donald Lupton's satiric characterization of rural constables in 1632 sketches some of his responsibilities:

Enforcement and Punishment

They have the command of four places of note: the stocks, the cage, the whipping post, and the cucking-stool. They appoint and command the watchmen with their rusty bills to walk circuit; and do also sound hue and cries after malefactors. They are much employed in four occasions: at musters, at pressing forth of soldiers, at quarter sessions, and assizes. Their office many times make them proud and crafty: if they be angry with a poor man, he is sure to be preferred [charged before the court] upon the next service. The alehouses had best hold correspondency with them; they are bugbears to them that wander without a pass. Poor soldiers are now and then helped to a lodging by their means. They'll visit an alehouse under color of search, but their desire is to get beer of the company.[14]

Punishments for minor offenses included fines, confiscations, or confinement in a pillory or stocks; slightly more serious offenses might be punished by whipping. Felonies were punishable by death, and even the theft of goods worth as little as a shilling was punishable as a felony. Execution was normally by hanging, although treasonous crimes might be punished by the cruelties of drawing and quartering for men or burning for women. Executions, as well as many lesser punishments, were conducted as public spectacles because authorities considered them an important form of social control.

Yet the use of judicial violence was dropping off markedly. As of 1600, a person accused of a felony stood about a 1 in 4 chance of being hanged; by the end of the century, the figure was around 1 in 10. Exceptional cruelties, such as punishment by mutilation (including branding or slitting the ear or nose), were likewise falling into disuse. At the same time, new forms of less violent punishment were on the rise. Imprisonment had traditionally not been used much as a form of punishment: long-term

Figure 2.2 The ducking stool at work (Furnivall 1877).

prisoners were usually either debtors, held until they discharged their debts, or political prisoners whom the crown wished to keep out of circulation. However, over the course of the century, a growing number of minor malefactors were being sent to "houses of correction"—equivalents of the modern prison. In the latter half of the century, it was becoming common for courts to punish felons with deportation to the American colonies instead of hanging.

As of the beginning of the seventeenth century, torture was still in use in major political cases—it was applied in the case of Guy Fawkes, the leading figure in the Gunpowder Plot of 1605—but already by the middle of the century, it was no longer being condoned; 1641 was the last year in which the state officially ordered its use on a political prisoner. Changes in attitudes toward judicial violence—just one facet of larger cultural trends—were reflected in the provision against "cruel and unusual punishments" in the Bill of Rights in 1689, an indicator of an important, if still incomplete, trend toward humanity in the English legal system.[15]

NOTES

1. On the population, see Keith Wrightson, *Earthly Necessities: Economic Lives in Early Modern Britain* (New Haven: Yale University Press, 2000), 229; Jeremy

Boulton, *Neighbourhood and Society: A London Suburb in the Seventeenth Century* (Cambridge: Cambridge University Press, 1987), 3; E. A. Wrigley and R. S. Schofield, *The Population History of England 1541–1871* (Cambridge, MA: Harvard University Press, 1981), 208–9.

2. Angus Fraser, *The Gypsies* (Cambridge: Blackwell, 1992), 133, 139.

3. On crime, see Keith Wrightson, *English Society, 1580–1680* (New Brunswick, NJ: Rutgers University Press, 1982), 162ff.; J. A. Sharpe, *Crime in Early Modern England, 1550–1750* (London and New York: Longman, 1984).

4. For a contemporary elite perspective on the poor, see Edward Chamberlayne, *Angliæ Notitia, or, the Present State of England* (London: J. Martyn, 1669), 43.

5. John Locke, *Two Treatises of Government*, ed. Peter Laslett (Cambridge: Cambridge University Press, 1966).

6. Ellen A. MacArthur, "Women Petitioners and the Long Parliament," *The English Historical Review* 24, no. 96 (Oct. 1909): 707; Christopher Hill, *The World Turned Upside-Down: Radical Ideas during the English Revolution* (New York: Viking Press, 1972), 250ff.; Lawrence Stone, *The Family, Sex, and Marriage in England 1500–1800* (New York: Harper and Row, 1977), 339ff.

7. On seventeenth-century radicalism in general, see Hill, *World Turned Upside-Down.*

8. Thomas Edwardes, *Gangraena* (London: Ralph Smith, 1646), 3.156.

9. On the sects, see Chamberlayne, *Angliæ Notitia*, 39.

10. Barry Coward, *The Stuart Age: A History of England 1603–1714* (London and New York: Longman, 1980), 425.

11. Julian Hoppit, *A Land of Liberty? England 1689–1727* (Oxford: Clarendon Press, 2000), 221; Coward, *The Stuart Age*, 253, 272.

12. Chamberlayne, *Angliæ Notitia*, 24.

13. Lady Anne Clifford, *The Diaries of Lady Anne Clifford*, ed. D. J. H. Clifford (Stroud: Alan Sutton, 1990), 39.

14. Donald Lupton, *London and the Country Carbonadoed* (London: N. Okes, 1632), 136.

15. See Chamberlayne, *Angliæ Notitia*, 50ff., 55; Stone, *Family*, 237. On government and law in general, see also Chamberlayne, *Angliæ Notitia*; Michael Dalton, *The Country Justice, containing the Practice of the Justices of the Peace out of their Sessions* (London: William Rawlins and Samuel Roycroft, 1690); Sir Matthew Hale, *Pleas of the Crown* (London: William Shrewsbury and John Leigh, 1678); Guy Miege, *The New State of England under our Present Monarch King William III* (London: R. Clavel, H. Mortlock, and J. Robinson, 1699), 3.1ff., 31ff., 69ff; J. A. Sharpe, *Crime in Early Modern England, 1550–1750* (London and New York: Longman, 1984); William Sheppard, *The Whole Office of the Country Justice of Peace* (London: W. Lee, D. Pateman, G. Beadell, 1650); Arthur Underhill, "Law," in *Shakespeare's England* (Oxford: Clarendon Press, 1916), 1.381–412.

3

HOUSEHOLDS AND THE LIFE CYCLE

In the Stuart age as today, the household was one of the fundamental building blocks of social organization. We often imagine preindustrial households as extended families, with multiple generations and perhaps various family branches living under a single roof. This was not uncommon among the aristocracy, but for most Englishmen, the household was based on the nuclear family, consisting of only one cohabiting couple and their children, though with the addition of servants, who would remain a part of ordinary households in Western society well into the industrial age. The typical family might consist of the parents, two or three children, and perhaps a servant or two; the home might also be occupied by a lodger or two.

At the core of the household was the married couple—the householder and his wife. The marital relationship was perhaps the most important factor in shaping the lives of Stuart women. The home was seen as the primary female domain, **Women and Men** and even the minority of women who never married were expected to operate within a domestic environment where their role was heavily informed by the hierarchy of the family.

The English translation of Comenius,[1] accompanying the image in Figure 3.1 of a wedding ceremony, offers a representative portrait of the prevailing understanding of marriage:

The Society betwixt Man and Wife

Marriage was appointed by God in Paradise, for mutual help, and the propagation of mankind. A young man (a single man) being to be married, should be furnished

Figure 3.1 A marriage (Comenius 1887).

either with wealth, or a trade and science, which may serve for getting a living, that he may be able to maintain a family. Then he chooseth himself a maid that is marriageable (or a widow) whom he loveth, where nevertheless a greater regard is to be had of virtue and honesty than of beauty or portion. Afterwards, he doth not betroth her to himself closely, but entreateth for her as a wooer, first to the father (1), and then the mother (2), or the guardians and kin-folks, by such as help to make the match (3). When she is espoused to him he becometh the bride-groom (4) and she the bride (5), and the contract is made, and an instrument of the dowry (6) is written. At the last the wedding is made, where they are joined together by the priest (7), giving their hands (8) one to another, and wedding rings (9), then they feast with the witnesses that are invited. After this they are called husband and wife; when she is dead he becometh a widower.[2]

Officially, marital relations were firmly hierarchical, with the husband standing in the position of feudal superior to his wife. Certainly, the distribution of power between the sexes in marriage was very uneven. Women had limited standing before the law, no right to participate in public office or political decision making, and restricted property rights within marriage. William Mather in 1699 described succinctly the legal limitations on women:

The woman at marriage becomes wholly the man's, together with all her movable goods, and if goods be given to a married woman, they all immediately become her husband's; she cannot let, sell, give away, or alienate any thing without her husband's consent.[3]

This disempowerment left women vulnerable if they ended up with cruel husbands. Elizabeth Freke, a woman of upper-class family, was secretly married in 1671 to a man of lower social standing, with whom she had evidently fallen in love; but Ralph Freke proved to be neglectful and exploitative, as she recorded in her "Remembrances of my misfortunes have attended me in my unhappy life since I were married":

Thus was three of my unhappy years spent in London . . . and I never had, as I remember, the command of five pounds of my fortune. Where I miscarried twice, and had very little of my husband's company, which was no small grief to me, I being only governed by my affections in this my marrying, and without the consent of any of my friends.[4]

A very different perspective is offered by Ann Lady Fanshawe, who recalled for her son the life she shared with her deceased husband:

It makes my eyes gush out with tears, and cuts me to the soul, to remember and in part express the joys I was blessed with in him. Glory be to God, we never had but one mind throughout our lives, our souls were wrapped up in each other, our aims and designs one, our loves one, and our resentments one. We so studied one the other that we knew each other's mind by our looks; whatever was real happiness, God gave it me in him.[5]

Lady Fanshawe had married the prominent royalist Sir Richard Fanshawe in 1644, in the middle of the Civil Wars, and had apparently also married for love, for she showed herself deeply loyal and supportive during the following difficult years; not only did she endure hard quarters, hunger, and exile, but she also traveled on her husband's behalf, smuggling documents and raising money for him at times when he was at risk of being apprehended by parliamentary authorities.

Lady Fanshawe's adventures were exceptional, but at every level of society, women played an important role in managing household affairs, and most women contributed significantly to the household economy. They tended the home garden, managed the domestic animals, and often did some wage-earning outside of the home. Even upper-class women were responsible for running the household establishment, an undertaking not unlike the management of a small business enterprise today.

A characteristic example toward the lower end of society is the case of Margaret Knowsley of Nantwich, a laborer's wife in Cheshire, who in 1626 was recorded as being pregnant and already having three young children, including a baby, but who nonetheless worked as a domestic servant, cleaning, laundering, gardening, and fetching fuel and water for the parish priest; she also took seasonal agricultural work, knitted, and provided medical services.[6] Such economic activity was naturally a source of some domestic empowerment, though still limited relative to the work of men, which was generally more lucrative and essential to the family's income: a typical daily wage for a laboring man was about 8–10d., while his wife might earn only 4d.

Women had primary responsibility for management of the household, including cooking and cleaning, basic medical care, provisioning, and managing household finances and personnel. Because all children were in the domestic sphere until age five or so, the woman of the house had responsibility not only for their care, but also for the basics of socialization and education. In a family of any social standing, the woman was also expected to manage charitable works on behalf of the household. Ann Lady Fanshawe recalled her mother's virtues:

My dear mother was of excellent beauty and understanding, a loving wife and most tender mother, very pious, and charitable to that degree that she relieved (besides the offal [leftovers] of the table which she constantly gave to the poor) many with her own hand daily out of her purse, and dressed many wounds of miserable people, when she had her health; and when that failed, as it did often, she caused her servant to supply that place.[7]

The man was the chief generator of cash income and had legal responsibility for the conduct of those under his charge. The male head of household was regarded as the ruler of the miniature state of the home, but as the Stuarts discovered over the course of the century, theoretical sovereignty was not the same thing as absolute power. Samuel Pepys's diary offers an intimate glimpse of the domestic politics of seventeenth-century married life. On one occasion, he scolded his wife Elizabeth for immodest dress:

At noon home to dinner, where my wife and I fell out, I being displeased with her cutting away a lace handkerchief so wide about the neck, down to her breasts almost, out of a belief (but without reason) that it is the fashion. Here we did give one another the lie [call each other liars] too much, but were presently friends.[8]

Yet Pepys himself, though he scolded his wife for her décolletage, indulged in a series of extramarital liaisons of various duration over a period of years, until Elizabeth finally caught him with the household servant Deb, "embracing the girl *con* my hand *sub su* coats."[9] In the ensuing months of domestic turmoil, Pepys was "sorry and ashamed," and Elizabeth took out her anger with alternating fury and silence, leaving her husband "mightily grieved and vexed." In the end the couple weathered their difficulties, but Pepys had learned something of the limits of his authority in marriage.[10]

Stuart gender relations ultimately need to be understood in the context of a culture where hierarchy was deeply ingrained as a fundamental principle of social organization. People in Stuart England were raised to be obedient: first, to their parents, as children; and later, to a master, during a period of domestic service. At adulthood, women were expected to become subject to their husbands, and men were subject to the civil authorities. As with other aspects of the hierarchy, individuals may have chafed when their will was overruled, but most people were able to function within the established system, and the example of Pepys suggests that the day-to-day operation of marital relations may not have been as different from modern experience as the hierarchical theory might make it seem. Nonetheless, as in the political domain, there were signs that some people were questioning the validity of that hierarchy: during the 1650s, there were already some calls for equality of the sexes, although such views were widely regarded as dangerously radical.

Perhaps the most unfamiliar feature of the Stuart household to the modern eye is the omnipresence of servants. Even a family **Servants** of rather modest means—the household of a tradesman or husbandman—might include a servant or two; statistics of the period suggest that about a third of households had servants.[11] Gregory King late in the century estimated that servants accounted for about 10 percent of the population in the country and a bit higher in the city; modern statistical studies show figures in about the same range, with servants accounting for about half the hired workforce. Servants did the same kinds of work that might otherwise be done by hired laborers or other employees: male servants assisted the householder with his work, and female servants helped the woman of the house with hers. The key feature that distinguished service from other forms of employment was that servants were hired by the year and generally became resident members of the employer's household.[12]

Servants were often young people in their teens to twenties: a period of work as a servant was a common experience for many people who were old enough to leave their homes, but not yet able to set up a household of their own. For ordinary people, service was a way for the young to earn their keep, but service also fulfilled a number of additional functions. Servants generally took work in households of higher status than their own family, and their time in service helped complete their socialization, improve their social network, and learn new skills to serve their future personal and professional lives. Again, Comenius offers a summary perspective of the role of servants in the household:

The Society betwixt Masters and Servants

The Master, the goodman of the house (1) hath men-servants (2); the Mistress, the good wife of the house (3), maidens (4). They appoint these their work (6), and divide them their tasks (5), which are faithfully to be done by them without murmuring and loss; for which their wages, and meat and drink, is allowed them.[13]

Figure 3.2 Servants (Comenius 1887).

Servants were in many ways regarded as "hired children": they were under the householders' authority in much the same way as the house-holders' own children, living in the home and fulfilling economic roles that might be carried out by the family children once they were old enough. For maidservants, this typically meant assisting the woman of the house in domestic chores, whereas menservants were usually taken on to assist the man in his professional work. Resident servants were by definition single people, although some married servants might live outside the home, essentially serving as long-term contractual employees.

Servants were usually hired on an annual contract, typically after the harvest in October or November. Because they were to become part of the household, it was important to verify their good character, so a prospective employer would expect to see a letter from the previous master attesting to the servant's good conduct. It was common for parents to maintain ongoing contact with their children in service—in part to make sure they were treated well. This was not hard to do given that servants often worked in the region where their parents lived.

THE COURSE OF LIFE

A typical woman at the time of her first marriage might have about 12 to 15 years of childbearing ahead of her and perhaps six or seven pregnancies. The total number of children produced in a marriage was commonly around five or six, but high mortality rates for the young meant that many of these would not survive childhood: only about two or three would live to see their twentieth year. Mortality rates were highest for infants and declined over the years of childhood. About one baby in seven died before their first birthday, and only about half the children born lived to adulthood. Overall, high rates of mortality meant that a very large part of the population at any time was made up of children: it has been estimated that over a tenth of the population were under five, and a quarter under 20.[14]

Like so much of the Stuart woman's experience of life, childbearing was a domestic activity. When birth was imminent, neighboring women were summoned to assist, often including a midwife (who in some cases might actually be a man). Occasionally, a physician might be brought instead, but this was exceptional and was usually limited to situations where a medical complication was involved. Throughout the 1600s, the childbed remained a predominantly female domain. Elizabeth Freke left us an unusually blunt narrative of her son's birth in 1675:

My dear son, Mr. Ralph Freke, was born about three o'clock in the afternoon at my father's at Hannington, and by him, with my aunt Freke and Sir George Norton, he was christened Ralph Freke, of my dear father's name. I were 4 or 5—five—days in labor of him, and had for him four midwives about me when he was born, the man-midwife affirming he had been long dead in me to my husband and aunt [and] sister Norton, with my Lady Thynne, all who were with me several days in this my extremity. At last the result was that he should be taken in pieces from me or I should not live one hour, which consideration of my life, all consented to the taking away my dead child from me in pieces. But whilst the man-midwife was putting on his butcher's habit to come about me, my great and good God that never failed me (or denied my reasonable request) raised me up a good woman midwife who came in at this juncture of time, and for about two or three hours in her shift [shirt] worked, till by my God's mercy and providence to me I was safely delivered . . . He was the same night christened by my dear father's name, Ralph Freke.[15]

Many women were less fortunate than Freke, though they did not die in childbirth as often as is sometimes imagined. Seventeenth-century maternal mortality in England is believed to have peaked during the reign of Charles II at 15.7 per 1,000 births, a rate that would be quite high even in the modern developing world: the figure is similar to that estimated for Niger in 2000, and the corresponding figure for Nigeria was 8 in 1,000.[16]

Within a few days of the child's birth, it would be brought to the parish church for christening, as described in the diary of the London lawyer John Greene in March 1644:

My eldest son . . . was baptized on Friday the 15th . . . by my uncle, Doctor Jermyn [a clergyman], in the house. . . . My own father and my Father Jermyn and my Grandmother Blanchard were gossips [godparents]. My Father Jermyn would have had it named John Alexander, but my father had no great mind to it, so it was named only John. I had a great banquet; stood me in about £4. I had not much company. Goodwife Aylett should have nursed him, but she came to town and fell sick, so we sent her down, and she commended one Goodwife Smith, whom we used, and gave 15s. a month. . . . On the last of this month my wife came down to dinner . . . [April] 3rd. My wife at lecture [sermon] and churched.[17]

Customarily, three godparents spoke for the child at the baptismal font, two of them being of the same sex as the child; this practice, dating from the Middle Ages, traditionally symbolized the Holy Trinity. The christening marked the child's public admission into the community of the church and was also the occasion for the bestowal of a name, with the name of one of the godparents or of some blood relative often being chosen. Middle names were rare—and Greene's father evidently didn't think much of this innovation.

The baptism was recorded in the parish register. Although baptism normally took place at church, it might be performed at home if there were fears that the child might not survive—or if the family were outside of the religious mainstream and wanted the child baptized into their own church. The biological parents had minimal involvement in the baptismal ceremony, but like John Greene, they might host a feast afterward to commemorate the event.

According to the traditional practices of the English church, a few weeks after the birth, the mother went to church for a ceremony variously known as "purification," "thanksgiving," or "churching." Traditionally, this ritual had been seen as purifying the woman of the sexual stain associated with her pregnancy, but by the 1600s, the English church had generally reinterpreted it as a ceremony of thanks for her safe delivery from the childbed. Many reformists rejected the ceremony altogether.

Infants and Toddlers   The experience of childhood is again excellently summarized in Comenius:

The Society betwixt Parents and Children

Married persons (by the blessing of God) have issue, and become parents. The father (1) begetteth, and the mother (2) beareth sons (3) and daughters (4)—sometimes twins. The infant (5) is wrapped in swaddling-clothes (6), is laid in a cradle (7), is suckled by the mother with her breasts (8) and fed with pap (9). Afterwards it learneth to go by a standing stool (10), playeth with rattles (11), and beginneth to speak. As it beginneth to grow older, it is accustomed to piety (12) and labour (13), and is chastised (14) if it be not dutiful. Children owe to parents reverence and service. The father maintaineth his children by taking pains (15).[18]

Figure 3.3 Parents and children (Comenius 1887).

Human infants are entirely dependent on adult care, which in the seventeenth century meant care by an adult woman. Children were normally breast-fed for their first year or so. In most cases, the mother did this, but a woman of means might choose to hire a "wet-nurse" instead. Many people criticized the use of wet-nurses: not only did moralists decry the practice, but also, in 1628, Elizabeth Clinton, countess of Lincoln, published a treatise encouraging mothers to breast-feed their own children. A wet-nurse needed to be lactating, so she would necessarily also have given birth recently and either had lost the child or was willing to take on a second one for the sake of the extra income. There were alternatives to breast-feeding—a leather nipple might be attached to a cow's horn to provide a feeding bottle—but these were only implemented in cases of medical need.

To clothe the infant, a linen cloth or "clout" was laid through the legs as a diaper, and the child was laid in "swaddling"—bands of cloth that were wrapped around the child in the fashion of a mummy, leaving only the face exposed. There were multiple reasons behind this practice. At a theoretical level, it was traditionally believed that swaddling helped the limbs to grow straight. More realistically, swaddling kept the infant insulated against the drafty environment of the Stuart home, as well as facilitating infant care for the woman, who probably had many other tasks to perform

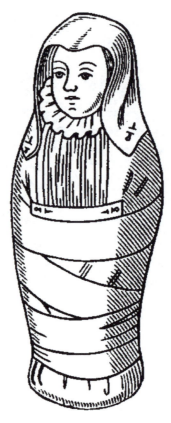

Figure 3.4 An infant in swaddling clothes (Clinch 1910).

while keeping an eye on the baby. By the end of the century, John Locke
was arguing against the practice.

By about four months, the upper part of the infant's swaddling would
be left off to allow mobility for the arms. At about a year, the child was
weaned from breast-feeding onto soft pap and eventually to solid foods.
At this point, the child was learning to walk, and the swaddling was
replaced by a long gown (known as "coats") that still provided warmth
but also allowed the child to move about—while retaining convenient
access to the "clout" when necessary. In many cases, the coats had long
bands sewn in at the shoulders. These imitated the look of old-fashioned
adult gowns with hanging sleeves, but simultaneously served as a child-
harness when needed—and could be tied to the woman's apron-strings
when she needed her hands free. The child also wore a bonnet similar to a
woman's coif, which again provided warmth.

In 1671, Jane Sharpe, having practiced as a midwife for 30 years, gave some general advice on the handling of infants and young children:

The midwife must handle it very gently and wash the body with warm wine; when it is dry, roll it up with soft cloths and lay it in the cradle. But in the swaddling of it be sure that all parts be bound up in their due place and order without any crookedness or rugged foldings, for infants are tender twigs, and as you use them, so they shall grow straight or crooked . . . Keep it not waking longer than it will, but use means to provoke it to sleep, by rocking it in the cradle and singing lullabies to it; carry it often in the arms, and dance it, to keep it from rickets and other diseases. Let it suck not too much at once, but often suckle as it can digest it. . . . Give it some pap of barley bread steeped a while in water and then boiled in milk . . . and thus they should be dieted till they breed teeth. . . . The stronger the child is, the sooner he is ready to be weaned, some at twelve months old, some not till fifteen or eighteen months; you may stay two years if you please, but use the child to other foods by degrees, till it be acquainted with it. . . . I cannot tell which may do most hurt: too much play, as children are prone to, will overheat the blood, and want of play and idleness will make them dull. Some parents are too fond of their children, and leave them to their own wills; some are too froward [ill-tempered], and dishearten their children. The mean is best for them both.

As Sharpe suggests, play was an important part of the life of Stuart children. The typical first toy of the Stuart child was a rattle. The high-end version was made of silver, with bells attached, sometimes a whistle, and a piece of polished coral that could be chewed on while the child was teething. Less expensive versions replaced the coral with a polished boar's tooth. Various types of supports and walkers were fashioned of wood to help the child to stand and walk; the child might also wear a padded roll around the head that protected against the inevitable stumbles of the toddler.

The naturalist Francis Willughby in the 1660s described some of the entertainments of young children:

The first things children play with are:

1. Whistles . . .
2. Rattles, made of round pieces of wood, painted & hollow, with peas or anything in them to rattle.
[3.] Babies, made of clouts [rags] sewed up in the shapes of men, dogs, horses &c., or made of wood painted . . .

When they begin to be able to run up and down, they play at "Put Pin," thrusting 2 pins towards one another till they can thrust them across. He that thrusts them across first wins & takes them up both. They must put or thrust by turns.

"Heads and Points" is when one hides 2 pins in his hand clutched. If both the heads lie one way, they are called Heads, if contrary ways, Points. He asks the other, Heads or Points? If he answer right he must have them. If wrong, as Heads when they are Points, Points when they are Heads, he must give him that held them 2.[19]

Although child mortality was high, most parents were very attached to their children. A striking glimpse of parental feelings is offered in John Evelyn's diary account of a domestic incident in 1654:

My little son Richard, now about 2 years old, as he was fed with broth in the morning, a square but broad and pointed bone, of some part of a rack of mutton, stuck so fast in the child's throat and across his weason [windpipe], that it had certainly choked him, had not my wife and I been at home; for his maid being alone with him above in the nursery, was fallen down in a swoon, when we below (going to prayers) heard an unusual groaning over our head, upon which we went up, and saw them both gasping on the floor, nor had the wench any power to say what the child ailed, or call for any help . . . The poor babe now near expiring, I hold its head down, incite it to vomit, it had no strength. In this despair, and my wife almost as dead as the child, and near despair . . . it pleased God, that on the sudden effort, and as it were struggling his last for life, he cast forth a bone . . . O my gracious God, out of what a tender fear and sad heart, into what joy did thy goodness now revive us.[20]

In addition to learning basic physical skills, the toddler would also begin to learn the fundamentals of religious belief: by age five, a child was expected to have learned the Lord's Prayer, the Ten Commandments, the Creed, and some basic prayers for daily use. By law, the parish priest was required to provide weekly catechism on Sundays for the local children, in addition to the expectation of religious instruction at home from the parents. Children also learned the fundamentals of etiquette, so that they would be ready to function in the world of adults. The following verses from a children's primer give an idea of the expectations:

When down to the table thy parents shall sit,
Be ready in place for purpose most fit.
Be meek in thy carriage, stare none in the face,
First hold up thy hands, and then say thy grace.
The grace being said, if able thou be,
To serve at the table it will become thee.
If thou canst not wait, presume in no case,
But in sitting down to betters give place.
Then suffer each man first served to be,
For it is a point of great courtesy,
Thy tongue suffer not at table to walk,
And do not of any thing jangle or talk.[21]

Raising children necessarily involved some form of discipline. It is difficult to quantify the level of physical punishment used with children, but it was certainly more prevalent than in the modern West: even children who failed to learn their lessons at school might expect to feel the birch rod. Robert Burton in 1622 discussed the topic in terms that suggest widespread reliance on physical discipline, but also an increasing tendency to question its use:

Parents, and such as have the tuition and oversight of children, offend many times in that they are too stern, always threatening, chiding, brawling, whipping, or striking; by means of which their poor children are so disheartened and cowed that they never after have any courage, a merry hour in their lives, or take pleasure in anything.[22]

John Locke at the end of the century felt that moderate use of physical punishments might be of use before a child reached the age of reason, but argued that adults should rely more on psychological inducements with older children.[23] His treatise on education went through numerous editions over the following decades, suggesting that his point of view resonated with many readers.

A spirited image of children's life in the home is offered in the following passage from a Latin dialogue book intended for a grammar-school audience:

C [Cornelia, the sister].	Get up, you errand sluggard.
D [Dionysius, the brother].	Alas, trouble me not.
C.	Will you sleep all the day? Get up I say, that I may make the bed.
D.	What do you say now?
C.	That you get up.
D.	Is it time?
C.	Your Master is gone into the school, and do you ask whether it be time or no?
D.	How long is it since he went in?
C.	A pretty while ago.
D.	What o'clock is it then?
C.	It is about seven . . . Make haste to get you ready, unless you will be knocked.
D.	Who shall do that?
C.	The Master of the school.
D.	Hang the school, and the Master too.

C.	Is that the beginning of your prayers?
D.	What shall I pray? I have more mind to curse.
C.	O most excellent principles of honesty!
D.	I pray you get you gone, and mind your kitchen-business.
C.	That shall be looked to well enough when you are dead and rotten.
D.	I pray you get you gone presently, I cannot put on my clothes whilst you are by.
C.	Are you become so bashful on a sudden?[24]

Childhood: Education and Professional Skills

For their first few years, all children were similarly dressed, under the care of women, and learning more or less the same repertoire of basic skills. At about age six, the experience of boys and girls diverged substantially. At this point, boys began wearing miniature versions of men's clothing and started learning the skills that would be expected of them as adult men. For most boys, this meant beginning to assist in the father's work: even a five-year-old was ready to help sweep the shop floor or scare birds away from the newly planted fields.

For boys of more privileged standing, this was the age at which formal schooling began. The typical first stage was the "petty school," at which children learned reading, writing, and basic numeracy. The traditional vehicle for learning letters was the hornbook, a piece of wood to which was pasted a printed sheet of paper with the alphabet, the Lord's Prayer, and sample combinations of letters; over the paper was tacked a thin transparent sheet of horn to protect it. But this was an age of educational experimentation, at least among some educators, who felt that the traditional modes of schooling did not work for all children. The educational theorist Charles Hoole offers a glimpse of some alternative approaches:

Some have got twenty-four piece of ivory cut in the shape of dice, with a letter engraven upon each of them, and with these have played at vacant hours with a child, till he hath known them all distinctly. . . . Some likewise have had pictures and letters printed . . . on the back side of a pack of cards, to entice children, that naturally love that sport, to the love of learning their books.[25]

Most children at petty schools were boys, but there were a few girls, and a small number of schools took only girls. Petty schools could be

Figure 3.5 A horn book (Godfrey 1903).

found in or near most communities. Formal schoolhouses did exist, but many schools were held in rooms rented for the purpose. The crucial component of the petty school was the master. Ideally, he was a university graduate with a bachelor's degree, and in theory all teachers were supposed to be licensed by the diocese. In practice, anyone who possessed the skills might set up a school if he could find scholars. Some petty schools were run by women, and in many rural parishes, the priest taught promising local boys. Charges were usually modest, and some schools even had endowments that allowed children to attend without charge.[26]

Nonetheless, only a minority of families considered it important or practical to have their children learn to read. Historical literacy is difficult to measure, in part because it is difficult to define—there was a broad spectrum of facility with the written word. Modern estimates suggest that in the middle part of the century, perhaps about 30 percent of men and about

10 percent of women may have attained at least basic literacy. Literacy rates were significantly higher in the towns, particularly in London: estimates suggest that about half the population in the larger towns and almost three-fifths the population in London had some literacy.[27]

The next stage of education, typically beginning somewhere around age eight, and possibly continuing until about age 15, was the grammar school, which was exclusively the preserve of boys. "Grammar" in this case meant Latin grammar: the chief subject of study was Latin language and literature (and sometimes a bit of Greek), still widely regarded as the foundation of all higher learning. This seemingly archaic system actually functioned much like a liberal arts education today: students read and wrote about a canon of "great literature" and in doing so acquired a discipline of thought and expression that gave them the intellectual tools they needed to fulfill positions of leadership in their society. Some grammar schools also offered additional instruction in more contemporary subjects such as modern languages and geography.

A portrait of a seventeenth-century grammar school is offered by Comenius:

A School

A school (1) is a shop, in which young wits are fashioned to virtue, and it is distinguished into Forms. The Master (2) sitteth in a chair (3); the scholars (4) in forms (5); he teacheth, they learn. Some things are writ down before them with chalk on a

Figure 3.6 A schoolroom (Comenius 1887).

table (6). Some sit at a table, and write (7): he mendeth their faults. Some stand and rehearse things committed to memory (9). Some talk together (10), and behave themselves wantonly and carelessly; these are chastised with a ferula [paddle] (11) and a rod (12).[28]

The typical grammar school schedule ran from about 8 A.M. to 11, breaking for dinner and then reassembling from one to five in the afternoon (but ending earlier in the dark season of the winter). Schools commonly met from Monday to Saturday morning, with Saturday afternoon and Sunday off, and perhaps Thursday afternoon as well. The "forms" mentioned by Comenius were benches: students of various ages were taught simultaneously in a single room, so each level of student was seated on a different bench. Many of the smaller grammar schools included the function of a petty school as well: the master taught the advanced students, and a younger "usher" was delegated to instruct the younger ones.

Grammar schools were less widespread than petty schools, but they could be found in most market towns. As with the petty schools, most students had to pay tuition, but there were also endowed scholarships that made grammar-school education available to some poorer boys who showed intellectual promise. Upper-class families generally preferred not to have their children rubbing shoulders with commoners, so they tended to send them to more exclusive schools or have them educated at home by tutors.

At about age 16 or 17, a select few boys continued on to university at Oxford or Cambridge. University education was much less common, and less important, than it is today. Some boys went to university in order to prepare for a career in the church: this was one of the ways in which a bright boy of modest origins might move up in the world, and there were scholarships and "work-study" arrangements available to make a university education possible for boys of this sort. The universities also served as a sort of finishing school for boys of the upper classes, who might go for a few years without subjecting themselves to the requirements for an actual degree.

The basic course of university study lasted four years, culminating in the degree of Bachelor of Arts, which was considered an appropriate level of education for a schoolteacher. The curriculum at this level focused heavily on the classics in Greek and Latin, including Homer, Aristotle, Ovid, Virgil, and Cicero, with subject matter relating to grammar, logic, history, and science. The Master of Arts required three additional years. Beyond that there were advanced degrees available in civil law, medicine, and divinity, requiring an additional four years or more, depending on the subject. Some Englishmen chose to pursue advanced studies on the Continent, particularly in areas such as medicine, where Italian universities were more highly reputed than Oxford or Cambridge.

The alternative English institution for higher education was the Inns of Court in London. These residential institutions provided a venue in which boys could obtain instruction in the law. Knowledge of the law was naturally of importance to those pursuing legal careers, but it was also a valuable skill for the landowning class in general, and many young gentlemen spent at least a year or two at the Inns gaining a grounding in the complexities of English law.

In addition to these longstanding institutions, important towns also supported thriving communities of tutors outside of the formal education system, who offered instruction in a variety of disciplines and skills, including modern languages, geography, mathematics, sciences, fencing, and dancing.

Vocational Training
Most boys never went to petty school, and even those who did were more likely to go on to work than to further schooling. Boys up to the age of 14 or so might do various kinds of light work, and by age 14, they were integrated in earnest into the working world. This process might take one of several forms. The sons of established urban tradesmen or craftsmen often were apprenticed to some shop outside of the home. The duration of apprenticeship depended on the trade—seven years was the official minimum, but not all apprentices completed their term. The apprentice, like a servant, was equivalent to the child of his master, who had legal authority over and responsibility for his apprentice. Conditions of apprenticeship were regulated by the urban guilds, which imposed rigorous codes of conduct—although these were not always obeyed. The terms of the apprenticeship were formalized in a written contract between the master and the boy's father, and they invariably included some sort of payment to the master for taking the boy into his keeping. The apprentice worked for room and board and perhaps a bit of pocket money, but the most important benefit was the opportunity to learn a trade that would support him in later life; apprenticeship was a privileged position that offered significant opportunities for later economic advancement. However, formal apprenticeship was in decline during the 1600s, reflecting the decline of the guild system itself: industrial production was shifting away from the old medieval towns and toward newer urban and rural centers that were not bound by existing guild structures. At the beginning of the century, about 15 percent of the population of London may have been apprentices, but by the end the figure had fallen to 5 percent.[29]

A common alternative to apprenticeship for a teenage boy was service or some other less structured form of employment; in fact, an apprentice was sometimes hard to distinguish from a servant. The exact nature of the employment varied greatly depending on the status of the employer and of the boy. A privileged teenager might secure a position in the employ of a prominent landowner, merchant, or craftsman, learning skills and making social connections that would help him on the path to a prosperous adulthood. Most boys were more likely to end up as ordinary servants or day-laborers. Even these boys learned some skills in their work that would improve their earning capacity over time, but they were unlikely ever to rise out of the laboring class. In many cases, the boy remained with his parents: statistics from Swindon in 1697 show two-thirds of those aged 15 to 19 living with their parents, and half of them lived with parents in their early twenties.[30]

A glimpse of the life of girls is offered by Lady Fanshawe, recall- **Girls** ing her childhood days as Ann Harrison:

> It is necessary to say something of my mother's education of me, which was with all the advantages that time afforded, both for working all sorts of fine works with my needle, and learning French, singing, lute, the virginals, and dancing; and not-withstanding I learned as well as most did, yet was I wild to that degree, that the hours of my beloved recreation took up too much of my time; for I loved riding in the first place, and running, and all active pastimes; and in fine I was that which we graver people call a "hoyting girl." But to be just to myself, I never did mischief to myself or [other] people, nor one immodest action or word in my life; but skipping and activity was my delight. But upon my mother's death, I then began to reflect, and as an offering to her memory I flung away those little childishnesses that had formerly possessed me, and by my father's command took upon me the charge of his house and family.

Lady Fanshawe had been fortunate in her privileged upbringing, but was not atypical in her love of childish sports or in the responsibilities placed on her at a young age. Some girls attended petty schools, but they were not admitted into grammar schools or institutions of higher learning. Privileged girls like the young Ann Harrison might have tutors or attend a girls' school to give them something analogous to a grammar-school education. These schools often emphasized French over Latin and included instruction in "feminine" skills such as those mentioned by Lady Fanshawe. By the latter part of the century, a number of people were beginning to advocate and promote better schooling for girls. John Locke argued in favor of a more academic education for women, given their responsibility for early childhood education.[31] One mistress of a girl's school, Bathsua Makin, published a vigorous defense of female education in 1673; at Makin's school outside of London, girls could pay a tuition of £20 a year to learn Latin, Greek, Hebrew, French, Spanish, and Italian, as well as writing, arithmetic, music, dancing, and needlework.[32]

Most girls received no formal education. Once a girl was old enough, she was expected to begin helping her mother with household duties, which not only facilitated the mother's work, but also taught the girl the domestic skills she would be expected to have mastered by the time she reached adulthood. As a teenager, she would leave home to work as a servant or laborer. As with boys, the nature of the employment depended on the girl's social standing. Ordinary girls could expect only menial positions involving fairly demanding physical labor, whereas a girl of more privileged standing, already educated in the appropriate personal graces and skills, might secure a more promising position, perhaps as a companion to a well-to-do woman, doing only very light work and being chiefly responsible for keeping her mistress company. The girl's years of service were an opportunity to learn skills and broaden her social network, until such time as she found a husband and set up a household of her own.

Aside from her unusual level of education, the story of the prolific author Hannah Woolley was in many ways typical. Woolley had been a schoolmistress, governess, and wife of an usher at a boys' school. At age 52, she recalled her early years, learning feminine skills at home, expanding those skills through service, and ultimately finding a suitable marriage:

My mother and elder sisters were very well skilled in physic and chirurgery, from whom I learned a little, and at the age of seventeen I had the fortune to belong to a noble lady of this kingdom, till I married, which was at twenty-four years. . . . She finding my genius, and being of a charitable temper to do good amongst her poor neighbors, I had her purse at command to buy what ingredients might be required to make balsams, salves, ointments. . . . When I was married to Mr. Woolley, we lived together at Newport Pond in Essex, near Saffron Walden, seven years, my husband having been Master of that Free School fourteen years before. We having many boarders, my skill was often exercised among them, for often times they got mishaps when they were playing.[33]

Girls rarely went into a trade that involved apprenticeship, although there were exceptions. Leonard Wheatcroft's diary in 1681 notes,

Upon September 5, 1681 I had occasion to go to Chesterfield, where I met with a bone-lace-weaver, with whom I bargained to take a daughter of mine apprentice, Elizabeth by name. So for three pounds ten shillings we agreed, and bound she was . . . for four years.[34]

The actual experience of a day in the life of a girl is outlined in Hannah Woolley's instructions to schoolgirls:

Rise early; having dressed yourself with decency and cleanliness, prostrate yourself in all humility upon your bended knees before God Almighty . . . Having said your prayers, then on your knees ask your parents' blessing; and what they shall appoint for your breakfast, do you by no means dislike or grumble at. Waste not too much time in eating thereof, but hasten to school . . . When you come to school, salute your misteress in a reverent manner, and be sure to mind what she enjoys you to do or observe . . . Returning from school, make haste home, not gaping on every idle object you meet with by the way. Coming into the house, apply yourself immediately to your parents, and having saluted them according to your duty, acquaint them with what proficiency you have made in your learning that day; be not absent when dinner is on the table, but present when grace is said, and sit not down before you have done your obeisance to your parents and the company then present . . . Going to bed, make no noise that may disturb any of the family, but more especially your parents, and before you betake yourself to rest, commit yourself into the hands of the Almighty.[35]

Entry into the rights and responsibilities of adulthood was a gradual process. Confirmation, the ritual by which a **Adulthood** child became an adult member of the church, generally took place around age 14. At 16, a boy became subject to service in the military, and all children became legally responsible for their own actions. Full entry into all the rights of adulthood came at age 21.[36]

Arrival at adulthood also marked the escape from the most dangerous years of mortality. Life expectancy at birth was about 35 to 40 years, but this figure was heavily skewed by the high rates of death among infants and children. An individual who lived to 21 had a good chance of living into old age, and the life expectancy for a 30-year old was about another 30 years.

For most people, adulthood involved getting married and setting up an independent home of their own. Yet contact between parents and children normally continued, and a solicitous parent might occasionally try to help out, as Elizabeth Freke's father did after years of watching his daughter suffer from a neglectful and grasping husband:

August 15. And on my looking a little melancholy on some past reflections, he fancied it was my want of money; and my dear father, without saying a word to me, went up into his closet and brought me down presently in two bags two hundred pounds, which £200 he charged me to keep private from my husband's knowledge, and buy needles and pins with it. This was very kind in my father; and which the very next post I informed Mr. Freke of, who presently found a use for it . . .

January 1. My dear father sent me . . . a hundred pounds for a New Year's gift, it being my unhappy birthday, and ordered me that if Mr. Freke meddled with it, it should be lost, or he to answer it, with the . . . interest, to my son. But Mr. Freke took it from me.[37]

Elizabeth herself was later greatly distressed that her only son and his bride went to live near his wife's parents, a hundred miles away from her, complaining that "they had ten children [and] might have as well trusted me with one at least to have lived in twenty miles of me."[38]

The most important rite of passage into adulthood was marriage, which marked the point at which individuals **Marriage** moved from a state of subordination within someone else's family into positions of authority in households of their own. Marriage ages were not greatly different from those common today. Technically, girls could marry at age 12 and boys at 14, but marriages under the age of 21 required the consent of the parent or guardian. In practice, such young marriages were extremely rare. For aristocrats, the typical ages were around 19 for women and 24 for men. For most people, marriage had to wait until the individual was economically capable of supporting a family. This meant that the typical age for a first marriage was around 26 for women and a year or two older for men.[39] A significant minority of people, particularly among the poor, never married at all—perhaps about a fifth of the overall population.

A young person's freedom in choosing a spouse varied inversely with their status in society. Royal marriages were governed by affairs of state, and aristocratic marriages were important in consolidating the economic and social status of the families. Ordinary couples were still expected to secure their parents' consent before marrying, but it was normal for them to initiate the choice of partner. Nonetheless, across society, there were strong cultural and practical pressures constraining that choice. Marriages that crossed substantial class boundaries were discouraged, and choosing the wrong spouse could lead to a substantial deterioration in a person's economic status. A typical perspective on the choice of partner is offered by a treatise of 1696:

To complete a true and happy marriage are required virtuous inclinations, hearty love, and true liking, so that they may both be of the same mind, and have one and the same interest; and to make this up, there must be suitable agreement in ages, humours, breeding, religion, families, and fortune, which when they concur, we may expect all the satisfaction this world can afford; but when any of these are wanting, marriage but seldom proves comfortable.[40]

The complex realities of partner choice and parental approval can be seen in a memorandum by one disappointed parent in 1649:

Know all men that I, Sir John Oglander, Knight, do acknowledge that the match between Sir Robert Eyton's son and my daughter Bridget was never with my approbation or good liking. It was her importunity that induced me to give way unto it, and she was resolved to have him whatsoever became of her . . . I confess I never liked Sir Robert, or his estate, a swearing, profane man. I beseech God to bless them and to make her happy, which I much doubt.[41]

Courtship between young couples tended to follow established cultural patterns. Leonard Wheatcroft, a Derbyshire yeoman, composed a lively narrative of his own courtship. He first heard of his future wife Elizabeth Hawley in 1655 at a "wake" (a parish festival), where he met one of her relatives, who spoke highly of her. Later in the day, he met the girl herself. At the time, he was 28, a typical age for a first marriage, but she was rather young at 18. Elizabeth was not the first girl Leonard had courted—there had been at least two before—but the previous romances evidently had led nowhere.

Leonard and Elizabeth seem to have fancied each other from the start, for they subsequently exchanged a series of letters—his tone is buoyantly romantic, hers at first rather more circumspect. A suitor was expected to visit the young woman's household for supervised time together, as well as a chance to win the favor of the family: Leonard spent time with Elizabeth at her family's home and obtained permission from her parents to take her to other local festivals. He described one of these visits to the Hawley household:

Coming to her father's house again, I stayed all night again with my dear and chief delight, using unto her many sweet expressions of my love. On the next morrow I set forth to come home, and she like a loving and kind soul came awayward with me about a mile or more. Then like two loving souls we sat down where many passengers [passers-by] came by and viewed us, yet nevertheless they did no whit hinder our discourse . . . At last we arose and lovingly saluted each other and departed for that time, wishing many joys to each other.[42]

Although Wheatcroft's account does not mention any exchange of gifts during the courtship, these were also a common feature of the process— the man in particular was expected to show his generosity and economic prosperity in this way. The Yorkshire farmer Henry Best in 1642 offered a detailed budget for a suitor:

The third time that he visiteth, he perhaps giveth her a 10s. piece of gold, or a ring of that price, or perhaps a 20s. piece, or a ring of that price; then the next time, or next after that, a pair of gloves of 6s. 8d. or 10s. a pair; and after that, each other time some conceited toy or novelty of less value.[43]

Eventually, the young man might seek permission from the woman's father to ask for her hand in marriage. For Wheatcroft, as for many suitors, this appears to have been the easy part. The couple had evidently decided to marry by the middle of 1656, but the marriage had to wait another year while Leonard negotiated with Elizabeth's father over the financial arrangements. Marriage was a major economic undertaking, and among families with any kind of property, there were invariably earnest negotiations over the financial arrangements of the marriage contract. Both Elizabeth and her father came to Leonard's home in Ashcroft to have a look at his estates, and the two men spent the better part of a year wrangling over the marriage contract. A woman was expected to bring some form of property into the marriage as a dowry, and the man was also expected to bring some amount of property to the marriage, of which a contracted component would go to the woman if she were made a widow. For young couples, securing this property depended on the goodwill of their families, which constituted an important point of leverage for enforcing parental consent. In Wheatcroft's case, the contract was not signed until a week after Easter 1657.

Already during the Christmas season in 1656, Leonard and Elizabeth had set a wedding date of May 20. Prior to the wedding, the proposed union had to be announced in the couple's respective parish churches on three successive Sundays, to allow any potential impediments to the marriage to be raised; Leonard and Elizabeth had done this back in October 1656. Alternatively, a couple could pay to receive a marriage license from their bishop—this option was often chosen by aristocratic families who preferred not to have their family matters publicized by announcement in church.

Mainstream belief and practice insisted that the wedding had to be performed by a clergyman, and it was also considered highly irregular, though still binding, to perform the ceremony anywhere but publicly in a church. The bride and groom were expected to wear their best clothing—ideally a newly made outfit: shortly after their marriage contract was signed, Leonard and Elizabeth went to a nearby town market to buy wool and linen fabric for their wedding outfits. On the day of the wedding, the couple were decked out with ribbons, flowers, and greenery; similar festive accessories were worn by the wedding guests; and the site of the wedding and wedding feast were likewise decorated. A few friends of the couple assisted as bridesmaids and groomsmen.

The wedding ritual as prescribed by the church involved an exchange of vows, and the groom placed a wedding ring on his bride's hand. The married woman took her husband's surname, and the marriage was recorded in the parish register. After Leonard and Elizabeth's ceremony, there was a typical wedding banquet—he tells us there were 14 tables for guests that filled up two or three times during the course of the day, as well as various entertainments that included bell-ringing, horse-racing, and a form of jousting at a target known as a "quintain."[44]

Sex Contemporary morality frowned on sex outside of wedlock, which was punishable through the church courts. The seriousness of the punishment varied considerably. Adultery by a married woman was regarded as a very grave offense because it could call into question the legitimacy of the offspring of the marriage. Other forms of nonmarital sex did not threaten the fabric of heredity, although they were still punishable by law. Overall, the illegitimacy rate appears to have been about 1 in 50 births. Sex between a couple who had contracted to marry but were not yet wedded was officially disapproved, but in practice it was acknowledged as a common and minor form of misconduct. Prenuptial pregnancies, in which the couple married after initiating sexual activity, may have accounted for some 25 to 30 percent of births.[45]

Not all sexual activity was restricted to male–female procreative sex. Homosexuality was widely recognized as present in society, if largely surreptitious—still classed as felonies, homosexual acts could carry the death penalty.[46] Sexual aids can be documented from at least the 1660s. For heterosexual partners who wished to avoid pregnancy, prophylactics such as condoms were known: examples recovered by excavations at Dudley Castle in the west Midlands were made from animal intestines. Contraceptive and abortive recipes were also among the stock in trade of the practitioners of folk medicine.[47]

The specifics of one man's sexual life are richly documented in Samuel Pepys's diary. The diarist recorded numerous examples of sexual encounters with women aside from his wife—usually women of lower social status who had in some way been won over through gifts. In Stuart society, these sorts of encounters were the typical cause of illegitimate offspring, and concerns over pregnancy seemed to shape these relationships in the case of Pepys: the women generally restricted the interaction to sexual stimulation in forms that fell short of actual coitus, though Pepys apparently wished for more. In the diary Pepys even recounts his sexual fantasies and a passing obsession with a pamphlet of French pornography— "a mighty lewd book, but yet not amiss for a sober man once to read over to inform himself in the villany of the world."[48]

Divorce Divorce was extremely rare and almost impossible to obtain, requiring a special act of Parliament. Judicial separation was available through the church courts on such grounds as adultery, violence, or desertion, but this did not permit the couple to remarry.[49] Widowhood, however, was fairly common, given high mortality rates, so individuals who lived to old age were likely to have more than one spouse during their lifetime, and many families included not just two parents and their children, but stepsiblings as well. Widowhood could be an advantageous position for a woman because it was the one situation in which she could truly be said to hold property in her own right: a woman was normally entitled to a third of her husband's property and a third of the fruits of her husband's landholdings, retaining her right to these even if she remarried. However, for a woman who lacked property, widowhood could mean extreme economic vulnerability because of her relatively limited earning potential: for such women, remarriage was often a matter of survival.

Old Age About a tenth of the overall population was over 60, the age at which a person was considered to have passed out of their prime productive years; this was the point at which men were no longer subject to military service or jury duty. The actual experience of old age was heavily shaped by class and gender. In principle, the elderly were considered to deserve special respect in light of their age and experience. In practice, an old person's actual quality of life depended on access to the means of subsistence. Those who had the resources—cash, land, or other sources of income—might at this age retire from their working life. But for many people, growing too old for the workforce meant loss of income, impoverishment, and hardship. Elderly women were especially vulnerable to poverty.

Married elderly parents rarely lived with married children, although widowed parents might. Care of elderly parents often fell on single children—unmarried daughters, in particular. There were also some charitable institutions for the support of the elderly poor. Known as "hospitals," these communities had originated in the Middle Ages and were in many ways similar to monasteries: inhabitants lived in monastic-style buildings (sometimes actual monasteries, converted after the Reformation), wore uniform clothing, and were required to adhere to strict codes of conduct. In spite of the regimented lifestyle, there was always plenty of demand for the security and stability provided by these residences, which were chronically inadequate to meet the demand among the indigent elderly.

Death
Death, when it came, was a much more familiar event than it generally is for Westerners today. Mortality rates were high for people in all age groups, and people rarely died in isolation from their social environment. No person could reach adulthood without having seen multiple corpses in their day, and by age 30, many people if not most had lost at least one parent, spouse, or child.

Death by sickness or old age normally happened at home. The family were expected to notify the parish sexton, who was required to ring the parish bell to mark the impending death. After death, the corpse would be washed, clad in a shirt, and wrapped with sprigs of rosemary in a shroud or winding sheet—a large cloth (often chosen from among the household bedlinens) that covered the entire body. The wrapped corpse would be laid out on a table in the house, so that friends and relatives could come to pay their respects and sit with the body; the visitors were typically given refreshments by the family. Embalming was used only by the wealthy, who had the means to afford this expensive procedure and who often needed to preserve the body long enough to make arrangements for a suitably elaborate funeral.

Between the moment of death and the time of burial, it was common to have one or more people watch over the corpse—partly a holdover from earlier Catholic traditions and partly a mark of respect and a practical means of ensuring that nothing went amiss with the deceased's earthly remains. Samuel Pepys mentioned watching over a corpse in 1661:

My uncle's corpse in a coffin standing upon joint stools in the chimney in the hall; but it begun to smell so I caused it to be set forth in the yard all night, and watched by my aunt.[50]

In most cases, the body would be buried within a few days, before putrefaction could set in; it was often buried on the very day the person died. When it was time for the funeral, the parish bell was rung again, and the corpse was laid on a bier, covered with a cloth called a pall, and carried to the churchyard, where it was met by the priest who would perform the burial ritual. Before being covered with the pall, the corpse might be laid in a wooden coffin; this usually belonged to the parish and was only a temporary housing for the body, used for all the parish funerals. Only the wealthy could afford a personal coffin that would be buried with the deceased.

The body was typically laid in an unmarked grave in the yard on the south side of the church (suicides and excommunicates were officially not allowed to be buried within the churchyard at all). Grave monuments were normally used only for people of very high standing, who were buried inside the church itself. A few outdoor graves had markers of wood or stone, but headstones were still rare as of the second half of the century and did not become common until the 1700s. After centuries of interments, many churchyards were getting quite full, so sometimes digging a new grave required moving the bones from prior burials into a charnel house.

The family of the deceased might mark the occasion by hosting a funeral banquet after the ceremony and possibly by distributing mourning accessories (such as sprigs of rosemary, black ribbons, or pins) to those who attended the burial. Family and friends were expected to observe a period of mourning, perhaps lasting up to a year, during which they wore black mourning attire. The funeral might also include the distribution of a "dole"—money or food given to the poor. This custom was another hold-over from the Middle Ages, serving both as a form of almsgiving and to draw larger numbers of people to the ceremony. The father of yeoman Adam Martindale at his death in 1658 had left such spending entirely up to his children:

Considering how good a father he had been, and how fashionably he . . . had lived among his neighbors, we thought it convenient to bring him home handsomely out of his own, and so we did. For all that came to the house to fetch his corpse thence (beggars not excepted) were entertained with good meat, piping hot, and strong ale in good plenty.[51]

Death also involved some legal ramifications: the burial was recorded in the parish register; an inventory was taken of the deceased's goods; if there was a will, it was implemented by the chosen executor; and if the circumstances of the death were at all dubious—whether by apparent accident or by known foul play—the coroner was called in to inspect the body and make a report to the authorities.[52]

Traditionally, funeral arrangements had been in the hands of the family and church, but by the end of the century, wealthy Englishmen were turning to the assistance of hired "undertakers," who undertook to handle these matters on the family's behalf. In death as in life, the English of the seventeenth century were entering a recognizably modern world.

Figure 3.7 A burial procession (Jackson 1885).

NOTES

1. Johannes Amos Comenius, *Orbis Sensualium Pictus,* trans. Charles Hoole (London: J. Kirton, 1659). This illustrated vocabulary book for children learning Latin was originally published in a German version in 1658. Comenius's pioneering work was soon translated into multiple European languages, and English versions and revisions continued to be issued into the 1800s.

2. Comenius, *Orbis,* 240–41.

3. William Mather, *The Young Man's Companion* (London: S. Clarke, 1699), 135.

4. Elizabeth Freke, *The Remembrances of Elizabeth Freke 1671–1714,* ed. Raymond A. Anselment (London: Cambridge University Press for the Royal Historical Society, 2001), 39.

5. Ann, Lady Fanshawe, *The Memoirs of Ann Lady Fanshawe* (London and New York: John Lane, 1907), 5–6.

6. Keith Wrightson, *Earthly Necessities: Economic Lives in Early Modern Britain* (New Haven: Yale University Press, 2000), 198.

7. Fanshawe, *Memoirs,* 19–20.

8. Samuel Pepys, *The Diary of Samuel Pepys,* ed. Robert Latham and William Matthews (Berkeley and Los Angeles: University of California Press, 1983), 7.379.

9. Pepys, *Diary,* 9.337. Pepys typically inserts non-English words when discussing sexual matters.

10. Pepys, *Diary,* 9.439.

11. Ralph A. Houlbrooke, *The English Family, 1450–1700* (London and New York: Longman, 1984), 173.

12. On servants, see Henry Best, *The Farm and Memorandum Books of Henry Best of Elmswell, 1642,* ed. Donald Woodward, Records of Social and Economic History New Series 8 (London: Oxford University Press for the British Academy, 1984), 138ff.; Guy Miege, *The New State of England under our Present Monarch King William III* (London: R. Clavel, H. Mortlock, and J. Robinson, 1699), 2.168ff.; Hannah Woolley, *The Compleat Servant-Maid* (London: Thomas Passenger, 1691); Hannah Woolley, *The Queen-Like Closet, or a Rich Cabinet Stored with All Manner of Rare Receipts,* 3rd ed. (London: Richard Lowndes, 1675), 332ff.

13. Comenius, *Orbis,* 146–47.

14. E. A. Wrigley and R. S. Schofield, *The Population History of England 1541–1871* (Cambridge, MA: Harvard University Press, 1981), 218; Jeremy Boulton, *Neighbourhood and Society: A London Suburb in the Seventeenth Century* (Cambridge: Cambridge University Press, 1987), 18.

15. Freke, *Remembrances*, 41.

16. David Cressy, *Birth, Marriage, and Death. Ritual, Religion, and the Life-Cycle in Tudor and Stuart England* (Oxford: Oxford University Press, 1997), 30. On childbirth and women's health in general, see R. Bunworth, *The Doctresse* (London: printed for Nicolas Bourne, 1656); Nicholas Fonteyn, *The Woman's Doctour* (London: John Blague and Samuel Howes, 1652); John Pechey, *The Compleat Midwifes Practice Enlarged*, 5th ed. (London: H. Rhodes, J. Philips, J. Taylor, and K. Bentley, 1698); John Pechey, *A General Treatise of the Diseases of Maids, Bigbellied Women, Child-bed-women, and Widows* (London: Henry Bonwick, 1696); Jane Sharp, *The Midwives Book* (London: Simon Miller, 1671).

17. Ralph A. Houlbrooke, ed. *English Family Life, 1576–1716: An Anthology from Diaries* (Oxford and New York: Basil Blackwell, 1988), 110.

18. Comenius, *Orbis*, 244–45. On the lives of children, see also John Pechey, *A General Treatise of the Diseases of Infants and Children* (London: R. Wellington, 1697); Miege, *New State*, 2.167–68ff.

19. Francis Willughby, *Francis Willughby's Book of Games: A Seventeenth-Century Treatise on Sports, Games, and Pastimes*, ed. David Cram, Jeffrey L. Forgeng, and Dorothy Johnston (Aldershot: Ashgate Press, 2003), 217–18. For more on children's toys and games, see chapter 8.

20. John Evelyn, *The Diary of John Evelyn*, ed. E. S. de Beer (London, New York, Toronto: Oxford University Press, 1959), 356; cf. Paul Seaver, *Wallington's World: A Puritan Artisan in Seventeenth-Century London* (Stanford: Stanford University Press, 1985), 87, 89.

21. *The English School-Master Completed* (London: John Hawkins and Ichabod Dawks, 1692), 71.

22. Cited Stone, *Family*, 169; see also 167ff., 439ff.

23. John Locke, *Some Thoughts Concerning Education*, ed. John W. and Jean S. Yolton (Oxford: Clarendon Press, 1989), 117, 144.

24. Charles Hoole, *Children's Talk* (London: Company of Stationers, 1697), 21ff. On childhood, see also Wrightson, *English Society*, 106ff.

25. Charles Hoole, *The Petty Schoole* (London: Andrew Crook, 1659), 7–8. For other sources on education, see John Brinsley, *Ludus Literarius, or, The Grammar Schoole* (London: Thomas Man, 1612); David Cressy, *Education in Tudor and Stuart England* (London: Edward Arnold, 1975); Charles Hoole, *A New Discovery of the Old Art of Teaching School* (London: Andrew Crook, 1660); John Newton, *The English Academy, or a Brief Introduction to the Seven Liberal Arts* (London: Thomas Passenger, 1677); John Newton, *School Pastime for Young Children, or the Rudiments of Grammar, in an Easie and Delightful Method for Teaching of Children to Read English Distinctly, and Write it Truly* (London: Robert Walton, 1669); John Newton, *The Countrey School-Master, or the Art of Teaching Fair Writing and All the Useful Parts of Practical Arithmetick* (London: Robert Walton, 1673); Wrightson, *English Society*, 184ff.

26. On petty schools, see David Cressy, *Literacy and the Social Order: Reading and Writing in Tudor and Stuart England* (Cambridge: Cambridge University Press, 1980), 35ff.

27. Cressy, *Literacy and the Social Order*, 72–75, 176.

28. Comenius, *Orbis*, 198–99.

29. Houlbrooke, *The English Family*, 173.

30. Houlbrooke, *The English Family*, 173.

31. Stone, *Family*, 345.

32. Bathsua Makin, *An Essay to Revive the Antient Education of Gentlewomen* (London: Thomas Parkhurst, 1673), 42; see also Hannah Woolley, *The Gentlewoman's Companion, or a Guide to the Female Sex* (London: Dorman Newman, 1673), 1; Cressy, *Education in Tudor and Stuart England*, 112–13; Stone, *Family*, 347.

33. Hannah Woolley, *A Supplement to the Queen-Like Closet, or a Little of Everything* (London: Richard Lowndes, 1674), 10–12.

34. Houlbrooke, *English Family Life*, 189.

35. Woolley, *Gentlewoman's Companion*, 17–20. On Woolley, see Woolley, *Gentlewoman's Companion*, 10ff.; Woolley, *Supplement*, 10ff.; Stone, *Family*, 344.

36. William Mather, *The Young Man's Companion* (London: S. Clarke, 1699), 136.

37. Freke, *Remembrances*, 49–50.

38. Freke, *Remembrances*, 231.

39. E. A. Wrigley and R. S. Schofield, *The Population History of England 1541–1871* (Cambridge, MA: Harvard University Press, 1981), 255.

40. N. H., *The Ladies Dictionary* (London: John Dunton, 1694), 198–99, 323.

41. Cited Houlbrooke, *English Family Life*, 18.

42. Leonard Wheatcroft, *The Courtship Narrative of Leonard Wheatcroft, Derbyshire Yeoman*, ed. George Parfitt and Ralph Houlbrooke (Reading: The Whiteknights Press, 1986), 53. On courtship, see also the description in Best, *Farm Books*, 122–23.

43. Best, *Farm Books*, 122–23.

44. Wheatcroft, *Courtship*, 86; John Aubrey, *Three Prose Works: Miscellanies, Remaines of Gentilisme and Judaisme, Observations*, ed. John Buchanan-Brown (Carbondale: Southern Illinois University Press, 1972), 169. On weddings, see also Aubrey, *Three Prose Works*, 168ff.; Best, *Farm Books*, 123.

45. David Cressy, *Birth, Marriage, and Death: Ritual, Religion, and the Life-Cycle in Tudor and Stuart England* (Oxford: Oxford University Press, 1997), 73, 277; G. R. Quaife, *Wanton Wenches and Wayward Wives: Peasants and Illicit Sex in Early Seventeenth Century England* (New Brunswick, NJ: Rutgers University Press, 1979), 56–57.

46. Quaife, *Wanton Wenches*, 175ff.; Stone, *Family*, 492; John Spurr, *England in the 1670s: "This Masquerading Age"* (Oxford: Blackwell, 2000), 185.

47. David Gaimster et al., "The Archaeology of Private Life: The Dudley Castle Condoms," *Post-Medieval Archaeology* 30 (1996): 129–42. Stone, *Family*, 422, 536, and passim.

48. Pepys, *Diary*, 4.230, 234; 5.17, 346, 351; 6.202, 318; 9.58–59, 337ff., 439.

49. On divorce, see Wrightson, *English Society*, 100; Susan Amussen, *An Ordered Society: Gender and Class in Early Modern England* (Oxford and New York: Blackwell, 1988), 57; Mather, *Young Man's Companion*, 136.

50. Pepys, *Diary*, 2.133.

51. Cited Houlbrooke, *The English Family*, 204.

52. On death and burial, see also Clare Gittings, *Death, Burial, and the Individual in Early Modern England* (London and Sydney: Croom Helm, 1984); Aubrey, *Three Prose Works*, 172ff.

4

MATERIAL CULTURE

The material culture of Stuart England can be seen as a part of the fullest flowering of the preindustrial material culture of Europe. By 1600, a highly developed technology was in place, capable of producing a broad range of high-quality goods in substantial numbers: the key differences between what was possible in the 1600s and what became possible in the 1800s lay in automation of repetitive manufacturing tasks, in precision engineering, and in the capacity to mass-produce iron and steel.[1] This chapter begins with the processes of cloth-making and production of ferrous metals (iron and steel) as the two most pivotal points in the technology and economics underlying seventeenth-century material culture.

Based on the number of people involved, cloth-making was without doubt the dominant industry in Stuart England, involving large numbers of both men and women of multiple specializations in the numerous stages from raw material to finished product—perhaps accounting for over a twentieth of the total workforce.[2] Each summer, an enormous quantity of raw wool was generated in the English countryside in the form of fleeces (Gregory King late in the century estimated there were 10 million being produced each year): these fleeces were dirty, tangled, and greasy and needed several stages of processing before their wool could be converted into thread. Washing was the first step: the fleeces were soaked in a lye solution to rid them of dirt and grease. Once they were clean, they could be carded: this involved brushing the fiber between a pair of wire-toothed combs that would untangle them

Cloth-Making

Figure 4.1 Tradesmen in the middle part of the century (Unwin 1904).

and lay them parallel in preparation for spinning. The process of spinning fed the fibers onto a rotating spindle to twist them around each other, while maintaining tension to draw out the twisting fibers into thread. The most old-fashioned way to do this was with a drop-spindle, where tension was created by the weight of the rotating spindle; this method of spinning was rare by the 1600s. For spinning ordinary wool, the usual means was the "great wheel," a form of spinning wheel in which the spindle was attached by a drive belt to a large drive wheel. The spinner gave the large wheel a turn to start the rotation and then walked backward as she spun out the thread. The most complex version of the spinning wheel was the treadle wheel, operated by the spinner's foot as she sat; this form of wheel had been in use for some time, but was only suitable for the finer types of wool.

Spinning was proverbially women's work in the 1600s and was often done at home as a means of supplementing family income; the household

Figure 4.2 Spinning flax fibers into linen thread. The processes are roughly analogous to those for wool: on the left, women are cleaning and combing out the fibers, and on the right, a woman is using a drop spindle; next to her is a spinning wheel (Comenius 1887).

daughters in particular might be expected to contribute to the family coffers this way, which is how unmarried girls came to be known as spinsters. The wool might come from the family farm, but in many cases it was received from an entrepreneur (called a clothier) through a traveling agent, or "factor," who would collect the finished product at the end and pay the woman for her labor.

The weaver might work independently, but again, it was increasingly common for him to be engaged by a factor who provided the thread and collected the woven cloth. The weaver would attach the warp (lengthwise thread) to his loom and then weave the weft (crosswise thread) back and forth through the warp to create the cloth. The weft could follow a number of patterns in going over and under the warp threads, depending on the kind of cloth desired—plain-woven broadcloth, diagonally patterned twill, V-patterned herringbone; the pattern was controlled by pedals at the weaver's feet. After weaving, the cloth was "fulled": this involved agitating it in water with various chemical additives to clean the fabric and fluff out the threads, filling the gaps between them and thickening the cloth. Fulling left the cloth roughly matted, so the cloth then went to a shearman who used a pair of shears to trim the surface.

The material could be dyed at a number of stages in the process. A variety of domestically grown plants yielded dyestuffs, including woad for blue, madder for red, and weld for yellow. Other colors could be achieved by dyeing with several dyestuffs in succession or to some degree by using the natural variations in wool colors, though dark wools tend to be more coarse than light ones. The domestic dyes tended to yield muted colors and to fade easily. More expensive dyes were imported from abroad, included cochineal for a more brilliant red and indigo for a superior blue. The finished cloth might be turned into ready-made garments or purchased by a retail customer, who could take it to a tailor to have it made up into clothing.

The cloth-making industry was seeing important long-term changes during the 1600s. The traditional sturdy "broadcloth" was giving way to lighter fabrics known as the "new draperies." These were cheaper and less durable than the traditional wools, akin to modern suiting fabric; they were particularly suitable for an age when the fashion in clothing was changing at an increasing rate. A growing global market in cloth was also having an impact: in the latter part of the century, the importation of cotton fabrics from India was creating a market for "calico" (a type of cotton cloth originally produced in the city of Calicut on the Malabar coast), encouraging the domestic production of cotton fabrics that would eventually become one of the driving forces of the Industrial Revolution.

Figure 4.3 Weaving (Comenius 1887).

Ironworking did not involve nearly as many people as cloth
production, but it was one of the most developed crafts in early   **Iron and**
modern Europe, and as in many cultures, the capacity to pro-   **Steel**
duce useful metals in quantity was a determining factor in all
areas of material culture, given that most other technologies relied to some
degree on metal implements.[3]

Iron is usually found in nature in iron ore, consisting of an iron oxide
(iron chemically combined with oxygen) and some combination of impurities such as sulfur, clay, stone, lime, water, and sand. The process of
producing iron began with mining the ore from the ground. Some iron
was derived from bogs, but most of the supply in Stuart England came
from underground mines. After centuries of mining, the shafts were being
dug deeper into the earth, making the mines more likely to flood, and
seventeenth-century entrepreneurs were actively searching for a means
of pumping water out of these deep mines—one of the chief forces
behind the development of primitive versions of the steam engine late in
the century.

In order to obtain usable metal, the contaminants had to be physically
removed from the ore and the iron chemically separated from the oxygen.
The initial stages of ore processing were aimed at removal of impurities
by physically breaking up and sorting out the ore according to the metal-
lic content; after this, some of the impurities might be washed or roasted
out. Once the ore was sufficiently purified, it was subjected to smelting,
a chemical process that detached the oxygen from the iron. The simplest
means of achieving this was the bloomery technique, in which the iron
oxide was strongly heated in the presence of carbon; the burning carbon
formed carbon monoxide gas, which would bond with oxygen from the
iron oxide to form carbon dioxide gas. The bloomery technique produced
small batches of iron in the form of a spongy lump or "bloom," consisting
of small globules of iron with trace quantities of other metals in a mass of
slag (waste material, chiefly consisting of silicon) and cinders. After smelting, the bloom was repeatedly reheated and beaten to drive out most of
the slag and cinders. This was the product known as wrought iron.

The bloomery process was a small-scale but labor-intensive operation
that could be practiced by an independent craftsman. By the 1600s, bloom-
eries were common only in the old and declining iron-producing regions,
such as the Weald in Kent. Most iron was being produced by "indirect
reduction," a more efficient process in which the ore passed through an
intermediate stage as cast iron. A bloomery in the mid-1600s might extract
only 55 percent of the iron in the ore, whereas indirect reduction might
yield as much as 92 percent.[4] There were also economies of scale because
a bloomery might produce up to 60–70 kilograms at a time, but cast iron
could be produced in batches of 300–900 kilograms.[5]

Melting iron required much higher temperatures than was possible
on a bloomery hearth and was achieved using a blast furnace, a major

industrial installation that vastly increased iron output: there were at least 78 of these in operation by the middle part of the century. Iron ore, charcoal, and lime were poured into a tall narrow furnace. The carbon in the charcoal reduced the melting point of the iron, and the temperature in the furnace was increased with the aid of water-powered bellows. As the iron-carbon mixture melted, impurities rose to the top, where they were poured off as slag. The molten iron (containing about 2.5 to 4% carbon) flowed out through a hole at the bottom of the furnace, branching out into a row of troughs dug into the sand floor. There it hardened as cast iron, and because the row of cast iron ingots looked like a litter of piglets suckling at a sow, the material came to be known as pig iron. Blast-furnace smelting was in many ways a very modern industry. The furnace had to be worked continuously because it took several days to get up to its working temperature when it was allowed to stop. Laborers typically worked in two teams, each taking a 12-hour shift.

Cast iron has its own applications, but it is extremely hard and brittle and impossible to reshape once it has solidified. For the iron to be usable for tools or weapons, the surplus carbon had to be removed through a process called fining. The cast iron bar was introduced to a fire that was hot enough to melt the surface. Molten cast iron would drip off the end of the bar, and a bellows blasted air at the falling drops, so that the excess carbon would combine with oxygen, leaving fairly pure iron that solidified as it fell to form a bloom at the bottom of the hearth.

Figure 4.4 A blacksmith at work (Comenius 1887).

Because the discovery of the system of elements still lay in the future, nobody actually understood the chemical processes behind smelting: the procedure was based on millennia of trial and error. Individual ironworkers had their own recipes for producing the best results, and their craft might be likened to that of a skilled chef: like the chef, they worked with chemical processes, but the means were an art rather than a science.

Iron production had been further industrialized in the sixteenth century with the first rolling and slitting mills, resembling an oversized pasta machine. The thick wrought-iron bar was heated and passed between a series of progressively smaller water-driven rollers to make it thinner; the resulting iron plate could then be passed through the slitter, which cut it into rods. Between the blast furnace and the rolling mill, iron processing represented the apogee of industrial techniques in early modern Europe.

Iron is tough, but if subjected to sufficient strain or impact, it will lose its shape. To some degree, it can be hardened by repeated beating, a process known as hammer-hardening or work-hardening. However, for a sharp tool or weapon, steel is far more suitable. Steel is iron mixed with .01–1.7 percent carbon, which makes it harder (and more fragile) than ordinary iron, but less so than cast iron. No means of mass-producing steel was found until the 1800s. In seventeenth-century Europe, the usual way to produce steel was to heat iron in the presence of charcoal or some other organic (and therefore carbonaceous) material, a technique known as case-hardening; the carbon would diffuse into the iron, converting at least the outer layer into steel.

Other Materials

Seventeenth-century craftsmen made use of a wide variety of other materials for producing consumer goods. Many of these began as by-products of farming. From livestock came not only such obvious materials as wool and leather, but also horsehair, used to stuff furniture; fats used for lighting fuel; bone, which is similar in properties to ivory; and horn, which was in many ways analogous to modern plastic—it was cheap, light, and resistant to breakage, it could be made translucent, and it could be partially molded by subjecting it to heat. Plant products included dyestuffs and medicinal materials; straw, used for such products as hats, baskets, and stuffing for mattresses; and various fibers such as flax for linen fabric and hemp for canvas and rope. Wood served for construction, furnishings, and fuel; fuel wood used in industrial applications such as brewing and metal working would be partially burned first to remove impurities, leaving charcoal, a substance that consists of almost pure carbon. Wood produced in England was generally from deciduous trees, especially oak. Pine and fir woods were used as well, but had to be imported, chiefly from Scandinavia.[6]

Important inorganic materials included coal for fuel, sand for glassmaking, clay for ceramics, and a variety of metals. Gold and silver were imported and were then worked by the highest level of craftsmen for decorative accessories and furnishings used by the wealthy. More ordinary metals included bronze and latten, both of which were copper alloys valued for their gold-like color and their resistance to rust. Copper by itself, being soft and rather expensive, was not much used. Lead was also soft, but it was the cheapest metal available and not subject to rust: its most important applications were for covering or sealing roofs and for water conduits and drains—the term "plumber" literally means a person who works with lead. For other purposes, lead could be alloyed with tin to make pewter, a harder metal with a silvery color and much used for tableware. Tin itself was moderately expensive and fairly soft, like copper, but it was often used as a coating for iron to protect it from rust; tinned iron was much used for cheap domestic wares.[7]

The Home   The late Middle Ages and early modern period had seen a substantial rise in the overall standard of living in England, manifested dramatically in English housing: new houses tended to be both larger and better constructed than those built before 1400. Nonetheless, the underlying techniques of construction remained the same, and most buildings in the seventeenth century, whether new or old, were constructed on the "timber-frame" model. The basic shape of the house was created by a frame of heavy oak beams, normally resting on some sort of stone foundation to keep groundwater from seeping into the timbers and rotting them. Such oak frames were highly durable: many of those standing in the 1600s were built in previous centuries, and quite a few of those built in the 1600s are still standing today. Once the frame was in place, the roof could be covered with thatch. The materials for this varied by locality: reed made the best thatch but was only available in regions with access to marshy ground. Alternatives included straw, ferns, and gorse. However, thatch was not the only roofing option. Slate provided better resistance to fire, although it was significantly more expensive and generally was used only by the well-to-do or in regions where slate was produced. Tiles also offered better resistance to fire than thatching; they were easier to produce locally, but were still relatively expensive. The very poorest houses lacked floors, having nothing but a floor of packed dirt, but any household of even moderate means would normally have a wooden or tiled floor and possibly a cellar beneath, particularly in urban houses where space was at a premium.[8]

Once the roof was in place, the walls could be filled in. A base was created by weaving a latticework of sticks or light wood (called wattle) in the areas between the timbers; this was then covered with material called daub. The exact recipe for daub varied by locality, but the components typically included clay for strength, manure for resilience, fibers such as horsehair or straw to hold the material together, and sand for filler. The daub was susceptible to water, so a finishing coat of limewash was applied to provide a hard surface. Limewash was also applied to the interior of the building; this not only made for a smooth and hard interior surface, but because the wash was usually white, it also helped brighten the interior. Wealthier households were likely to have homes of brick, again reducing the risk of fire, and areas rich in stone tended to have stone houses. A well-appointed house would also have wooden wainscoting and a plastered ceiling. Doors were hinged into the frame of the house and could be fitted with locks for security.

Fireplaces and windows were essential to houses in an age when fire was needed for heat and cooking, and daylight was the most effective and inexpensive way to illuminate a home. The number of fireplaces in a home was a good indicator of **Heat and Light** the wealth of the household: a prosperous family might have a fireplace in every inhabited room, whereas the poorest might have one only in the kitchen. Even in a wealthy household, rooms tended to be drafty, with a very uneven distribution of heat. Fires had to be banked at night to reduce the risk of burning the building while the household slept, so even a prosperous home could get quite cold on a winter's morning—one of the functions of the household servants was to light the fires before the householders ventured from their beds. The fuel did not normally consist of logs: heavy timbers were a valuable commodity in a country that had seen substantial deforestation over the past millennium. Instead, smaller branches were cut while leaving the body of the tree intact, and the individual sticks were bound together in bundles to provide more substantial fuel for the domestic fire. However, by 1650, wood had been replaced by coal as the chief source of domestic fuel, though the process was more advanced in the towns than in the country.[9] Chimneys had a tendency to smoke, and even when they were drawing properly, the seventeenth-century household would have had a distinctly smoky odor about it to a modern visitor.

Windows were always a trade-off: the more window space there was, the better the light during the day, but the worse the draft. Well-to-do households typically had glass window panes, which let in all the light but significantly reduced the draft. Less expensive options included horn panes and panes made of linen or paper soaked in oil. Because windows were usually kept small to reduce the draft, the interior tended to be rather dim in comparison with a modern home.

Additional light was provided by the fireplace and by smaller domestic lights using various fuels. Candles were the most common. The best candles were made of beeswax, which burned brightly and cleanly. The more economical alternative was tallow candles, made from animal fat, but tallow smoke tended to leave an oily residue. In 1664, Samuel Pepys, feeling increasingly prosperous in his civil service job, decided "to burn wax candles in my closet [small room] at the office, to try the charge and to see whether the smoke offends like that of tallow candles."[10] Candles took some maintenance: as a candle burned down, the wick became exposed, and it eventually had to be trimmed—not until the 1800s was a self-consuming wick invented. Candles were not the only form of artificial lighting, however; other options included rushlights (rushes dipped in animal fat) and oil lamps. Not every room in a house necessarily had lights in it, and outdoor lighting was minimal, so lanterns were also an essential domestic item—the panes were most often made of horn. Well-to-do men like Samuel Pepys often hired a servant to carry a link, or torch, to light their way after dark.[11]

Even something as simple as lighting a fire took a measure of skill in the seventeenth century. The typical means was a "flint and striker"—a sharpened piece of flint that was struck against a hard piece of steel. The flint shaved tiny specks of steel off the striker, heating them white-hot in the process. If the sparks were caught on a light and flammable material (charred linen cloth and tow were common), they could yield embers, and these could be used to ignite a "match"—a strip of thin cardboard whose tip had been coated in sulfur. Once lit, the match worked much as a modern match. Overall, the process was tricky and potentially aggravating, which is one of the reasons fires were banked rather than extinguished at night. A housewife who found her coals had died out in the morning might choose to get some from a neighbor rather than starting from scratch—to alleviate the fire hazard, local bylaws typically forbade transporting coals from one house to another in an uncovered container.

Water and Sanitation One of the most fundamental differences between a Stuart home and a modern one is the lack of running water or sanitation facilities. Water always had to be brought in from outside, whether the householders fetched it themselves from a well or stream, as was normal in the country, or purchased it from water-carriers in the city; the household would keep water barrels or cisterns to store what it needed. Getting waste out of the household also required more effort than it does today. The typical ways for dealing with bodily waste were the chamber-pot and the privy. The chamber-pot was a clay vessel kept in the bedroom ("chamber"), which could be dumped as it was filled. It might be hidden away in a "close-stool," a kind of portable toilet consisting of a seat with a hole in it with a space underneath for the pot. The privy was a permanent structure equivalent to a modern outhouse; it could be either attached to the side of a building or placed at the far end of the domestic garden—close enough for convenient access, but far enough to cut down on the smell. It rested over a cesspit, which would need to be emptied from time to time—a job given to professional "jakes farmers" in the city, while in the country, someone from the household would cart the old waste out to the fields. The cesspit was also a convenient place to dispose of other household waste, although organic materials would usually go to a muck-heap where they could decompose to provide fertilizer for the household garden. For toilet paper, a variety of options were used, including scrap paper and bundles of straw. When necessary, people just managed as best they could. Samuel Pepys recorded rising at night during one Christmas season: "I lacked a pot, but there was none, and bitter cold, so was forced to rise and piss in the chimney, and to bed again."[12]

Although conditions were rough by modern standards, maintaining a clean home was considered an important responsibility for the woman of the household, whether she did it in person or supervised servants who did the work. A satiric ballad of about 1630 describes the outrageous shortcomings of a fictional bad housewife, who swept the house only four times a year and washed the dishes only once a month—and if she lacked a dishcloth, "she set them for the dog to lick, and wipe them with his tail."[13]

Nonetheless, poor sanitation and vermin remained a problem in the Stuart household, most especially in the cities, where the problems were exacerbated by overcrowding and an underdeveloped urban infrastructure. Rats, mice, fleas, and lice were chronic problems. Professional rat-catchers used terriers, ferrets, and poisons to deal with larger vermin; smaller ones called for use of herbs, cleaning, and picking by hand when they made an appearance. Samuel Pepys recorded an unwelcome visitation in 1669:

So to my wife's chamber, and there supped and got her cut my hair and look [at] my shirt, for I have itched mightily these six or seven days; and when all came to all, she finds that I am lousy, having found in my head and body above 20 lice, little and great; which I wonder at, being more than I have had, I believe, almost these 20 years. I did think I might have got them from the little boy, but they did presently look [at] him, and found none—so how they came, I know not; but presently did shift myself, and shall be rid of them, and cut my hair close to my head.[14]

Overall, the seventeenth century was witnessing a rising standard of living in England, at least for those who could find steady employment; as one contemporary observed, "The mean mechanicks and ordinary husbandmen want not silver spoons, or some silver plate in their houses."[15] Nonetheless, people of this age owned far less movable property than their counterparts today: each domestic furnishing and personal accouterment had to be made by hand, in most cases by a skilled craftsman, and therefore represented a significant cost in labor, not to mention the value of the materials.

Furnishings

The best furniture was mostly of oak, and the finest was made by joiners, who specialized in jointed and paneled furniture. Slightly more economical was turner's work, often used for stools, consisting largely of shafts turned on a lathe. The simplest furnishings were "boarded"— simple planks nailed or pegged together, work that was often done by a carpenter. More ephemeral furnishings were made of wickerwork, including baskets, cradles, animal cages, and even chairs.

The typical furnishings of an ordinary Stuart parlor—the chief public space of the house, where meals were served and guests were entertained—included a table, a few sideboards or cupboards, benches or stools, and perhaps a single chair, reserved for the householder or a privileged guest (which is why the term "chair" is still used for the head of an organization). To make the seating more comfortable, people usually laid cushions on the seats. Wealthier families were less likely to rely on stools and more likely to have upholstered chairs for all the family and their guests.

The most important furnishings of the bedchamber were the bed itself and storage furniture such as chests. The seventeenth-century bed was based on an oak frame, which for any person of standing normally had a canopy and curtains to keep out the cold night air of the unheated chamber. The rectangular bedframe supported a layer of boards or a woven network of ropes that provided the lowest layer of the sleeping surface; above that there were mattresses consisting essentially of large stuffed sacks (ticks). A fully appointed bed would have at least two of these mattresses (the softest naturally on top); in ascending order of comfort and expense, the stuffing might be straw, chaff, wool, or feathers (ideally goose down). The typical fabric for these mattresses was striped "ticking," still sometimes found in bed furnishings today. The sleeper's head was supported by a long bolster running across the top of the bed, usually stuffed with a coarser material like wool, on top of which were finer pillows, which were likely to be stuffed with down. The bolster and pillow supported the upper body in a semi-upright position, one of the reasons surviving beds of the period seem short to modern eyes. The sheets were normally of linen, although canvas was used in poorer households. Warmth was provided by blankets and coverlets made of materials including woolen fabric, quilted fabric stuffed with wool, and long-pile coverlets known as "rugs." Children and servants might sleep on a "pallet"—a simple tick set out on the floor at night.

The traditional means for storing personal possessions was in chests—these could be made fairly cheaply by carpenter's work or could be quite elaborate carved and painted items. In the Middle Ages, chests had been practical for the poor because they were cheap and for the rich because they could be moved from one estate to another as the household traveled. By the 1600s, the trend was toward permanent standing furniture, and households of middling means or better tended to rely more heavily on cupboards, chests of drawers, and other less mobile storage furniture. A chest might have a small lockable "till" inside it, or valuables might be kept in a small metalbound coffer. The bedchamber also had a washbasin and pitcher, used for daily washing of the face and hands.

Throughout the home, floors might be covered with mats made of straw or rushes; these were woven with colors and patterns for decorative effect. Carpets were too valuable for walking on, but were found in wealthy households adorning the walls or tables; tapestries were also hung on walls, providing decoration as well as cutting down on the draft. Other fashionable decorations for the walls included paintings, portraits, maps, and prints.

THE MATERIAL ECONOMY

The complex material culture of Stuart England was made possible by a high degree of artisanal specialization. In the country, the household might produce a certain amount of goods for its own use, but both urban and rural households relied heavily on specialized providers for crafted goods; even domestic spinning was largely done to generate cash rather than to provide thread for "homespun" clothing.[16] People could purchase these goods from shops in the town, and in many cases, the craftsman who produced the goods maintained the shop, although smaller items such as tableware and clothing accessories might be retailed by mercers who carried a wide range of minor goods. Other sources of artisanal wares included weekly markets and annual fairs and, in the country, peddlers who carried mercery wares from village to village.

Because materials and crafted items were relatively expensive, there was a great deal of reuse and recycling. Then as now, many people bought clothing and other domestic items used rather than new; when a shirt wore out, smaller pieces could be salvaged for handkerchiefs, and completely worn out linen could be sold to itinerant "rag and bone men," who could then resell it to a papermaker. The wardrobe of Samuel Pepys, by no means a poor man, included a coat made from one of his wife's old skirts.[17] Recycling was even more typical for metal goods, where the material was valuable and highly amenable to reuse.

At the opening of the 1600s, all official coinage was in the form of precious metals—gold and silver—and the value of a coin was directly based on the value of the metal it contained. This system had some serious drawbacks because the high cost of silver meant that the smallest coin—the halfpenny, a mere half an inch across—was enough to buy a quart of ale. Copper coins or tokens, generally valued at a halfpenny, farthing, or half-farthing, circulated unofficially or semiofficially throughout the century, but not until 1672 did Charles II begin issuing copper halfpennies and farthings as coin of the realm. These copper coins were particularly susceptible to counterfeiting, and the shortage of small change persisted into the following century.[18]

Money and Other Assets

There was no paper money, although banking houses and other commercial firms issued letters of credit that could be redeemed at other offices of the firm. By 1600, the medieval stigma attached to charging interest for moneylending was largely a thing of the past. Usury was still condemned, but had been redefined to refer to the charging of excessive rates of interest: the accepted rate varied over the century, but a law of

Figure 4.5 Coins of Charles II: silver shilling, top; silver penny, middle; copper farthing, bottom (Brooke 1932).

1623 set 8 percent as the statutory maximum. Banking services in England were commonly provided by goldsmiths, who were accustomed to dealing with large quantities of precious metals; people would deposit money with a goldsmith, who would then issue a receipt for the deposit. Only at the very end of the century did England acquire a national bank, and that served to underwrite the debts of the government, rather than to provide banking services to individuals. At the more ordinary level, borrowing and lending was a very common activity for most people: pawnbrokers lent money at interest, based on the surety of some kind of personal property, and even one's neighbors might be a source of short-term cash. Purchasing on credit was also quite common, at least for those who were well known to (and trusted by) the vendors.

Then as now, cash and cash equivalents were not the only significant form of financial resource. Land was still regarded as one of the most important forms of long-term investment, offering not only relatively stable economic return, but also social status. The principle of the joint stock company was well established, both for short-term and long-term enterprises, and many entrepreneurs had a significant portion of their assets in this form. Both landed property and stock were largely restricted to the wealthy, but for ordinary people, there were also tangible forms of investment aside from money. The furnishings and personal property in a household represented a significant part of the household's wealth— this was especially true of furnishings in precious metals such as silver tableware, but furniture, clothing, and other salable personal property were often taken to pawnbrokers as a means of generating short-term cash when necessary.

It is difficult, and potentially misleading, to compare the values of currency in the 1600s with the currency used today: the value of a penny depended on what you were trying to buy. Overall, labor cost less than it does today, and crafted goods cost more. The situation was complicated by a volatile market economy: whereas the prices of domestic goods and services in a modern developed economy remain relatively stable, they could fluctuate substantially in seventeenth-century England, particularly in response to fluctuations in the harvest: the actual yield of grain in any given year could vary dramatically as a result of weather conditions, and in a society economically dominated by grain farming, these fluctuations rippled across the economy at large. England saw years of severe hardship after crop failures in the early 1620s, around 1630, and in the late 1640s, though the economy was much more stable in the second half of the century. Overall, the trend in the first half of the century was inflationary, with prices rising about 40 percent between 1600 and 1650, but they remained fairly stable in the latter half of the century, even showing a slight decline between 1650 and 1700.[19]

Tables 4.1 and 4.2 give an idea of the coins circulating during the century; the exact denominations being minted at any given time varied over the course of the century.

Wages and salaries were rarely as straightforward as they are today. For laborers, income could fluctuate significantly; different tasks were paid at different rates, and wages also fluctuated seasonally, with higher pay available in harvest time and lower pay in winter. Room and board were often included as a part of wages. The actual income of a salaried officeholder can also be difficult to judge. On the one hand, many officials were expected to dip into their salary to pay for certain professional costs, including the hiring of subordinates, and on the other, they often collected various perquisites in their duties—fines, emoluments, and other tangential sources of income—to supplement their quarterly wages. For a civil servant like Samuel Pepys, it could be difficult to distinguish between personal and public money, a situation that did little to curb corruption in the Stuart government.

Table 4.1
Approximate Values of Seventeenth-Century Money

	Denomination	Value	Purchase Value	Equivalent
Copper coins	farthing (q.)	¼ of a penny	1 pint of ale	$.50
Copper or silver coins	halfpenny (ob.)	½ of a penny	1 quart of ale	$1
Silver coins	penny (d.)	7 ²/₃ grains silver at .925 fine (sterling)	1 loaf of bread	$2
	twopenny (half-groat)	2d.	1 pint of wine	$4
	threepenny	3d.	1 oz. of pepper	$6
	fourpence (groat)	4d.	1 meal at a country inn	$8
	sixpence	6d.	1 meal at a London inn	$12
	shilling (s.)	12d.	1 day's income for a laborer	$25
Silver or gold coins	half-crown / quarter angel	2s. 6d.	1 day's income for a master craftsman	$60
	crown / angelet / half-angel / quarter-laurel	5s.	1 day's income for a substantial yeoman	$100
Gold coins	noble	6s. 8d.	1 week's income for a craftsman	$150
	half-sovereign / angel / half-laurel	10s.	1 sword	$250
	sovereign / unite / laurel / guinea	20s. (£1)	1 day's income for a manor lord	$500
Moneys of account	mark (marc.)	13s. 4d. (2/3 of £1)	1 year's income for a female servant	$350
	pound (li., modern £)	20s.	1 carthorse	$500

Table 4.2
Sample Prices

Fine ale or beer (1 pint)	½ d.	Small ale or beer (1 pint)	¼ d.
Wine (1 quart)	4d.	Butter (1 lb.)	5d.
Horse	£5–10	12 oz. wheat loaf	1d.
Cheese (1 lb.)	4d.	Eggs (12)	4d.
Tallow candles (12 lb.)	4s.	Wax candles (1 lb.)	1s. 6d.
Wine (1 gal.)	3s.	Cinnamon (1 oz.)	4d.
Sugar (1 lb.)	1s.	Shoes	1s. 6d.
Shirt linen (1 yd.)	1s.	Woolen cloth (1 yd.)	2s.
Penknife	6d.	Silk stockings	28s.
Joint stool	1s. 6d.	Hedging bill	10d.
Musket	14s	Sword and belt	7s
Lantern	1s. 6d.	Bible	6s.
Clock	£11	Coach	£40
Deck of cards	6d.	Portrait	£6
Laborer's food for a day	4d.	Ordinary meal at an inn	4–6d.
30-acre leasehold (with home pasture, meadows, commons rights)	£20/year	Cottage and croft	10s./year
Cheap 2 or 3 room apartment in Southwark	40–60s./year	Small 3-story house with one bedroom in Southwark	£4–5/year plus £20–25 entry fee

Source: Adapted from James E. Thorold Rogers, *A History of Agriculture and Prices in England* (Oxford: Clarendon Press, 1882), 6.256ff., 313ff., 330ff., 416ff., 426ff., 529ff., 552, 586ff., 713ff.; Jeremy Boulton, *Neighbourhood and Society: A London Suburb in the Seventeenth Century* (Cambridge: Cambridge University Press, 1987), 194. The system of measures in use in the period was also complex: see Hubert Hall and Frieda Nicholas, *Select Tracts and Table Books Relating to English Weights and Measures 1100–1742* (London: Camden Society, 1929).

CLOTHING

Clothing was one of the most important components of Stuart material culture: a person's clothes were not merely practical protection against the elements, but a statement of their position in society (or at least how they wanted to be seen), as well as an occasionally significant financial asset and one of the chief engines driving the English economy. The fashion

Table 4.3
Sample Wages and Incomes

Boy laborer	4d./day
	20s./year with room and board
Girl servant	14s./year with room and board
Servant	8d./day
	50s./year with room and board
Unskilled rural laborer	8d./day
Female laborer or servant	6d./day
	16s./year with room and board
Skilled rural laborer	10d./day
	50s./year
Laborer	1s./day
Journeyman craftsman	1s. 4d./day
	£8/year with room and board
Master craftsman	2s./day
Yeoman	£40-50/year
Country parson	£50/year
Esquire	£400/year
Knight	£800/year
Nobleman	£6000/year

Source: Adapted from Rogers, *Prices,* 6.630ff., 692ff.

in clothing varied significantly from decade to decade over the course of
the century, and numerous contemporaries decried the English obsession
with clothing styles, largely imported from abroad:

The English ... have in this one age worn out all the fashions of France and all
the nations of Europe, and tired their own inventions, which are no less busy in
finding out new and ridiculous fashions, than in scraping up money for such idle
expenses; yea, the tailors and shopkeepers daily invent fantastical fashions for
hats, and like new fashions and names for stuffs.[20]

Although the forms changed, the underlying component parts were for
the most part fairly stable, and the materials were largely consistent. The
chief fibers were wool and linen. Wool served for the outer layers of clothing: it is water-resistant, offers good insulation against the cold, and is
amenable to dyeing. Linen, which dyes poorly but is easier to wash than

wool, was used for most parts of the wardrobe in contact with the skin: shirts, collars, drawers, and sometimes stockings. The wealthy also used fabrics made of silk in various forms (including velvet and satin), elaborate ones for external layers, plainer types for the interior layers. In the latter part of the century, cotton cloth was becoming increasingly important, first as an import from the growing English commercial contacts with India and eventually as a domestic product based on imported raw materials. Most fabrics were woven, but knitted garments were also a standard feature of the wardrobe, particularly for stockings, hats, and gloves.

The innermost layer for both men and women consisted of a shirt and drawers; linen was the typical fabric for both of these, **Linens** though cheap and sturdy shirts could be made from hempen fabric, and finer shirts and drawers were made of silk and sometimes adorned with embroidery or lacework. A man's shirt generally reached to his upper legs and had a V-neck to pull over the head, tying shut at the throat. A woman's shirt, called a shift or smock, extended to the ankles and was sometimes cut like a man's shirt, or sometimes with an open neckline to go with the decolleté style of the outer garment. Drawers were tied at the waist, and were similar to modern boxer shorts. Drawers were not worn by women as universally as by men: traditionally, English women had gone without them because their shirts were

Figure 4.6 Stitching and laundering linens (Comenius 1887).

so much longer than those of men, but it became more common for women to wear them over the course of the century—Samuel Pepys's wife was wearing them by the 1660s.[21]

Stockings were essentially undergarments in the case of women, who did not show their legs in public, but outer garments in the case of men. Knitted wool was a typical material for these, with silk for those who could afford it. To keep the stockings in place, both men and women wore a pair of garters—typically narrow bands of fabric—that tied just below the knee.

All of these garments were fairly simple and not particularly subject to rapid change over time or to very great variation between male and female versions. The remainder of the outer layers were where fashion and gender played a major role.

Men's Clothes For men throughout the century, the basic garment for the lower body was a pair of breeches, equivalent to a pair of trousers cut short just below the knee. In the early part of the century, these breeches tended to be voluminous, but the trend over the course of the century was for them to be cut closer to the body. In the first half of the century, the breeches were usually attached to the upper-body garment, either by laces (called "points") passing through eyelet holes or by hooks and eyes; after mid-century, the breeches were generally independent.

The upper-body garment changed even more substantially over the decades. In the first half of the century, the usual garment was called a doublet; it was high waisted and relatively short and was adorned with small skirt-pieces called pickadills. A fashionable doublet was often slashed to reveal a fine lining fabric underneath. To keep one's neck and hair from soiling the doublet, a separate collar called a "falling band" was pinned into the neck of the doublet. Since the falling band needed to be washable, it was made of the same sorts of materials as the undergarments; in some cases, it was incorporated directly into the shirt in the modern fashion. The more fashionable might also wear a pair of linen or silk cuffs pinned into the ends of their doublet sleeves. Early in the century, a man might wear a ruff instead of a falling band, but this style was already becoming old-fashioned.

In the early decades of the century, a man might also wear a sleeveless jerkin, similar to the doublet, on top, for added warmth or display of wealth; this garment sometimes had false sleeves falling from the shoulders. The jerkin was again a holdover from the previous century and fell out of favor by about 1620. Additional warmth could be provided by a "waistcoat," similar to a modern knitted vest, worn over the shirt and under the doublet: Charles I insisted on wearing a waistcoat on his way to the scaffold, lest by shivering in the January cold he should give the impression of fear.

By mid-century, the doublet was starting to give way to the coat, which lacked the attached pickadills and instead had a body that extended down to the thighs and, by the latter part of the century, had a turned-back cuff at the sleeve. Men were also starting to wear this coat open, with a fabric

Figure 4.7 High fashion in the early 1600s (Besant 1904).

waistcoat showing underneath it; this style of waistcoat was similar in cut to the main coat but lacked sleeves. By this time, the falling band was being replaced by a strip of cloth that was tied around the neck, known as a cravat. By the end of the century, the essential components of the modern three-piece suit were in place—even if the look was rather different.

For a woman, the next layer above the shift was the "stays" or bodice. This garment essentially combined the functions of a modern bra and corset, as well as providing a foundation for the outer garments that followed the fashionable line of the day. The degree of restriction and stiffening in the stays varied significantly: upper-class stays emphasized fashion, whereas those of working women had to be more practical. Stiffening was achieved with a combination of heavy fabrics and interlining, with channels to accommodate reeds or strips of baleen; the front had a larger channel for a solid strip known as a busk, made of metal, bone, ivory, or wood. A fashionable

Women's Clothes

Figure 4.8 A well-dressed couple of the late 1600s (Clark 1907).

woman's stays laced up the back—a style that presupposed the assistance of a servant in dressing. For ordinary women, the garment was more likely to lace up the front; the gap at the opening could be covered with a separate decorative piece called a stomacher.

The stays were often fitted with eyelet holes around the base to which the skirts were tied. Ordinary women tended to wear very full skirts of woolen cloth, sometimes in multiple layers, and supported by a "roll"—a fabric tube that tied around the waist to imitate the look of fashionable skirts and that also freed up the legs. For fashionable women, the profile of the skirts was one of the chief features of one's ensemble: this profile changed over the decades and was originally achieved by the use of a farthingale or hoop skirt as the base layer—a skirt with inserts of wire or some similar material to give it the desired shape. Later in the century, the trend was to achieve fullness through multiple layers of skirts. The topmost shirt would be left open in front to reveal the contrasting (and preferably costly) fabric underneath. As the farthingale went out of fashion for upper-class women, the roll also fell out of use among ordinary women.

The main upper-body garment for a woman was most often called a bodice and was cut close to the shape of the stays underneath. Most styles ended at the waist, though in the latter part of the century some styles included long skirts somewhat analogous to a man's coat. By mid-century, the trend for women was to wear an open-fronted robe on top of a skirt and a close-fitting bodice. Early in the century, a woman might wear a ruff at the neck and wrists. By the middle decades of the century, the fashionable style of bodice was low-cut, and women who wanted to observe modesty as well as fashion added a neckcloth, pinned around the shoulders to cover the décolletage. Middle- and lower-class women also tended to wear an apron.

Headgear was an integral part of the ensemble for both men and women; one would never venture out without it, and it was generally worn indoors as well. The most common man's hat throughout the century was some variant on the broad-brimmed hat, made of woolen felt or (if one could afford it) beaverskin. The shape of the crown and the depth and curve of the brim varied from decade to decade; the tendency toward the latter part of the century was to "cock" or curl up some part of the brim. By the end of the century this had given rise to the tricorn cocked hat characteristic of the 1700s.

Accessories

Ordinary women usually wore some sort of linen head-covering, known as a coif, which was never actually removed in public; fashionable women often left their hair uncovered to emphasize their elaborate coiffures. On top of this, a woman might also wear a loose hood or hat when she was outdoors; the hat was usually a smaller version of that worn by men. Both men's and women's hats were invariably adorned with hatbands, and the more stylish men might also add feathers or other adornments to the band.[22]

The last component of the basic outfit was the shoes. These were made of leather, and over the course of the century, the trend was toward more lift in the heels. For most of the century, the usual fastening was a lace, but tongue-and-buckle fastenings began to come into style in the latter part of the century; Pepys recorded adopting the fashion in 1660.[23] Men on horseback generally wore high boots to provide protection against the rigors of riding, and low boots were worn by working men, particularly in the country. By the middle part of the century, boots had also become quite common for ordinary wear among fashionable men, the upper leathers being artfully folded down over themselves for style and convenience.

In addition to these basic garments, a range of additional ones existed for specialized purposes. Loose coats and capes provided extra protection against wet or cold. Handwear was used both for practical purposes and as a fashion statement: for working people, gloves or mittens made of leather or knitted wool provided protection against cold and when working outdoors, and for fashionable people, gloves of fine leather such as kidskin were another opportunity for personal adornment. Specialized robes and caps for indoor use were also becoming increasingly fashionable over the course of the century. Because these did not have the hard use of outdoor garments, they could be made of richer and more delicate fabrics than ordinary garments, emphasizing the wealth of the wearer.

Fashionable women might complete their look with a variety of small accessories, including muffs, fans, and hanging mirrors and watches. Jewelry was also worn by women across the social spectrum, the degree varying by wealth and status: items included brooches, rings, necklaces, and pendants, crafted from precious metals and stones, pearls, and enamel. Many of the same accessories were worn by men, including rings, watches, and sometimes muffs.[24] A distinctively male accessory was the sword, worn on a specialized sword-belt and, during the early part of the century, often accompanied by a matching dagger. The style of sword changed over the course of the century as the long rapier gave way to the shorter and lighter smallsword. One male accessory that first came into fashion during the 1600s is the walking stick, which was occasionally seen before the Civil Wars and became widespread after the Restoration. Spectacles were also in use during this period, chiefly to assist in reading and other close work. Men's breeches generally had pockets in them; women wore purses suspended from a belt, sometimes under an overskirt. Coins and other small items could be kept in pouches of leather, cloth, or knitted fabric.

Grooming   Like clothing, the fashion in personal grooming changed over the course of the century. Men in the first half of the century were generally bearded, and fashionable men tended to wear their hair long. During the Civil Wars, hairstyle became proverbially a mark of a man's political affiliations, with the parliamentary party coming to be known as "Roundheads" on the basis of their supposedly shorter hairstyles. Like most stereotypes, this one was as much myth as reality (Oliver Cromwell's haircut would never pass muster in a modern army), but as with other elements of fashion, the manner of wearing one's hair was a statement of social position.

After the Restoration, the fashions changed significantly. Many men began to crop their hair short and cover it with a long wig called a periwig; this was obviously more expensive than natural hair, but it allowed for an endless variety of fashionable styling, and Pepys found it convenient because it simplified the maintenance of one's own hair. By this time, men were also clean-shaven, save in some cases for a very small moustache; by the end of the century, this too had vanished, and facial hair would not be seen on English men again until the 1800s. Men might shave themselves (Pepys tried this for a time to save money), but it was easier to leave shaving in the hands of a professional barber. For both men and women, grooming the hair was done with combs, which might be of wood, horn, bone, or ivory.[25]

For most ordinary women, hairstyle was fairly simple: the hair was braided and worn up under the coif, though unmarried girls might leave their hair uncovered. Fashionable women left their hair uncovered and kept it arranged in a suitably fashionable style; the mode in hairstyles was constantly changing. Fashionable women also wore cosmetics. The preferred look was pale, sometimes with a small "beauty spot" in the latter part of the century. Visor-style masks also became fashionable in upper-class circles for a time after the Restoration, providing an air of mystery for the wearer, as well as helping her to maintain a fashionably pale complexion.

As a rule, only the linen and silk undergarments that were in contact with the body were actually washed: outer garments were cleaned by brushing because none of the usual fabrics for them were amenable to launder-ing. The laundry might be done at home in the country, but in the city, it was often given to a professional laundress, who washed the garments with water and soap or lye, beating them with a paddle to loosen the grime (equivalent to the agitating action of a modern washing machine). After rinsing, the linens would be stretched out in the sun to dry and whiten them, and an iron, heated at the fire, could be used to press them. Collars and cuffs might also be starched after washing. It seems to have been common to launder once a week; this may suggest that in ordinary households, this was as long as one garment might be worn at a stretch without changing it.[26]

As in all societies, the wearing of clothing was governed by a complex framework of etiquette and custom. People were expected to remove their hats in the presence of a social superior; it was also very unusual for people to be seen in public without some outer garment over their shirt or shift, unless they were engaged in a very demanding physical activity such as tennis or laundering. Most ordinary people had two sets of clothing, a good one to wear on Sunday and an ordinary one for working days.

HEALTH

One of the biggest differences between modern life and that of the sev-enteenth century is the nature of health care available. Medicine today is largely based on our understanding of the workings of the human body, grounded in generations of study and experimentation. In the 1600s, this process of scientific study and experimentation was still in its infancy, and the mainstream of medical theory was still largely based on theoretical understandings of human physiology, derived from speculative scholar-ship of the ancient Greeks. At the same time, centuries of hands-on prac-tice had given rise to a body of practical medicine that was capable of achieving real effects even if there was no theoretical understanding of the processes behind them. This split between theory and practice permeated the medical system of the day.

Medical theory was above all the domain of the physician. Physicians were university-educated, the total time spent at an institution of higher learning typically being around 14 years, beginning with the usual undergraduate education and ending with a doctorate in medicine. Medical studies emphasized physiological theory based on traditional authorities. The dominant mode of understanding the human body was still based on the doctrine of the "four humors," expounded by the Greek physician Galen in the second century C.E. According to this view, the human body was composed of four substances called humors, each

Figure 4.9 A physician and an apothecary (Comenius 1887).

definable by a pair of properties: melancholy (cold and dry), phlegm (cold and wet), blood (hot and wet), and choler (hot and dry). The state of a person's health was thought to depend on the balance among these four humors, and the work of the doctor was to assess the state of that balance and to recommend remedial action: typical remedies included bloodletting, dietary change, and medicines prepared from a range of herbs and chemicals.[27]

The doctor was involved only in diagnosis and prescription. The actual preparation of remedies was the work of the apothecary, much as drugs are purchased from the pharmacist today. Any medical treatment requiring physical work on the body was the domain of the surgeon or his lower-status counterpart, the barber. Unlike the doctor, the apothecary and surgeon were not necessarily university-educated; their level of education was usually fairly high, but their chief means of learning their craft was through a seven-year apprenticeship to an experienced practitioner. In the highly structured class hierarchy of the day, the surgeon was lower in standing than the physician, although his overall standing in society might be fairly prestigious. The barber was accorded even less status; he was essentially a street practitioner equivalent to other tradesmen who sold goods and services; in addition to performing minor surgery such as setting broken bones, he might also provide dentistry—as well as the

Table 4.4
Humors, Elements, and Correspondences

Humor	Element	Qualities	Wind	Celestial Quarter	Time of Day / Gender	Zodiacal Sign	Body Part	Planet
Blood	Air	Hot, Moist	South	West	Day / Male	Gemini Libra Aquarius Shins, ankles	Shoulders, arms Loins, kidneys	Mercury Venus Saturn
Choler (Yellow bile)	Fire	Hot, Dry	East	East		Aries Leo Sagittarius	Head, face Heart, back Thighs, hips	Mars Sun Jupiter
Melancholy (Black bile)	Earth	Cold, Dry	North	South	Night / Female	Taurus Virgo Capricorn	Neck, throat Bowels, belly Knees, back of the thighs	Venus Mercury Saturn
Phlegm	Water	Cold, Moist	West	North		Cancer Scorpio Pisces	Breast, ribs, stomach Genitals, bladder Feet, toes	Moon Mars Jupiter

Note: This table illustrates the system of correspondence between various aspects of the physical universe as understood by traditional seventeenth-century science. The humors are the four substances that compose the human body; the elements are the substances that compose the physical world. All of these substances are integrated into an orderly scheme of associations, as shown here.

obvious shave and a haircut. In spite of the limitations of seventeenth-century medicine, practitioners were capable of significant medical achievements: Samuel Pepys had a kidney stone removed in 1658, but lived until his seventieth year in 1703.

A significant portion of day-to-day medicine was in the hands of non-specialists: basic medical care was one of the kinds of lore passed on from mother to daughter in the household and could be supplemented by recourse to local folk practitioners. Childbirth in particular was still largely in the hands of midwives, who also provided gynecological care in general. Hannah Woolley's recipe "for the cough or stopping of the breath" is typical of the sorts of medicines one finds in household books of the period: "Take syrup of horehound, hyssop, licorice, of each an ounce, and take thereof every morning a spoonful or two."[28]

Woolley's horehound, hyssop, and licorice are still used today for alleviating respiratory trouble. Somewhat less convincing is her recipe "for infection of the plague":

Take a spoonful of running water, a good quantity of treacle, to the bigness of a hazel-nut; temper all these together and heat it lukewarm, and drink it every four-and-twenty hours.[29]

Personal hygiene was considered important, although it was not as meticulous as today. People washed their faces and hands on a daily basis—typically first thing in the morning—as well as washing hands before and after a meal or after defecating. The best soap was imported from Spain and was known as "Castile soap"; it was based on a chemical mixture of olive oil and lye. English soap used animal fats instead of olive oil. Bathing the full body was not very frequent, nor was washing the hair; in an age of drafty houses and limited medical understanding, a bath could be a risky undertaking.[30] Teeth were cleaned with a toothpick and perhaps by rubbing with a cloth, a light abrasive (some recipes mention cuttlefish bone), and salt (which served as an antibacterial). When problems arose, one might have the teeth scaled by a professional practitioner. Overall, personal hygiene was chiefly aimed at removing perceptible uncleanliness, rather than at systematic cleanliness as part of an overall strategy of health.[31]

The medical situation was not helped by relatively unhealthy living conditions, particularly in the towns where large numbers of people were crowded together with questionable water supplies and inadequate sanitation; such conditions contributed to an urban death rate that exceeded the birth rate as well as to periodic epidemics. Diseases were an ongoing problem, including plague, smallpox, syphilis, typhus, dysentery, and tuberculosis. Among dietary illnesses, scurvy was one of the most common, since fresh fruits and vegetables were available for only part of the year. Nonetheless, seventeenth-century Englishmen were not the stunted dwarfs sometimes pictured in the modern imagination. Archeological study of human remains from the Stuart London show average heights of 5 feet 7 1/2 inches for men and 5 feet 2 1/4 inches for women—only about one and a half inches less than the heights modern figures and greater than those of the Industrial Revolution.[32]

The most notorious disease in Stuart England was the plague, which was endemic through the century, with major outbreaks in 1605, 1625, and above all, 1665. The mortality brought by the Great Plague in London in 1665 is thought to have been over 100,000, or a quarter of the city's total population. After this last major outbreak, the plague tapered off, the last known case being in 1679.

NOTES

1. Note throughout this chapter that the modern scholar needs to adhere to a consistent technical vocabulary in describing historical material culture, but historical usage was generally fluid: a given item might be described with multiple terms, or the same term might apply to multiple items.

2. Brian Murphy, *History of the British Economy* (London: Longman, 1973), 113; Joan Thirsk and J. P. Cooper, eds., *Seventeenth-Century Economic Documents* (Oxford: Clarendon Press, 1972), 783. On cloth-making, see Randle Holme, *Living and Working in Seventeenth-Century England: An Encyclopedia of Drawings and Descriptions from Randle Holme's Original Manuscripts for The Academy of Armory (1688)* [CD-ROM], ed. N. W. Alcock and Nancy Cox (London: British Library, 2001), Bk. 3, ch. 3, 6, 8, 20.

3. On ironworking, see Joseph Moxon, *Mechanick Exercises, or the Doctrine of Handy-Works, Applied to the Arts of Smithing, Joinery, Carpentry, Turning, Bricklayery* (London: Daniel Midwinter and Thomas Leigh, 1703), 1ff.; Holme, *Academy*, Bk. 3, ch. 4, 7; Murphy, *British Economy*, 245.

4. R. F. Tylecote, *A History of Metallurgy* (London: Metals Society, 1976), 302.

5. Charles Joseph Singer, ed., *A History of Technology* (Oxford: Clarendon Press, 1954–1978), 2.71.

6. On woodworking, leatherworking, and horn, see Holme, *Academy*, Bk. 3, ch. 4, 5, 8, 9, and passim.

7. On pewter, leadworking, tinworking, brass, and so on, see Holme, *Academy*, Bk. 3, ch. 3, 5, 7, and passim.

8. On buildings, see Henry Best, *The Farm and Memorandum Books of Henry Best of Elmswell, 1642*, ed. Donald Woodward, Records of Social and Economic History New Series 8 (London: Oxford University Press for the British Academy, 1984), 112ff., 144ff. Holme, *Academy*, Bk. 3, ch. 3, 5, 8, 9, and passim; Eric Mercer, *English Vernacular Houses* (London: Her Majesty's Stationery Office, 1975); Joan Thirsk, *The Agrarian History of England and Wales 1500–1750* (Cambridge: Cambridge University Press, 1967, 1984, 1985), 4.696ff., 5.ii.590ff.; Thornton, Peter, *Seventeenth-Century Interior Decoration in England, France and Holland* (New Haven: Yale University Press, 1978), 52ff.

9. Keith Wrightson, *Earthly Necessities: Economic Lives in Early Modern Britain* (New Haven: Yale University Press, 2000), 171.

10. Samuel Pepys, *The Diary of Samuel Pepys,* ed. Robert Latham and William Matthews (Berkeley and Los Angeles: University of California Press, 1983), 5.346. On candles, see Holme, *Academy,* Bk. 3, ch. 6. On lighting, see Thornton, *Decoration,* 268ff.

11. Pepys, *Diary,* 4.30.

12. Pepys, *Diary,* 5.357. On sanitation facilities, see Thornton, *Decoration,* 321ff.

13. William Chappell, ed., *The Roxburghe Ballads* (Hertford: Ballad Society, 1871–1899), 2.513.

14. Pepys, *Diary,* 9.424.

15. Edward Chamberlayne, *Angliæ Notitia, or, the Present State of England* (London: J. Martyn), 30. On furnishings in general, see Victor Chinnery, *Oak Furniture. The British Tradition* (Woodbridge, Suffolk: Antique Collectors' Club, 1979); Holme, *Academy,* Bk. 3, ch. 14; Eric Mercer, *Furniture 700–1700* (London: Weidenfeld & Nicolson, 1969); Peter Thornton, *Seventeenth-Century Interior Decoration in England, France and Holland* (New Haven: Yale University Press, 1978); S. W. Wolsey and R. W. P. Lanff, *Furniture in England: The Age of the Joiner* (New York: Praeger, 1968).

16. For an introduction to the Stuart economy, see George Unwin, "Commerce and Coinage," in *Shakespeare's England: An Account of the Life and Manners of his Age* (Oxford: Clarendon Press, 1916), 311–45; Keith Wrightson, *Earthly Necessities: Economic Lives in Early Modern Britain* (New Haven: Yale University Press, 2000); Julian Hoppit, *A Land of Liberty? England 1689–1727* (Oxford: Clarendon Press, 2000), ch. 10.

17. Pepys, *Diary,* 10.99.

18. On coinage, see George C. Brooke, *English Coins from the Seventh Century to the Present Day* (London: Methuen, 1932); C.H.V. Sutherland, *English Coinage 900–1900* (London: Batsford, 1973), ch. 10, 11; Fynes Moryson, *An Itinerary* (London: John Beale, 1617; reprinted Amsterdam and New York: Da Capo Press, Theatrum Orbis Terrarum, 1971), pp. xi–xii.

19. Joan Thirsk, *The Agrarian History of England and Wales* (Cambridge: Cambridge University Press), 4.593ff., 865, 5.ii.1ff., 879.

20. Fynes Moryson, *An Itinerary* (London: John Beale, 1617; reprinted Amsterdam and New York: Da Capo Press, Theatrum Orbis Terrarum, 1971), 3.177–78.

21. Pepys, *Diary,* 4.140, 172.

22. On headgear, see Holme, *Academy,* Bk. 3, ch. 1, 5, 18.

23. Pepys, *Diary,* 1.26. On footwear, see Holme, *Academy,* Bk. 3, ch. 1, 5.

24. On accessories, see Holme, *Academy,* Bk. 3, ch. 1, 2, and passim.

25. Holme, *Academy,* Bk. 3, ch. 3, no. 57, describes the work of a barber in considerable detail.

26. On laundering, see Holme, *Academy,* Bk. 3, ch. 3, no. 35; Hannah Woolley, *A Supplement to the Queen-like Closet, or a Little of Everything* (London: Richard Lowndes, 1674), 1ff.; Comenius, *Orbis,* 124–25.

27. On medicine, see Harold John Cook, *The Decline of the Old Medical Regime in Stuart London* (Ithaca: Cornell University Press, 1986); Nicholas Culpeper, *The English Physician Enlarged* (London: George Sawbridge, 1681); Doreen Evenden, *Popular Medicine in Seventeenth-Century England* (Bowling Green, OH: Bowling Green State University Popular Press, 1988); John Pechey, *The London Dispensatory,*

Reduced to the Practice of the London Physicians, wherein Are Contained the Medicines Both Galenical and Chymical That Are Now in Use (London: J. Lawrence, 1694); Roy Porter, *Disease, Medicine, and Society in England, 1550–1860* (Cambridge and New York: Cambridge University Press, 1995); Roy Porter and Dorothy Porter, *In Sickness and in Health: The British Experience, 1650–1850* (New York: Blackwell, 1989); Raymond Stanley Roberts, "The Personnel and Practice of Medicine in Tudor and Stuart England, Part 1: The Provinces," *Medical History* 6 (1962): 363–82; Raymond Stanley Roberts, "The Personnel and Practice of Medicine in Tudor and Stuart England, Part 2: London," *Medical History* 8 (1964): 217–34.

28. Hannah Woolley, *The Compleat Servant-Maid* (London: Thomas Passenger, 1691), 153–54.

29. Woolley, *Compleat Servant Maid*, 49.

30. On soap, see Holme, *Academy*, Bk. 3, ch. 21. On washing and bathing, see Thornton, *Decoration*, 315ff.

31. On teeth, see Karen Hess, *Martha Washington's Booke of Cookery* (New York: Columbia University Press, 1981), 442; Woolley, *Servant Maid*, 72; Woolley, *Supplement*, 10. On dentistry, see Arthur Ward Lufkin, *History of Dentistry* (London: Kimpton, 1948), 121ff.

32. Alex Werner, *London Bodies: The Changing Shape of Londoners from Prehistoric Times to the Present Day* (London: Museum of London, 1998), 108.

5

COUNTRY LIFE

England in the seventeenth century was still very much an agrarian country, although during the century, transformations in English agriculture were taking place that would ultimately change this long-standing reality of English life. About 80 percent of the population lived in rural settlements,[1] and even city-dwellers were never fully detached from country life: even in London, farmland was within easy walking distance, and most city folk had relatives in the country, if they were not indeed immigrants to the city themselves. In cultural terms, England still set considerable store by its rural traditions, whether in the form of popular festivals linked to the rhythms of agricultural life or in the preoccupation of the wealthy with acquiring rural land—the ultimate benchmark of social status.

As with many aspects of seventeenth-century life, the rural experience was shaped by traditional structures inherited from the Middle Ages, with an overlay of more recent changes that were fragmenting these structures. In order to understand Stuart country life, one must begin with the open-field village that was the "classical" form of rural settlement in the medieval period and which still remained a feature of the landscape in the 1600s; the example used here is the Gloucestershire village of Chedworth, in the western part of the Cotswolds and among the last villages in England to abandon open-field farming.[2]

Open-field lands were known as "champion" lands in the 1600s. The typical open-field village had a central cluster of houses and other buildings, surrounded by several hundred to a few thousand acres of farmland. The exact configuration depended on the lay of the land and the evolution

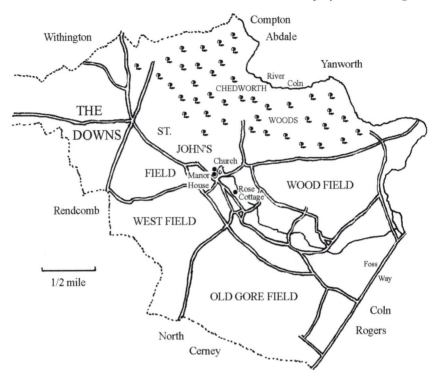

Map of Chedworth.

of the settlement—Chedworth had been continuously inhabited since at least the eighth century, and the remains of a Roman villa have been found north of the village. In Chedworth, the central village occupied a strip of high uneven ground; along its north side was a brook, fed by a spring at the upper end of the central village. This location ensured a plentiful supply of water for the villagers and minimized the use of good farming land for housing: the village fields were on flatter and lower ground surrounding the central village.

At the upper end of the central village were the manor house and the parish church; the village houses followed the brook eastward. At the eastern extremity of Chedworth, the brook joined the Coln, the river that formed the northeastern border of the village. At this point, the Coln was crossed by the old Roman road known as Foss Way, which formed Chedworth's southeastern border. Chedworth was a fairly average-sized village, numbering around four hundred people in about a hundred households; the village spanned about four miles east to west, and three and one-fourth miles north to south, for a total of nearly 4,000 acres. The adjoining villages were about three miles away, and there were a number of market towns within a day's walk: Cirencester was 5 miles to the south, Cheltenham 8 miles to the northeast, Stow-on-the-Wold 12 miles to the north, and Gloucester 12 miles to the west.

The central village was divided up into residential plots called "messuages," each of which included a house, garden, and service buildings. Each messuage was associated with a particular holding of land in the village fields, and the messuage with its associated farmland was passed through the generations from the farmer to his heirs. In some cases, the house had no associated landholding (in which case it was usually called a cottage), and the household had to rely on alternative sources of income. The specifics of each landholding were dictated by tradition, in most cases dating back to the Middle Ages: each landholding came with specific rights and responsibilities, falling within a few general types of "tenure."

The most advantageous form of holding was free tenure, also called a freehold. A freehold farmer held absolute right in perpetuity to his holding, to be passed on freely to his heirs. The freehold was in principle not actually owned by the farmer: it was rented, and in theory the freeholder might owe some sort of payment to the manor lord for his lands, but these rents had generally been established centuries before, and by the seventeenth century, they had become so nominal that they were rarely worth collecting, and the freeholder was effectively the owner of the holding.

Somewhat less secure was the copyhold. Copyholders occupied tenancies that centuries earlier had belonged to medieval serfs. Actual serfdom had died out in England by this time, but like his medieval predecessor, the copyholder was generally required to pay an actual rent to the manor lord—in the Middle Ages, the bulk of the rent had been paid in labor, but by the 1600s, labor payments had been converted to cash rents. The copyholder derived his name from holding a copy of the manorial records that stipulated the traditional rights and obligations of the tenancy. Copyhold tenure varied in duration, depending on the traditions associated with the holding and with the manor in general: it might be in perpetuity, or it might be for a specified number of lifetimes. At the death of the copyholder, his heir would usually have to pay a fee (often called an "entry fine") to take possession of the holding. A payment of about one or two years' rent was typical. Raising this fee excessively was one of the ways an unscrupulous landlord might drive copyholders out of their holdings, although major increases over traditional entry fines were sometimes successfully challenged in court.

By the 1600s, copyhold tenure was becoming less attractive to landlords. It was an artifact of medieval manorialism and had evolved as a means of ensuring a steady labor supply for the landlord in the underdeveloped economy of post-Roman Europe. For landlords of the Stuart age, accelerating economic change encouraged a trend toward more flexible forms of tenure in the form of leaseholdings and tenancies-at-will. The leaseholder occupied the holding on terms more or less familiar to us today, paying an annual rent in biannual or quarterly installments, for a period determined by the terms of the lease. Before 1600, it had been fairly common for a leasehold to run for one or more lifetimes (i.e., for the leaseholder and his heirs), but in the seventeenth century, it was becoming more common for leases to run for a term of years, typically between 7 and 21 years. Least secure of all were the tenants-at-will, who generally rented their land from quarter to quarter. Such people were highly vulnerable in an age when many landlords were looking to improve their incomes by more effective management of their estates.[3]

The terms of the holding were independent of its actual size: a free-holder might have a very small holding of land (this was particularly common for tradesmen such as millers or smiths, who derived their income mostly from their trade), whereas a leaseholder might occupy a large one. Depending on the quality of the land and the state of the economy, the break-even size of landholding was typically between 10 and 20 acres. Tenants who had this much land could support their households on the landholding, and if the holding was large enough, perhaps about 30 acres (a holding known as a "yardland"), they might lead a moderately pros-perous life, employing workers of their own to help till their lands. Ten-ants whose landholdings fell below the break-even size were unable to support a household on the landholding and needed to sell their labor in order to make ends meet. At the very base of village society were the land-less laborers, who held no land of their own and relied entirely on wage income to support themselves.[4]

At the opening of the century, there were upwards of 7 freehold tene-ments in Chedworth and 17 copyholds, the latter ranging in size from about 20 to 75 acres. Over the century, more of the copyholds were broken up and sold off as small freeholds; by the time of enclosure in 1803, there were 110 freeholdings in the parish, most of them having under 10 acres.

AGRICULTURE

The most important staple crop was wheat, but the traditional open-field village practiced a mixed form of agriculture that integrated multiple forms of farming. The classic form of Western European crop agriculture in this period is known to historians as the "three-field" system of crop rota-tion. Developed in the early Middle Ages, the three-field system divided the crop lands into three roughly equal parts and rotated them through a three-year cycle consisting of a winter crop (usually wheat), a spring crop (typically legumes such as peas or beans; barley was also a spring crop), and inactivity (called fallowing). The wheat was the most important cash crop: as the source of bread, it was the basis of England's diet and econ-omy. However, repeated crops of wheat exhaust the fertility of the soil, so the other two-thirds of the cycle helped revitalize the soil. The spring crop restored nitrogen to the soil, and even fallow land did not lie idle: the village livestock were pastured on this ground, providing grazing for the animals while refertilizing the soil with the animals' manure. The farmland of the village was typically divided into three or more large fields of a hundred acres or more, each of which would be allotted to one stage of the crop cycle. The actual implementation of this type of agriculture varied from one community to the next: in Chedworth there were in fact four principal fields, called Wood Field, Old Gore Field, West Field, and St. John's Field.

The arable lands of an open-field landholder were not all in one place, but scattered in small "furlongs" in the various fields of the village. A furlong might range from less than an acre to several acres—the stereotypical furlong was about an acre, which in theory was the area that could be plowed in a day, although the actual speed of plowing depended in part on the nature of the local soil. The scattering of each holding ensured that different qualities of ground were more or less equitably distributed among the landholders and that everyone would have a third of their land in each part of the crop cycle. Each furlong was recognizable by its topographical features, particularly the ditch or "furrow" that ran between one furlong and the next: a furlong was plowed in a manner that cast the soil toward the center, leaving a furrow at the outermost edges. There might also be boundary posts or stones, but there were no actual barriers between the furlongs, hence the name "open-field." Each field as a whole was surrounded by a hedge, cultivated over the centuries from plants such as hawthorn that make good barriers. These hedges were essential, since inactive fields were often used as pasturage

Figure 5.1 Threshing in the barn, plowing, sowing, harvesting, and haymaking (Comenius 1887).

for animals. Mobile fencing, called folds, was sometimes used to manage animals while they were on pasture, but hedges were the most important form of barrier because they cost nothing except the labor of maintaining them: they needed to be trimmed periodically, and the branches had to be interlaced to provide a stout enclosure for the animals. As with other aspects of English agriculture, the details varied from region to region: in the stony lands of northern England, drystone walling was often used as a barrier instead of hedges.[5]

In addition to the main crop-raising lands of the village, there were also secondary areas used for other farming purposes. Meadows were allowed to grow high each year so that the long grasses could be mowed and dried at the end of the summer as hay to provide winter fodder for the livestock. These meadows were often damp ground unsuitable for crop-raising, but excellent for growing hay; in Chedworth they mostly lay in a narrow strip along the brook north of the central village and in some small stretches by the Coln. Other land unsuitable for crops might serve as pasturage for the animals. In Chedworth, the "Downs," several hundred acres of rough high land to the northwest of the village, were the chief area of pasturage. This pasturage supported animals such as horses, cattle, and sheep.

The village pastures supported a variety of farm animals, chiefly horses, cattle, and sheep. Horses served principally as draft animals, pulling the farmers' plows, carts, and other farm equipment. Cattle had multiple purposes. Heifers (young females) were raised to become cows (mature females), for breeding and dairying. A few males were raised as breeding bulls, but most were gelded. A few of these nonbreeding bulls would be trained as working oxen, and the others would be sold off at a young age for meat—the seventeenth-century term for such meat cattle was "beeves" (the plural of "beef"); today they would be called steers. Sheep were an important source of cash, chiefly for their wool, which was shorn once a year. They also provided meat that could be sold or eaten by the house-hold. Sheep's milk was not much used in England, in contrast to some parts of Europe. Goats were relatively uncommon in English villages, but were found in some highland zones where the land was less hospitable to cattle.

Finally, a village might have marginal lands that were unsuitable for any of these purposes. Woods were essential for providing necessary resources such as fuel and building timber and could also support pigs, who could forage very efficiently in wooded areas. The Chedworth Woods on the north side of the village were substantial; in all there were about 629 acres of woods in the manor. Households also cultivated trees at the margins of some of the arable fields to provide wood for fuel and other domestic uses: only the lightest branches would be harvested, using techniques called coppicing and pollarding, which allowed the trunk and main branches to provide fresh wood each year.[6]

Additional farm work took place on the messuage. Keeping pigs, chickens, ducks, and geese was an efficient means of turning domestic waste like kitchen scraps into food for the table. Each household also had a garden to supply vegetables and herbs, adding flavor and nutritional variety to the staple grains and legumes raised in the village fields. The herb garden was also the villager's apothecary shop, providing the materials for the traditional folk remedies passed on from mother to daughter.

The freehold associated with the "Rose Cottage" in Chedworth is a good example of the landholding of a farmer of comfortable means in the period.[7] The cottage stood in the central village adjoining the brook, just down the street from the manor house and parish church. In addition to the house, the messuage included a barn, stable, garden, and orchard and 39 acres of arable land in Old Gore Field and Wood Field, divided into 25 parcels of varying sizes:

1. 3 acres in Old Gore Field, including a coppice
2. 6 acres in Old Gore Field
3. 1 1/2 acres at Coln Deans Way in Old Gore Field
4. 1/2 acre headland in Dead Furlong in Old Gore Field
5. 1/2 acre in Old Gore Field
6. 1 1/2 acres at Moor Gap in Old Gore Field
7. 2 acres at Chessel Bushes in Old Gore Field
8. 1/2 acres at Chessel Bushes in Old Gore Field
9. 1 farundell (1/4 acre) at White Walls in Old Gore Field
10. 5 farundells above Cortway in Old Gore Field
11. 3 farundells below Portway in Old Gore Field
12. 1 acre in Old Gore Field
13. 1/2 acre below Holly Lane Way in Old Gore Field
14. 2 acres in Wood Field
15. 4 acres on Sundays Hill in Wood Field
16. 2 acres on Red Hill in Wood Field
17. 3 farundells in Blackwells Bottom in Wood Field
18. 1/2 acre in Blackwells Bottom in Wood Field
19. 1/2 acre at Shillford in Wood Field
20. 1 1/2 acres at Coaks Grove in Wood Field
21. 1 acre on Entons Hill in Wood Field
22. 1 acre on Harmell Hill in Wood Field
23. 1 acre on Harmell Hill in Wood Field
24. 1/2 acre on Raybrook in Wood Field
25. 1 acre headland at Gibbes Hedge in Wood Field

The holding also included five acres of pasture and meadow land: one acre was known as "Home Close" and adjoined the cottage, and the other four were an enclosure in Wood Field, called "the Croft." Finally, as with most such holdings, the tenant had a right to keep a certain number of livestock on the common grazing land of the Downs—this was called a stint. In the case of the Rose Cottage, the stint was 65 sheep and 4 cattle. This was many more sheep than were necessary for the household, so the animals were clearly serving as a source of cash for the household, mostly from their wool (for which the Cotswolds were famous) and secondarily from mutton. The four cattle probably represented either a four-ox plow team or two draft oxen and a pair of milking cows.

This picture of the English village is necessarily somewhat simplified: the realities were inevitably more complex, depending on local tradition, history, and topography. Open-field farming was most typical of the central regions of England. Some areas, particularly Kent, the Southwest, the North, and Wales, had never developed a strong tradition of open-field farming: farms were more likely to be discrete units, and settlements were therefore more scattered. In the highland zones (the northern and western part of the country), the land was less likely to be suitable for crop husbandry, and a larger portion was devoted to grazing.

The situation was further complicated by economic trends that were undermining traditional open-field farming in favor of consolidated landholdings. One factor was the rise of wool as a cash crop. During the Middle Ages, the production of woolen cloth had come to drive much of the commercial economy of Europe, and England's role in this industry had increased dramatically, first as an exporter of superior wools for the use of Flemish and Italian weavers and then, by the 1500s, as a major producer of finished woolen cloth. The wool market was subject to dramatic swings and cooled off significantly after the mid-1500s, but still the production of wool could be an attractive option for an enterprising landowner in the 1600s: wool could fetch a good price in a favorable market, and sheep-raising was vastly less labor-intensive than crop-raising, which could mean a decrease in production costs and an increase in profit margin. Many landlords sought to bring manorial lands into their direct control so that they could create consolidated holdings for pasturage or other purposes.

The process of consolidating formerly open landholdings, known as enclosure, was one of the most fiery political topics of the Tudor and early Stuart age. Various specific tactics might be used, but overall, the trend was for the manor lord to evict or buy out tenants from all or part of their land and to separate the new consolidated holding from the remaining open fields with some sort of enclosure; in many cases, marginal lands including common pasture and waste were enclosed as well.

Although the process may have been legal, it aroused widespread hostility, for a variety of reasons. For one thing, the negotiation between a manor lord and tenant was far from an even playing field: political, legal, and economic power lay with the manor lord, and enclosure was naturally seen as coercive even when the law was not actually violated. Nor were those who gave up their landholdings the only ones affected. Depending on the customs of the community, every villager might have some rights of use of the open fields, commons, and waste, whether for collecting firewood or for pasturing animals on land not currently being used for crops. Once this land was enclosed, it was no longer accessible for such purposes, and many villages where enclosure took place witnessed riots where the enclosures were torn down by the dispossessed villagers. Last, even those who were not directly hurt by the process often decried its broader social impact. Enclosure swelled the ranks of landless laborers and fragmented the traditional structures by which village communities had lived for centuries. Many feared—and not without cause—that the unmaking of these structures would contribute to the fragmentation of society as a whole. Fynes Moryson, summarizing the agricultural state of his country in the early 1600s, expressed a view that was shared by many of his countrymen:

Daily [England's] plenty of corn [i.e., grain] decreaseth, by reason that private men, finding greater commodity in feeding of sheep and cattle, than in the plough, requiring the hands of many servants, can by no law be restrained from turning corn fields into enclosed pastures, especially since great men are the first to break these laws.[8]

Moryson's view was fairly commonplace for many of his contemporaries, but it was increasingly out of touch with reality. By the 1600s, the chief impetus for enclosure was no longer wool production, but agricultural innovation. The seventeenth century was an age of intense technological and scientific experimentation, and this trend encompassed farming as well. English landowners avidly read the latest self-help manuals on how to improve the economic productivity of their lands. One of the important developments of the century was the increased use of fertilizers, not only in the form of animal dung, but also marl and lime. Another innovation was the increased cultivation of cash crops other than the traditional grains and legumes: these included fibers such as flax and hemp, oil-bearing plants such as rapeseed (canola), and dyestuffs such as saffron, weld, woad, and madder. Such innovations were apparently having an impact in Chedworth, as suggested by the field-name "Hemplands" toward the east end of the village. The period also saw the first experimentation in what would eventually become the "four-course" form of crop rotation that helped feed the Industrial Revolution. In four-course rotation, the fields rotated among wheat, a root crop (typically turnips), barley or oats, and clover or rye. The land was under continual cultivation, and the turnips and clover provided more animal fodder, not only increasing meat and dairy capacity, but also increasing the supply of fertilizing manure.[9]

The transition to four-course husbandry was only just beginning by the end of the century, but the practice of agricultural entrepreneurialism was well established. Yet such changes were difficult to implement on the scattered holdings of an open-field village, and economies of scale favored large holdings over small ones. Over the course of the century, it became increasingly accepted that open-field farming was an obstacle to efficiency, and enclosure was being used not only by landlords but also by the villagers themselves in an effort to improve their economic potential. Farmers were actively buying, selling, and trading landholdings to consolidate them and then creating enclosures around their newly consolidated holdings. The trend can be documented in Chedworth as elsewhere: in the first half of the century, the vicar Nathaniel Aldworth and villager William Lawrence traded a quarter-acre of pasture near the village brook; Aldworth was then able to enclose his new land with two adjoining plots he already held.[10] By 1700, the enclosure issue had largely died as a matter of public debate, and a century later, almost all the remains of open-field farming would be swept away by parliamentary statute.

The Agricultural Year

Rural life in all societies has a substantially different rhythm from the life of the city. Whereas city-dwellers repeat the same work day after day, country life changes dramatically over the course of the year, following the cycle of the seasons. One of the best ways to understand the shape of Stuart village life is to follow the seasons from planting to harvest in the traditional cycle of three-field husbandry.[11]

The first stage of the cycle began around October, shortly after the end of the previous year's harvest, with the preparation of the winter fields for next year's crop. First, the field had to be plowed. Since ancient times, plowing had been the archetypical man's work. The plow might be pulled by horses or oxen: horses were generally faster and easier to graze, but they were more expensive to keep, and they plowed less well in certain types of soil, so the choice of draft animal often depended on local topography as well as on the finances of the farmer. A plow consisted of three chief working elements. First was the coulter, an iron blade toward the front of the plow that sliced vertically through the soil. Behind the coulter was the plowshare, a roughly wedge-shaped block of wood sheathed with iron to cut the soil horizontally. Last was the mouldboard, an angled plank that lifted the strip of sod cut by the coulter and plowshare and tossed it toward the side. The plow might be pulled by anywhere from two to six animals, with a plowman behind to steer the plow by the handles (a physically demanding job); often there was a second person in front—sometimes a boy—to guide the animals. Because an acre theoretically required a day to plow, a substantial farmer with 30 or 40 acres would require about two weeks of work to plow the third of his fields in each part of the crop cycle.

Plowing fulfilled two chief functions. It broke up weeds and the remains of the last harvest and turned them under the soil to become nutrients for future crops. It also broke up the soil itself, providing a suitable surface into which seed-grain could be cast. The casting of seed, or sowing, was the next step in the process: the sower would walk up and down with seed in a box, apron, or other container, tossing handfuls of grain into the prepared ground. This "broadcast" method of sowing wasted a good deal of grain, but planting each grain by hand would have been prohibitively time-consuming; systematic planting of grain had to wait until the invention of a mechanical seed-planter by Jethro Tull at the beginning of the 1700s. The broadcast grain was inevitably a magnet for birds, so here again a boy would have a chance to make himself useful and learn the ways of farming by gathering stones and throwing them at any scavenging wildfowl. After the grain was spread, a harrow would be dragged over the ground to cover it up: this was a wooden frame with spikes on the bottom, again pulled by draft animals.

The planting of wheat was proverbially supposed to be over by Martinmas, November 11. This was also the day traditionally associated with the slaughtering of animals for winter. In reality, relatively few animals were actually slaughtered. Sheep were able to forage until the snow got deep, although at this time of year, they were generally brought in from the more distant fields and pastured closer to the home. Cattle had to be foddered over the winter, but anyone who could afford to eat beef could also afford to have it fresh. The chief animals actually slaughtered were pigs, and these were mostly hogs (young neutered males); as with most meat animals, females (sows) were generally kept for breeding, and a small number of males were left unneutered (boars) for the same reason. Those parts of the pig that were amenable to salting or pickling would be preserved, and the parts that had to be eaten at once (chiefly the entrails) were made into sausages.

The central part of winter—from late November to early January—was one of the less demanding periods in the village work cycle. Relatively little agricultural labor could be done in midwinter, so this was a season for maintenance and preparation: mending hedges, cleaning ditches, gathering timber and firewood, repairing tools and buildings. In the middle of winter came the Christmas season, which across English society was one of the most important times of year for social activity and recreation.

In January, serious agricultural work began anew with the preparation of last year's winter fields for the spring crops. Plowing began in January, and the crops were to be in the ground by March. These were typically legumes such as beans or peas; beans, unlike grains, could be planted by hand (called dibbing or setting) because fewer seeds were involved. The women, in the meantime, began tending their orchards in preparation for the next growing season. February was also the beginning of lambing season, and the animals required extra attention to ensure a high survival rate. Gardening, another female responsibility, began in earnest in March. By this time, most of this year's lambs had been born, and livestock were moved from the home pasturage out to the village pastures. By April, the new lambs and calves were being weaned from their mothers' milk, and dairying could begin; it would generally continue until about November.

Between March and May, the fallow fields were spread with manure, cesspit waste, and other fertilizers and were plowed to make them ready for the next year; this process might be repeated during August and September. During May and June, the crop fields were weeded several times, using a hoe or weeding-hook. Late April to early June was another relative lull in the work cycle and again a traditional time of year for rural festivities, but whereas Christmas generally focused on friends and family, the summer festivities were traditionally community affairs, although communal village festivities were on the decline during the century (see chapter 9).

In late June, the pace of work picked up again with the arrival of sheep-shearing season. July was traditionally the time for haymaking, one of the most intense labors of the agricultural year. The mowers cut the tall grasses with a scythe; following them came the rakers, who spread the hay out on the ground to dry and then gathered it into haystacks. The process was moderately tricky: the farmer hoped for good weather so that the hay would dry properly. Then the hay was pitched onto carts and put under shelter as quickly as possible: a sudden rainstorm could ruin everything, hence the importance of "making hay while the sun shines." Once the meadows were mowed, livestock were moved there to graze.

After haymaking was over, the grain harvest began. The reapers worked their way through the fields with sickles, cutting off the stalks of grain toward the top; others would follow to gather up the stalks, tie them into bundles, and toss them onto carts to be taken into the barn. The remainder of the stalk could then be mowed with a scythe to provide straw, used for a wide variety of purposes, including basketry, bedding, floor mats, and headgear. The time pressures involved in both haymaking and harvesting meant that labor was at a premium from July to September: wages were higher, temporary hired help was engaged, and women and children assisted in the field work. Once the grain had been harvested, it was traditionally permissible for animals to be turned out on the common fields to feed on the stubble and scraps.

The grain came to the barn still on the stalk: several more stages were required before it was ready for consumption. First, it had to be threshed, pounded to break the grain free from the stalk and husk. The typical way to do this involved spreading the grain on the ground (typically a "threshing floor" inside the barn) and beating it with a heavy jointed staff called a flail. The grain could then be fanned and winnowed: large straw fans blew away the chaff from the heavier grain, and further refinement was possible by tossing the grain in a "winnowing basket" of straw that allowed the rest of the chaff to be blown away while the grain remained. Once the harvest had been reduced to the actual grains, it was ready to be stored, most for eventual consumption, but a part always set aside (typically about one-sixth to one-eighth of the crop) for next year's planting.

Grain was stored whole because it preserved better this way; it would only be ground into flour as needed. The process of grinding was one of the oldest industrialized technologies in Europe: by the end of the Middle Ages, almost all the flour produced in Europe was processed in a mill. A few parts of England, particularly the eastern counties, used windmills, but in most of the country, the mills were water-powered: a pair of heavy grindstones were mounted horizontally, and the top one was connected to a waterwheel by a system of wooden gears and shafts. The grain was poured into a hopper that automatically fed the grain between the stones; the top stone spinning above the stationary one broke open the kernels. The resulting mix could then be refined by sifting to remove the coarser parts of the grain from the fine flour.

The conclusion of harvest was traditionally celebrated with a harvest festival, often coinciding with Michaelmas (September 29). The period after the grain harvest was also traditionally a time for gathering nuts and fruits, as well as for harvesting peas and beans.

As with the depiction of the open-field village itself, this account of the agricultural year does not account for the wide variety of actual practices. There were significant regional variations: the three-field system of crop rotation was particularly characteristic of the open-field regions, whereas in the north, many localities used what is known as the "infield-outfield" system, in which there was an intensely cultivated area directly around the village and an area of shifting cultivation at the periphery. Newly evolving modes of agriculture like four-course rotation similarly dictated different cycles of work. Yet across the board, the overall pattern of annual cyclicality was, as it remains, a distinctive feature of rural life.

THE MESSUAGE

The rural household's living environment depended both on the family's resources and on the local tradition of material culture. In most parts of England, the typical farmhouse was a timber-framed structure with wattle-and-daub infill and a thatched roof; however, in stone-rich areas such as the Cotswolds, stone was the usual building material. The Rose Cottage, on Chedworth's central street, was built of Cotswold stone in the seventeenth century, probably replacing an earlier and simpler home and reflecting the prosperity of its owner. Although the material was particularly characteristic of the Cotswolds, the overall design of the

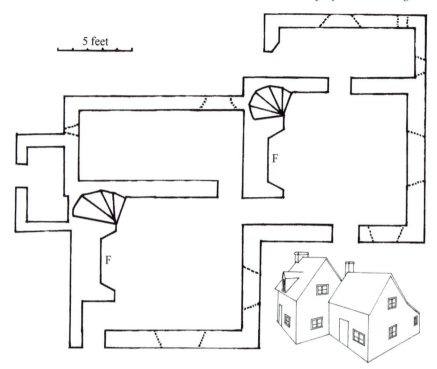

Figure 5.2 The ground floor of the Rose Cottage, with schematic view ("F" designates fireplaces). One of the main rooms on the ground floor served as a parlor (probably the one on the left), the other as a kitchen.

house was typical of homes of the more substantial farming families of the period.[12]

The Rose Cottage is typical of rural homes of the period in having two main rooms on the ground floor, with two others above these. One of the ground floor rooms would have been used as a kitchen, the other as a parlor (for dining and other social activities). The rooms above served as bedchambers. The Rose Cottage also has some service rooms attached at ground level, probably used for storage, dairying, and other similar functions; some rural houses had cellars, useful for cool storage.

The design of the house was heavily dependent on the means of the family. The poorest families might live in a tiny cottage of just one or two rooms, with loft space above for storage. The houses of wealthy rural families—those of substantial yeomen or gentry—were more diverse, but a classic form described by Gervase Markham featured a large central "hall," derived from the main room of the medieval manor house, flanked by two wings in an "H" pattern, one given to household functions, the other for the entertainment of visitors.

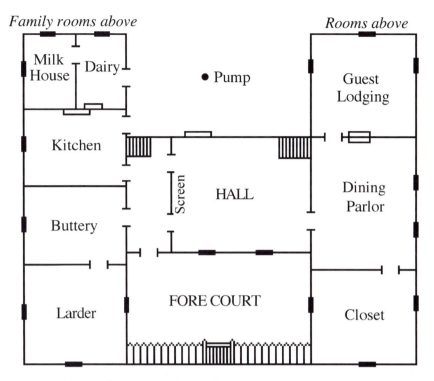

Family rooms above   *Rooms above*

Milk House   Dairy   • Pump   Guest Lodging

Kitchen   Screen   HALL   Dining Parlor

Buttery

Larder   FORE COURT   Closet

Figure 5.3 Plan of a country house for a prosperous yeoman or a minor gentleman, after a design in Gervase Markham's *The English Husbandman* (1613). The "closet" is a private room in the guest wing, the larder is for storing food, the buttery for drinks. Meals would normally take place in the dining parlor. The screen is a wooden partition dividing the hall from the passageway to the main door, the service rooms, and the family's rooms above—it served to cut down on drafts.

In addition to the home, the messuage might include a variety of service buildings. A good example of a well-appointed messuage is that of Chedworth's vicar, which in 1623 included a barn, two stables, a cowshed, a shelter for pigs, and a dovecote. The barn was essential for storing crops and for providing a dry indoor space for threshing. The stables accommodated draft horses and, in the case of a well-off villager like the vicar, almost certainly one or two others just for riding. There might also be a separate shed for a cart or wagon. In addition to the cowshed and pig shelter, many messuages included small houses for chickens, geese, and ducks; there might also be a beehive. The dovecote provided a roosting place to attract pigeons: the young could be pulled from the nests before they learned to fly, providing food for the table, and the bird's dung was highly prized as a fertilizer.[13] The messuage would also have cats and at least one dog, the former to prey on mice in the house and barn and the latter to protect the house and livestock.

Baking and brewing could pose fire hazards and were often relegated to a separate bakehouse and brewhouse on the messuage. Like all houses of the day, the Rose Cottage had a garden; it also had an orchard, a common feature of rural homes in this apple- and pear-growing section of England. Water might be available from a well on the messuage; the inhabitants of the Rose Cottage also had ready access to the village brook, which passed below the orchard, and to a communal well in the center of the village. Vegetable waste and the dung of herbivores would be piled on a dunghill, where it would decompose to provide rich soil for the garden. For human feces and other waste unsuitable for the garden, there would be a privy on the grounds of the messuage; its cesspit would be emptied periodically to fertilize the fields.

The village community also included a number of other facilities frequented by the villagers in general. A village needed at least one smithy and a mill. The blacksmith provided essential services in making and repairing the iron tools on which agriculture depended, as well as shoeing horses and oxen. The mill, as we have already seen, was a key component in the process of transforming the work of the fields into food for the farmer's table. Like many English villages, Chedworth had several mills, lying along the streams that ran through and around the village. As with other holdings in the village, the position of a smith or miller was generally passed on from father to son. Many villages also had one or more alehouses, generally a private home where the woman of the house brewed ale as a means of generating income. An alehouse could be opened by obtaining permission from two justices of the peace, although there were countless unlicensed alehouses in the countryside, many of them private homes temporarily serving guests when there was a surplus of ale in the household.[14] Finally, somewhere in the village there would usually be an enclosure for stray animals, called a pound: animals that got loose were brought here by the manorial official known as a pinner, to be recovered by their owners upon payment of a fine.

THE MANOR

The most elaborate homestead of the village was that of the manor lord, whose grounds typically included a substantial manor house with multiple service buildings, working and ornamental gardens, and a fishpond. Like other holdings in the community, the manor house had a holding of agricultural land associated with it, known as the "demesne": in the Middle Ages, the demesne had been the source of the manor lord's income and had been worked by the lord's serfs as labor service. The demesne at Chedworth in the early seventeenth century consisted of about 150 acres in the open fields, 85 acres of enclosed pasture and meadows, and the right to keep 300 sheep and other livestock on the Downs. Although serfdom had died out, the demesne continued to provide income to the manor lord; it was either worked by hired labor under the management of the manorial steward or let out to subtenants for cash rents.

The institution of the manor had been inherited from the Middle Ages: roughly speaking, a manor had once been the lands required to support a mounted and armored knight. By the 1600s, this military dimension had long since vanished, and the typical manor lord was not even necessarily a resident knight or squire living in the manor house: in many if not most cases, he was an entrepreneur who owned multiple manors, spending little time on any of them and buying and selling them as opportunities arose, leaving the actual administration of the manor to a hired steward.

The case of Chedworth is representative of the complexities of seventeenth-century manorial investment. At the opening of the century, the manor belonged to Sir John Tracy of Toddington, a village about 13 miles north of Chedworth; Tracy had acquired Chedworth manor by purchase. In 1608 Tracy sold the manor house and demesne land to a trio of London investors and the rights of the manor as a whole to William Higgs of London. In 1616 the investors sold the demesne to Sir Richard Grobham of Great Wishford, about 60 miles south in Wiltshire, and two years later, Grobham managed to purchase the entire manor. The manor remained in Grobham's family for the rest of the century, and in 1741 it became a lordship. The manor house at Chedworth had portions dating to the Middle Ages, and by the early 1600s, much of it was probably in a state of disrepair, as there had not been a resident manor lord for a century. Only for a while in the latter part of the 1600s did the manor house come to be used again as a residence for the Grobham family, at which time there was some remodeling of the building; for the most part, the family made their residence at nearby Withington or Stowell Park.

As was often the case, the village and parish of Chedworth did not cover precisely the same territory as the manor. In the northwest part of the parish, there was a separate estate of about four hundred acres called Woodlands. In the Middle Ages, this had been held as a sergeanty, supporting a feudal soldier of a lower level than a knight. In the 1600s, Woodlands also passed through the hands of a series of investors. Another part of the northwestern area of the parish had once been donated to Bruern Abbey and eventually ended up as part of the adjoining manor of Rendcomb.

The manor was one of the chief structures for local government. By custom, each manor held yearly manor courts, at which the villagers administered matters of shared concern. The manor court was largely self-governing, with little involvement from the manor lord: it consisted chiefly of a jury of villagers who issued bylaws for the manor and ruled in matters of dispute. The chief responsibilities of the court were the administration of communal agriculture and the smooth functioning of the village community: issues dealt with included boundary disputes among the villagers, complaints about unfulfilled responsibilities (such as maintenance of the hedges that protected the communal fields from stray animals), and misdemeanors of public concern, such as carrying uncovered coals from one house to another (which would put everyone at risk of fire).

THE PARISH

Aside from the manor house, the other very large building in the village was the parish church. The parish was an extremely important institution for the community, providing not only a spiritual life for the villagers, but also a communal identity and much of the political and social apparatus by which the village operated. National laws, such as the provisions for poor relief and the militia, were administered at the local level through the parish. The church and churchyard were one of the few genuinely public spaces in the village, and they traditionally served as the venue for meetings, festivities, and other public activities, although there was some decline in such practices in the face of Reformist Protestantism. The village church was rarely a modern building: most parish churches had been built in the 1400s at the latest, and many could trace their roots back more than half a millennium to Anglo-Saxon times. Chedworth's church was dedicated to St. Andrew, and parts of the structure dated to about 1100, though there had been multiple modifications over the centuries. The village church was generally built of stone, and often with a slate or tile roof.

Every parishioner was required by law to pay the church an annual tithe, consisting of a tenth of all income, to be rendered in cash or kind— tithable produce included crops from the villagers' fields and both lambs and fleeces produced by their sheep. Administrative authority over the local church was known as the rectory and included the right to appoint the parish priest, the right to collect tithes, and a landholding known as the "glebe." Over the course of the Middle Ages, parish rectories had typically ended up in the hands of someone outside the parish. By the late Middle Ages, the rectory of Chedworth had been acquired by the monastic establishment of Sheen Priory. After the dissolution of the monasteries by Henry VIII, the rectory was acquired by private investors, and by 1600, it had been donated to support the grammar school in Northleach, a bit northeast of Chedworth. The rectory consisted of about 100 acres of glebe lands, and two-thirds of the tithes of the parish, worth a total of about £80 a year by the end of the 1600s.

As Chedworth's rector, the grammar school was responsible for hiring a "vicar" to discharge the actual duties of the parish priest; in this case, the choice of vicar was actually made by Queen's College, Oxford, who had become patron of the school in 1606. The vicarage came with a house near the church; the vicar also received the residual third of the parish tithes and had a glebe of a few acres in closes, 90 acres of open field, and sheep pasturage. This was supplemented by an annual payment of £1 6s. 8d. out of the rectory. In all, the vicar's living was valued at £50 in 1650. In the Middle Ages, the parish priest might have been something of a peasant himself, working the land during the week, but by the 1600s, the level of education—and material expectations—of the clergy were significantly higher, and the priest would generally hire laborers to till his fields, or lease them out for cash income.

The administration of the parish church was in part the responsibility of the vestry, a body of substantial local landholders who chose from among themselves a number of churchwardens to act as executive officers of the parish. The vestry's responsibilities included overseeing the parish finances and maintaining parish facilities, such as the church, but they also appointed the officers who administered national laws at the local level. These included the overseers of the poor, who administered the poor laws, and constables, responsible for basic law enforcement. Like the vestry, these officials were chosen from among the leading local householders and were generally of yeoman status.

THE RURAL HOUSEHOLD

The rural household was a complex economic unit involving multiple people in diverse income-generating activities. Farming work was largely segregated by gender: generally speaking, field labor was done by the men, and work around the messuage was the domain of the women.

Both the man and the woman might be assisted in their work by children and hired help. Depending on the size of his landholding, the householder might work it himself, hire workers to do it for him, or leave the work entirely to the hired help while he devoted his time to other pursuits—ideally the economic betterment of the household through farm management and enterprise. In addition to the year-by-year hiring of servants, day laborers might be hired on a short-term basis for periods of intense work on the farm, particularly haymaking and harvesting. Such temporary workers lived a difficult and precarious life, traveling from one community to another in search of work, which could be hard to find during the slow seasons, although there was at least some ongoing demand for threshers throughout the year.

The role of women in the household was in many ways more complex than that of the men. Whereas most of the men's effort was taken up by the cycle of planting and harvesting, women had to perform a broad range of functions to keep the household running. In addition to the responsibilities common to all housewives of the period, the rural woman was expected to brew ale or beer, the staple drink of the English home as well as a source of cash for the household: both of these had a limited shelf-life, so whenever a batch was brewed, the surplus was sold. She also tended the garden and orchard and looked after the animals. Poultry did not require much attention, but dairy animals were another matter: during dairying season, they had to be milked, and the milk had to be converted to butter or cheese before it went bad. If a thrifty housewife could find the time, she might also do some spinning to generate more money as well.

Then as now, shopping was one of the responsibilities of the homemaker, but this was a more complex undertaking in a seventeenth-century village than it is today: a journey to a market town was an all-day affair and involved selling as well as buying, since surplus produce was an important source of cash for the family. There were a number of weekly markets within a day's journey of Chedworth: Gloucester had markets on Wednesdays and Saturdays, Cirencester had them on Mondays and Fridays, and on Thursdays there were markets in both Stow-on-the-Wold and Cheltenham. These market towns also hosted annual fairs: May 1 in Stow, June 24 in Gloucester, and October 21 in Cirencester. In part because of her role in provisioning the household, the woman bore a large part of the responsibility for managing the family's finances.

THE CHANGING RURAL LANDSCAPE

Overall, the seventeenth-century English village was a community in transition, where medieval features existed side-by-side with modernizing trends. Manorial structures were still very much in place, open-field farming was common in many parts of the country, and the medieval parish remained a defining structure in local administration and community identity. But market forces were fast undermining this integrated socioeconomic unit, as villagers consolidated their landholdings in order to take advantage of new entrepreneurial modes of agriculture. The once-vast communal fields of the open-field village were being broken up into individual holdings, and landless cottagers had to find alternative means to support themselves. Many turned toward craft production. In iron-rich areas such as the West Midlands, simple metalworking crafts like nail-making became an increasingly important part of the village economy. In sheep-rearing areas such as the Cotswolds, wool processing played a larger role—the sheriff of Somerset in 1622 remarked on the "multitude of poor cottages built upon the high ways and odd corners in every country parish ... stuffed with poor people ... that did get most of their living by spinning, carding, and such employments about wool and cloth."[15] Already by 1700, many rural districts of England were beginning to take on a semi-industrialized look, setting the stage for the country's definitive transformation from a rural to an industrial economy in the 1700s and 1800s. Once again, the transition can be seen in Chedworth: of 36 men inscribed in the village's militia rolls in 1608, 16 are husbandmen, and 2 are smiths, but there are also 2 masons (doubtless working the local Cotswold stone), 2 carpenters, 5 tailors, a weaver, a woolwinder, 2 shoemakers, and a glover.[16]

NOTES

1. Julian Hoppit, *A Land of Liberty? England 1689–1727* (Oxford: Clarendon Press, 2000), 53, 346.

2. Chedworth was among the villages enclosed by the parliamentary act that effectively ended open-field farming in 1803. Additional sources on Chedworth include the following: Sir Robert Atkyns, *The Ancient and Present State of Glostershire* (London: Robert Gosling, 1712); N. M. Herbert, ed., *The Victoria History of the County of Gloucester* (Oxford: Oxford University Press, 1987), 7.163–74; John Smith, *Men and Armour for Gloucestershire in 1608* (Gloucester: Alan Sutton, 1980), 253–54. I am also indebted to Greenfield Village Museum, Detroit, for access to their files on Chedworth, and to Mike Tovey for sharing his transcriptions of various Chedworth documents.

3. Donald Lupton, *London and the Countrey Carbonadoed* (London: N. Okes, 1632), 112–15.

4. On tenure and landholdings, see Samuel Hartlib, *The Compleat Husband-man* (London: Edward Brewster, 1659), 45; Lupton, *London*, 108ff.; Eric S. Wood, *Historical Britain* (London: Harvill Press, 1995), 52ff.; Keith Wrightson, *Earthly Necessities: Economic Lives in Early Modern Britain* (New Haven: Yale University Press, 2000), 184ff.

5. On hedges, walls, and so forth, see Joseph Blagrave, *The Epitome of the Art of Husbandry* (London: Benjamin Billingsley and Obadiah Blagrave, 1669), 38ff., 166; Wood, *Britain,* 78.

6. On coppicing and pollarding, see Wood, *Britain,* 17.

7. The landholding is detailed in a deed of 1748; it is possible that the distribution of the holding had changed since the 1600s, but the holding as described is consistent with holdings of the previous century. The Rose Cottage itself is one of very few English buildings of this period now in North America.

8. Fynes Moryson, *An Itinerary* (London: John Beale, 1617), 3.147. On enclosure, see also Hoppit, *Land,* 358–59.

9. On agricultural innovations and enclosure, see Blagrave, *Epitome,* 198ff.; Hartlib, *Husband-man*; Hoppit, *Land,* 361ff.; Wood, *Britain,* 73; Wrightson, *Necessities,* 162ff., 209ff., 233.

10. I am indebted to Mike Tovey for his transcription of the glebe terrier of 1623, GRO Ref P77 IN 3/1.

11. Particularly useful sources on the agricultural cycle include Joseph Blagrave, *The Epitome of the Art of Husbandry* (London: Benjamin Billingsley and Obadiah Blagrave, 1669); Thomas Tusser, *Five Hundred Points of Good Husbandry,* ed. Geoffrey Grigson (Oxford: Oxford University Press, 1984); and Dorothy Hartley, *Lost Country Life* (New York: Pantheon, 1979).

12. The name of the cottage is modern; it can be seen today at Greenfield Village Museum, outside of Detroit. It was brought to America in 1930 by Henry Ford, and the building has been somewhat modified since the seventeenth century, notably by the addition of porches to the main doors, but overall, its shape remains representative of seventeenth-century rural homes.

13. On dovecotes, see Wood, *Britain,* 100ff.; John McCann, "An Historical Inquiry into the Design and Use of Dovecotes," *Transactions of the Ancient Monuments Society* 35 (1991): 89–160.

14. On country alehouses, see Lupton, *London,* 127–31; Peter Clark, *The English Alehouse: A Social History 1200–1830* (London and New York: Longman, 1983); R. F. Bretherton, "Country Inns and Alehouses," in *Englishmen at Rest and Play: Some Phases of English Leisure 1558–1714* (Oxford: Clarendon Press, 1931), 145–202.

15. Wrightson, *Earthly Necessities,* 194.

16. John Smith, *Men and Armour for Gloucestershire in 1608* (Gloucester: Alan Sutton, 1980), 254.

6

CITY LIFE

Although the majority of the English population lived in the country, a growing proportion were living in urban communities. Historians believe that in 1600, some 8 percent of the population were living in towns of more than 5,000 people; by 1700, this figure had risen to 17 percent.[1] These urban communities still accounted for only a minority of the overall population, but their influence was greater than their actual numbers might suggest: they were the hubs around which the whole of the economic, social, and cultural life of the nation revolved. These towns spanned a broad spectrum, with populations ranging from the hundreds to the hundreds of thousands. For convenience, they can be classified as market towns, major towns, and London, which was in a class by itself.

The market town was the smallest and most numerous type of urban settlement: there were upwards of six hundred, and few places in England were more than 5 to 10 miles away from one of them. There were some seven hundred small market towns, with populations numbering from the hundreds to about 2,500 people. These towns chiefly provided focal points serving the surrounding rural communities. They hosted a weekly market at which farmers from the district could sell their wares, and they provided small centers of retail and craft production where rural families could purchase regularly needed goods and services that were not available in the villages.[2]

Major towns were lively urban communities in their own right and were less intimately connected with the countryside. They were hubs of domestic trade and centers for craft production. Many of these towns had fortifications, although these were mostly old, dating to the Middle Ages, and required substantial reworking during the Civil Wars in order to be effective against contemporary siege weapons. These towns were also important administrative centers. For the state, they served as seats of regional government, residences of administrators, and venues for regional courts. They were also ecclesiastical centers, particularly in the case of cathedral towns that served as the regional bishop's residence. There were about 37 towns numbering 2,500 to 5,000; about 30 over 5,000; and a handful of cities with populations over 10,000. The largest towns apart from London were Bristol and Norwich, at around 20,000 each.[3] As commercial centers, these large towns were focal points in the network of transportation, linked by major roads to other large towns, and they usually had good access to water transport by sea or river. These larger towns also had one or more weekly markets and were also the sites of annual fairs, bringing traders from around the country as well as from overseas. These fairs had been major commercial venues during the Middle Ages, but by the 1600s, they were losing much of their economic importance.[4]

LONDON

An enormous gap existed between even the largest of these major towns and London.[5] Home to some 200,000 souls at the beginning of the century, and 575,000 by the end, London accounted for about 5 percent of the entire population of England in 1600 and over 10 percent in 1700, and it grew from the third-largest city in Europe (after Paris and Naples) to the largest. London was also growing more rapidly than any other English city, although after 1650, this dominance was starting to wane, as regional urban centers began to grow more rapidly, presaging the pattern of the Industrial Revolution.[6] Beyond its sheer numbers, London dominated the political, cultural, and economic life of England. This chapter focuses in particular on London as the fullest manifestation of urban life in England, specifically through the London "suburb" of Southwark, the area at the south end of London Bridge, across the River Thames from the City proper.

Like a number of England's major cities, London had been an urban center in the Roman Empire, although the urban settlement was disrupted during the post-Roman period. Towns had reestablished themselves over the course of the Middle Ages, partly as administrative centers, partly as centers of craft production, and partly as hubs of trade. London was an episcopal seat and an important producer of manufactured goods, but its most important feature was its location: the city lay on the tidal waters of the Thames, with good access to ports on the Continent, and at the lowest point on the river capable of supporting a bridge, given the technology of the period. London Bridge was the gateway to the rich farmlands and important urban centers of southern England, and the city was above all a center for trade by both land and sea.

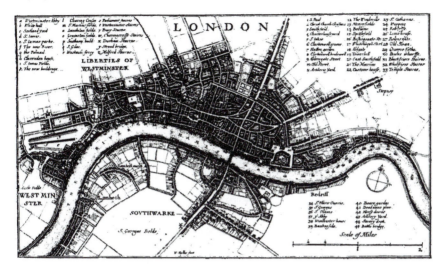

Wenceslaus Hollar's map of London before the Great Fire of 1666 (Hind 1922).

Stuart London was still small by modern standards: by the late 1600s, it was still only seven miles east to west, and only two and a half from the city's northernmost point to the south end of Blackman Street in Southwark.[7] At its core was the City of London proper, consisting of the area within the medieval city walls plus a few adjacent suburbs. The wall roughly encompassed the site of the Roman city and had about half a dozen gatehouses through which passed the major roads that connected London to the rest of the country.

The western end of the City was dominated by St. Paul's Cathedral, the seat of the bishop of London. The cathedral as it stood in 1600 was a Gothic church built during the Middle Ages, but this structure was destroyed in the Great Fire of 1666, and during the last quarter of the century, it was replaced by the domed structure that stands today, designed by Sir Christopher Wren. At the opposite end of the City was the Tower of London, initiated by William the Conqueror in the late eleventh century and expanded over the course of the Middle Ages. During the seventeenth century, the Tower not only was the nation's most important fortress, but also served as an arsenal, prison, government storehouse, and royal palace, and it was the location of the national mint, several government record offices, the royal menagerie, and the crown jewels. The massive structure of St. Paul's and the sprawling Tower complex were two of the nation's most important centers of church and state, and they dominated the skyline of London; between them were the spires of over a hundred parish churches.

Like most seventeenth-century cities, London's street plan had evolved organically during the Middle Ages. One important factor in the shape of a town was the major governmental and ecclesiastical centers, like the Tower and St. Paul's. The other major shaping force was the city's economic and transportation infrastructure. Market areas, wharves, guild-halls, and the gates out of the town were linked to each other by a complex pattern of meandering streets, making London's street system look like a network of overlapping spider webs.

One of the most important arteries leading out of London was the road across London Bridge, which led to Canterbury, Dover, and the other major towns and ports south of the Thames, as well as to the farmlands of Surrey, Kent, Sussex, and Hampshire. A traveler leaving London by the bridge would pass along a street lined with houses—with heavy traffic channeling across it every day, the bridge was a high-visibility commercial area, and the buildings on the bridge were some of the most expensive real estate in town. The bridge was a stone structure built in 1176–1209 to replace an earlier bridge of wood. Toward its southern end was a wooden drawbridge—long disused and now no longer functional—and a gate-house with a portcullis; like other gates to the city, it was shut at night as a security precaution. On top of the gatehouse were displayed the heads of executed political criminals, impaled on pikes—a grim welcome to the city and one that never failed to impress foreign visitors with its barbarity,

Figure 6.1 A view of the south end of London bridge, from a print of 1616 by Klaes van Visscher (Besant 1904).

though it doubtless served its function as a reminder of the state's power over the life and death of its subjects.

The drawbridge was one of the few points on the bridge from which one could actually see the Thames. Downriver to the east, there were large seagoing craft sailing to and from the wharves that linked London to the economic centers of Continental Europe and the emerging global trade routes. There were several wharves in Southwark frequented by vessels of this sort, and St. Olave's parish, on the seaward side of London Bridge, was home to a significant population of sailors. Upriver, countless smaller craft plied the waters: fishing boats taking fishes and eels from the Thames, barges carrying goods and travelers along the heavily populated Thames valley, and small rowboats called "wherries" ferrying pedestrians from point to point on London's riverbanks. It was estimated around the turn of the seventeenth century that there were some 2,000 of these wherries in London, and a 1622 survey of heads of households in the Bankside area of Southwark found that nearly half worked as watermen on some kind of river-going boat. The riverfront in Southwark was dotted with small docks and stairs down to the water, serving as boarding points for these craft. The basic rate for a wherry ride was 1d., but the fare could be higher for longer distances, and it tripled for a journey against the tide. Samuel Pepys, like most Londoners, made extensive use of wherries for getting about town, and he was a frequent visitor to the Southwark tavern known as the Bear at Bridge Foot, where he could enjoy a leisurely drink close to the wherries at Bridge Stairs while he waited for the tide to change.

SOUTHWARK

Whether by land or water, the traveler coming from the City to Southwark would often enter at the foot of the bridge, at the head of the street known as Long Southwark (today called Borough High Street). The geographical area of Southwark was organized around three main axes fanning out from the bridge. To the west was the Bankside, a riverside area of resort and entertainment frequented by Londoners from all parts of town. To the east was St. Olave's Street (now corrupted to Tooley Street), an area largely inhabited by lesser tradesmen and craftsmen, and increasingly by the poor toward its eastern end. To the south was Long Southwark, the commercial heart of Southwark, which led into the street called St. Margaret's Hill, which itself turned into Blackman Street further south. Branching off these main streets were innumerable alleys, yards, and closes (dead-end streets).

Like most urban communities of the period, Stuart Southwark was a patchwork of overlapping jurisdictions inherited from the Middle Ages. Because the relatively rigid structures of feudalism were not hospitable to the flourishing of crafts and commerce, towns had emerged in the Middle

City Government

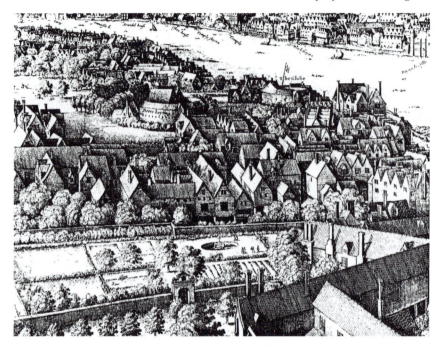

Figure 6.2 From Wenceslaus Hollar's perspective view of London in 1647, looking west toward the Bankside from the top of St. Saviour's church (Hind 1922).

Ages as zones of relative freedom from feudal control; feudal lords were often happy to grant these freedoms because of the income the towns could generate within their domains. Urban land was held from a feudal lord, but in a form known as "burgage tenure." Burgage land could be bought and sold freely without any involvement from the lord, and it carried with it no personal burdens or restrictions on the holder. However, within this general framework there were myriad variations depending on local history, and Southwark is an excellent example of the complexities that seventeenth-century towns inherited from their medieval past.

The feudal lords of London were the kings of England, who had granted considerable autonomy to this valuable commercial center over the course of the Middle Ages. The City of London was self-governing under the crown and was immensely rich and powerful. It was divided into 26 wards: in each ward, the guild masters elected an alderman who served for an unlimited term; the alderman was assisted by two deputies. Like many governmental posts of the period, the alderman was not paid for his services, and in spite of the powers the position offered, many of those elected chose to pay a fine rather than take on the burdens of the office.[8] The Court of Aldermen, the chief governing body of the City, included the 26 aldermen and the Lord Mayor, elected from among their number. The

Court was responsible for city government, finances, and law, and its chief executive officer was the City Sheriff.

Outside the City proper, there were two major suburbs. Westminster, about two miles upstream from the City, was the seat of national government, home to the houses of Parliament, the national law courts, and the royal palace of Whitehall. The other major suburb was Southwark: the economic and strategic importance of the bridge, combined with Southwark's distinctive situation as a semi-independent suburb directly adjoining the City, made Southwark a unique and very significant place in seventeenth-century England.

Stuart Southwark consisted of two general jurisdictions: the Borough, which was under the authority of the City of London, and the Bankside, which was not. The Borough of Southwark constituted the London ward of "Bridge Ward Without" (i.e., outside the City). Like other wards, Bridge Ward Without had its own alderman and two deputies. However, in contrast with other wards, the alderman was chosen by the Court of Aldermen, rather than by the guild masters of the ward itself, so the connection between the alderman and his ward was rather weak. Within Southwark, the alderman had theoretical responsibility for civil order, including such matters as policing and maintaining the streets. Yet in practice the alderman had limited impact on the life of Southwark because the main structures of administration and enforcement were based on the manor and the parish, not the city ward.[9]

The Borough of Southwark consisted of three manors, which had taken shape during the Middle Ages: Guildable Manor near the bridge, King's Manor to the south, and Great Liberty Manor to the east. The City of London had acquired Guildable Manor in the Middle Ages, and in 1550 it purchased the other two. Essentially, the City was the manor lord of the Borough of Southwark, and it was as manorial lord that the City exercised its real power. Although this manorial structure was anomalous within London, the actual operation of manorial administration within Southwark was typical of urban administration in Stuart towns.

The City's principal manorial officer was the steward, who was responsible for overseeing other manorial officers and the manorial courts. The courts were convened every October: each manor had its own court, consisting chiefly of a jury of about 15 to 20 jurors selected from the community. The jury was empowered to hear cases of civil and minor criminal matters and to issue bylaws for the manor: the chief areas of regulation were fire prevention, pollution, street maintenance, traffic control, and marketplace conduct. Typical of the yearly work of the manor courts were the efforts of the Guildable Manor jury in 1667, who spent two days wandering the streets of the manor to test the scales of shopkeepers and market stallholders against their own official sets. They issued a series of fines to various tradesmen for having deficient weights, as well as against the manorial bailiff for allowing a deficient weight in the meal market.

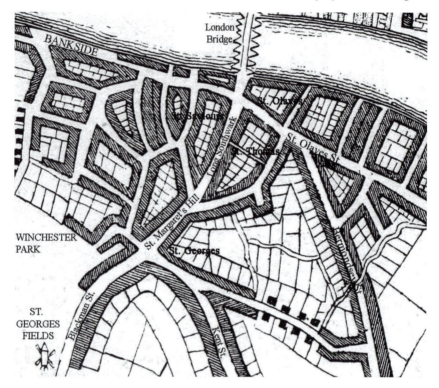

Map of Southwark.

The steward also supervised the "Pie-Powder" court held each year dur-ing Southwark Fair—this court was designed to administer swift justice for the fair's temporary population.[10]

The most important manorial officers under the steward were the con-stables, who were selected from the leading householders of the commu-nity; they were assisted by deputies in their work. The constables were unpaid officers responsible for basic law enforcement. They executed warrants, rounded up vagrants, reported unlicensed victualers, examined weights and measures, and responded to minor nuisances. They were also involved in organizing the local watch and militia (trained bands). There were 4 constables in Guildable manor, 5 in King's Manor, and 13 in Great Liberty Manor; each was assigned to a particular neighborhood within the manor.[11]

Each manor had other lesser officers as well. The aletasters, sometimes called aleconners, were principally responsible for enforcing regulations on ale and bread, the staples of the English diet. Surveyors of the flesh mar-ket were appointed to ensure that substandard meats were not being sold in the manor. Each manor had two scavengers, responsible for overseeing

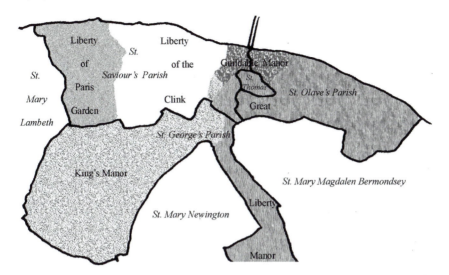

Figure 6.3 Southwark's manors and liberties (shaded areas) and parishes (in italics, outlined in black).

the collection of waste and the cleaning of the streets; they contracted "rakers" to do the actual work. The City also appointed a bailiff for Southwark, chiefly responsible for the administration of the law: he collected court fines and organized the manorial juries, in addition to such miscellaneous tasks as receiving the rents for the City's property in Southwark. Southwark sent two members to Parliament and was a "scot and lot" constituency, having as wide an electorate as was possible at the time—essentially, all householders wealthy enough to pay the "subsidy" or "scot and lot" taxes had the right to vote.[12]

ST. SAVIOUR'S CHURCH: THE URBAN PARISH

The single most prominent building as the visitor entered Southwark from the north was the parish church of St. Saviour's, a visible reminder of the continuing importance of the church in the lives of seventeenth-century Englishmen. St. Saviour's was a large Gothic church standing just west of the bridge, and it is one of the few structures in modern London that predates the fire of 1666. St. Saviour's had originally been the church for the Augustinian priory of St. Mary Overies, but with the dissolution of the monasteries by Henry VIII, the priory's property was sold off by the crown, and the church became a parish church.

There were four parishes in Southwark. St. Saviour's served the northwestern section, numbering about 7,000 parishioners at the beginning of the century and including neighborhoods in both the Borough and

Bankside. St. Olave's, a stone's throw downriver from the bridge, served the northeastern section, with about 8,000 people. St. George's served the southern section, with about 3,000. St. Thomas's served a small parish of about 500 in the immediate vicinity of St. Thomas's Hospital. In 1672 the Bankside manor of Paris Garden was removed from St. Saviour's to create Christchurch parish—a sign of the growing population of the Bankside.[13] These churches fell within the deanery of Southwark, which was part of the archdeaconry of Surrey, within the diocese of Winchester.

Everyone was theoretically expected to attend Sunday services at their own parish church under pain of fines, but this was never much enforced unless the nonattender was believed to be a Catholic or Separatist: in 1633, when the diocese inquired into nonattendance in the parish, the churchwardens of St. Saviour's responded that "the parish being very great, we know not who doth therein offend, and there is no money taken of any."[14] In fact, Southwark's parish churches would have been unable to accommodate the parishioners if they had all chosen to show up to any given service.

At least among the upper levels of the community, church attendance was probably fairly high, and indeed presence in church was an important means of asserting one's place in society. Being seated in the pews in the front of the church was a mark of high status and was much coveted by the socially aspirant. The assignment of pews was often a hotly contested issue. In 1639 the churchwardens of St. Saviour's complained to the Bishop of Winchester that "the pew wherein one Mrs. Ware sits and pretends to be placed, is and hath always been a pew for women of a far better rank and quality than she, and for such whose husbands pay far greater duties than hers."[15] In 1634 Marie Chambers of St. Saviour's was presented to the church courts "for refusing to sit in the pew where she is placed by the churchwardens, and procuring a key to be made to the lock of the pew from whence she was removed without the leave of any of the churchwardens, and striving to sit there still, having been by them warned to the contrary and placed in another decent pew."[16]

St. Saviour's was the most important and prosperous church in Southwark. As was usual, governance was in the hands of the vestry, consisting of 30 prominent parishioners. Vacant places in the vestry were filled by cooption, and a seat on the vestry was a mark of leadership in the community. The vestry selected four to six churchwardens, laymen who acted as executive officers of the parish. An unusual feature of St. Saviour's was that its two ministers were appointed by the churchwardens—it was more common for the rectory (including the right to appoint the vicar) to belong to someone other than the parish itself.

Supervision of the parish was partly through the church hierarchy, but civil authorities also played a part, since the parish played an important role in civil administration. Some parish officers, such as the overseers of the poor, were under the authority of the justices of the peace because their chief function was the implementation of national laws. The range of parish functions is suggested by the various records kept by St. Saviour's parish, which included vestry minutes, the churchwarden's account books, account books of the overseers of the poor, tithe books, pew placement books, a book of leases of parish property, and records of marriages, baptisms, and burials. The parish also had some responsibility for the surveyors of the highways, who ensured that the roads were properly maintained, and the parish additionally kept and maintained equipment for the trained bands.[17]

One of the most important civil functions of the parish was relief of the poor, mandated by national Poor Laws **Relief of the** passed during the reign of Elizabeth and administered by **Poor** the "overseers of the poor." St. Saviour's had four overseers of the poor, drawn from the vestry.[18] Poor relief was supported by the Poor Rate, a tax levied on the more well-off parish householders; this money was supplemented by other parish funds and by the occasional bequest. Relief was disbursed for both long-term and short-term needs. The long-term poor, including the elderly and the infirm, widows, and abandoned wives, were assisted by ongoing weekly payments. Short-term support was handed out for extraordinary circumstances. The sums were small and not really sufficient to support the recipient without additional income: typical pensions in Southwark were about 7–9d. a week, well less than the 14d. a laborer might expect to make in a day.

The parishes also had responsibility for permanent charitable establishments for supporting the long-term poor. One of the most important in St. Saviour's parish was the "College of the Poor," which housed 16 people: residents were selected by the parish administration, priority being given to those who were aged past the point of work, followed in order by the lame and sick, the blind, those "despoiled of their goods and brought from riches to poverty by any sudden casualty," the chronically sick, and families "overcharged with a burthen of children."[19] Residents received 20d. a week in addition to free fuel, bread, and lodging, as well as extra payments at Easter, at Christmas, in cold weather, and during sickness. Their life was strictly regulated: they were required to wear distinctive gowns and a badge; they were not allowed to marry; they were expected to work to the degree that they were able; and they could be fined or expelled for improper conduct, including tippling, begging, swearing, and railing.[20] The life of such people is illustrated by the petition of the widow Ann Tedder to be admitted to the college: she was

above three score and twelve years of age and past labor, and hath nothing to live on but a pension of 8d. a week, and not able to pay any rent for dwelling, and destitute of friends to relieve her living in extreme need and misery. Wherefore she humbly beseecheth your worships in respect she is a lone woman and hath been long acquainted with Goody Coleman, being now also a lone woman living in the College where there are two rooms with chimneys in them, that your worships will be pleased to suffer her to dwell in the house with the said Goody Coleman.[21]

The able-bodied poor might be sent to a workhouse: Southwark authorities regularly purchased hemp and flax for such people to work on.[22] Other charitable foundations were independent of the parish. Across the street from St. Saviour's church was St. Thomas's Hospital, a medieval establishment that cared for the elderly and permanently infirm who were too poor to support themselves. In 1629 it housed some three hundred residents, attended to by 13 "sisters" (nurses), a physician, an apothecary, three surgeons, and an herb-woman. Support might also be available from a guild: John Norgate, a stationer of St. Saviour's parish, wealthy enough to contribute to the poor rate in 1621–1622, received charitable support from the Stationers' Company in 1636. Many of the chronic poor had to resort to begging: according to certain St. Saviour's residents in 1619, the wife of a local poulterer, "having but one eye and going with a staff[,] did live by begging, and with Agnes Cooper alias Shell did daily beg together."[23]

Because the Poor Laws mandated that the poor were the responsibility of the local parish, there was a strong incentive to keep poor people from moving into the neighborhood: in 1631 some three hundred vagrants were expelled from the Borough in a six-month period. Christopher Fawcett, an agent hired by St. Saviour's parish in the early 1600s to seek out newcomers and force them to pay a bond or leave, reported a typical instance: "William Price with his wife and two children being come from St. George to dwell in Fishmonger Alley, I took a constable with me, and went to them, and told them that either they must put in sureties to discharge the parish, or be gone again; when being unable to put in sureties, went again out of the parish, and so we were rid of them."[24]

Schools The parish was also involved in education. Primary schooling was provided by petty schools, either private or attached to one of the local churches: John Hawkins, schoolmaster at St. George's, published a textbook for schoolboys in 1692. For more advanced students, there were two grammar schools in Southwark, one associated with St. Saviour's, the other with St. Olave's. These were supported in part by rents collected from properties donated by benefactors.[25]

Private tutors were also abundantly available in London for a wide range of subjects: one author in the late 1600s mentioned languages, geography, navigation, surgery, chemistry, calligraphy, shorthand, riding, fencing, dancing, military, fireworks, limning, painting, sculpture, architecture, heraldry, music, and arithmetic.[26] There was no university in London, but at the west end of the City, outside the walls, were the Inns of Court, which were essentially colleges where young men could get training in the law.

St. Saviour's church and parish leaned toward Puritanism, as was common in communities with a large proportion of petty tradesmen and craftsmen. In addi- **Nonconformity** tion to the official church, early seventeenth-century Southwark was also a center of the suppressed sect of Brownists, an early form of Congrega- tionalists named after Robert Browne, who had once taught at St. Olave's School. By 1672, there were five Congregationalist or Presbyterian meeting houses, as well as one each for the Quakers and Baptists.[27] Stephen Harris, an agent of the government responsible for the detection of several Sepa- ratist churches in Southwark, petitioned to the Privy Council in 1662 that because of his service to the government "your petitioner hath quite lost his trade, living in the Borough of Southwark amongst the most numerous factious people . . . and consequently ruined himself by being marked out by them as a Saul or persecutor of the people, as they term him."[28] Among the Puritan-minded families of seventeenth-century Southwark was that of John Harvard, son of a Long Southwark butcher and vestryman, who attended St. Saviour's School and later Emmanuel College, Cambridge. In 1637, Harvard immigrated to Boston, where his legacy would help found America's first university.

LONG SOUTHWARK: URBAN DEMOGRAPHICS AND ECONOMY

Passing St. Saviour's along Long Southwark, travelers would find themselves in the heart of the Borough on a street thronging with people and commercial activity. The population of Southwark at the beginning of the century was around 20,000; by century's end, it had increased to over 30,000. Newcomers were attracted to the city because of its rela- tively fluid labor market and economic opportunities: wages in South- wark tended to be 50–100 percent higher than in the country, although this was at least partially offset by higher prices. The increasing popu- lation reflected a constant stream of immigration into the city from the countryside and from smaller towns, as well as some immigration from overseas. In fact, living conditions in the seventeenth-century city were so unhealthy that the death rate exceeded the birth rate, and this was exacerbated periodically by epidemic disease, particularly the great plague of 1665. London as a whole appears to have required 6,000 immi- grants every year to maintain its rate of growth, and in St. Saviour's parish in 1636, it is estimated that 1 householder in 22 had been resident for less than a year.[29]

Foreign immigrants to England tended to gravitate toward London, and Southwark in particular, because of the economic opportunities there. These were mostly Protestant refugees from France and the Low Countries, and they tended to be relatively skilled and well educated. St. Thomas's parish had a particularly high number of foreigners, perhaps as high as one-sixth of the population, with St. Olave's next at 1 in 25; other parts of Southwark were around the London norm of 1–2 percent.[30]

The Market   Much of Southwark's life, as that of any city, took place in its streets. The streets were packed with people going to and fro about their work, travelers coming in and out of the city, and carriers transporting the goods that London needed to support its growing population. Long Southwark was an especially broad street, and it was not only a major national artery, but also the site of a market on Mondays, Wednesdays, Fridays, and Saturdays. The market was held on the west side of the street, and it extended about two hundred yards from the end of London Bridge to Market House, a small structure in the middle of the street from which the market was supervised and where a public weighing-beam was kept to ensure that flour was sold by proper measures. An ordinance of 1624 assigned the north end of the market to vendors from the country, including women selling butter and farmers with veal, lamb, pork, and bacon. After this came the sellers of fresh fish; then local victualers, including bakers and vendors of fruits, vegetables, and flowers; then the flour market; and finally the butchers.[31] The market opened before dawn and lasted until midafternoon (slightly longer in the summer and shorter in the winter).

Southwark market was frequented by vendors from London, Middlesex, Essex, Kent, and Surrey, as well as locals. For people like Nathaniel Drury, a cobbler who lived by St. Saviour's church, a stall in the market was a means of getting better visibility for his wares than was possible from his home shop, although like many other stallholders, his aggressive sales techniques brought him afoul of the authorities: in 1620 he was called before the manorial court "for hanging shoes out beyond the edge of his stall to the annoyance of his neighbours."[32] In fact, the location of the market along a major national road was inevitably a traffic problem because the market tended to clog up the street, and many people felt that it needed to be relocated. The issue was exacerbated by the market's tendency to expand in time as well as space: an order had to be issued in 1676 that the market was to take place only on its appointed days.[33]

Inns and Victualing Houses   In most of the buildings fronting main streets such as Long Southwark, the ground floor was given over to some sort of commercial establishment. On Long Southwark, about half of these belonged to producers and retailers of food and drink, and a significant number of the rest were inns. Because Southwark lay on the principal road between London and the south, there were an enormous number of inns in the area. The best inns were found on Long Southwark. Among them was the Tabard Inn, on the east side of the street, just where it fed into St. Margaret's Hill: the Tabard had been famous since the fourteenth century as the starting place of the pilgrims in Geoffrey Chaucer's *Canterbury Tales.* Just north of the Tabard was the George, a portion of which survives today.[34] As well as the large inns, there were smaller victualing houses (restaurants), taverns, and alehouses; Southwark was believed to have 350 alehouses in 1604.[35]

The inns typically had an archway fronting on the street, big enough to accommodate wagons as they came into the innyard; surrounding the yard were not only lodgings and dining rooms, but also warehouses. London's inns were frequented by carriers, the wagon-drivers who brought goods and passengers to and from the city. Because carriers tended to do their business at the inn where they were staying, the inns doubled as centers for commerce and transportation. One guidebook from 1637 lists the inns where the carriers from the various towns in England could be found: "to the George in Southwark come every Thursday the carriers from Guilford, Wonersh, Goudhurst, and Chiddingfold in Surrey, also thither come out of Sussex (on the same days weekly) the carriers of Battle, Sandwich, and Hastings."[36] Commerce of this sort outside of the public market was called "forestalling the market" and had been illegal since the Middle Ages: Guildable Manor in 1624 ordered that no "persons buy any provisions in any inn or private warehouse but in the open market." Yet the challenge of feeding London's rapidly growing population made it more practical for buyers and sellers to prearrange regular shipments of goods into the city, to be handled in these innyards. There seems to have been some official recognition of these changing economic realities: also in 1624, the court in King's Manor ordered that inns "keep beams and scales in their yards that they have their measures sealed by the clerk of the market and chained with a chain, that every traveler may have the full measure of their cattle [i.e., goods]."[37]

Most of the remaining building fronts on Long Southwark were given over to the shops of craftsmen and tradesmen. Crafts were also important in the urban economy; a full range was represented in Southwark, although like other urban communities, Southwark particularly specialized in a few areas. Because Southwark was especially well served with streams, it was home to a number of industries that required substantial supplies of water. Brewers were numerous, and leather-making was also an important local industry, mostly in the Boroughside area of St. Saviour's parish, which was the center of London's leather industry. Dyers were numerous in the Bankside, close to the plentiful water supply of the Thames. There were also grist mills over a few of the larger streams where they poured into the Thames. Practitioners of a particular trade often clustered in the same neighborhood. Butchers congregated on the west side of Long Southwark, an arrangement intended to keep the unpleasant by-products of their trade from fouling the community in general. Baking, glassblowing, and soapmaking establishments were numerous in St. Saviour's, as were cloth-making businesses in St. Olave's. A survey of heads of households in St. Saviour's in 1622 found

Crafts and Trades

Figure 6.4 A procession in a London street in 1638 (Furnivall 1877).

a preponderance of butchers, weavers, shoemakers, victualers, and porters in the Borough, with weavers, tailors, leatherworkers, smiths, and victualers in the Bankside.[38]

In the areas under the jurisdiction of the City, the practice of a trade or craft was theoretically controlled by the London guilds, called "companies." Within any town, each trade had its own company. The companies had authority over working conditions, training requirements, and product quality; in large measure, they served to restrict access to the trade and to ensure that excessive competition did not undermine the livelihoods of its members. Membership in the companies conferred the status of citizenship in the city of London; it tended to be passed on in the family, and it was relatively difficult for outsiders to acquire. Most of the wealthiest residents of Southwark belonged to one of the London guilds, although they were not always in the guild of the trade they actually plied: of 24 members of the Drapers' Company living in Southwark in 1641, only 3 were actually tailors. This situation could cause problems in enforcing regulations: in 1639 the Feltmakers' Company attempted to search the house of a Southwark felt-maker named Peter Robinson, but Robinson barred his doors and denied their authority, claiming to be of the Haberdashers' Company.[39]

The restrictive effect of the companies was often at odds with economic and demographic pressures, as a substantial population of newcomers to the city sought a living for themselves and as rapidly growing and changing markets were creating demands not met by the existing guild structures. Southwark was an important player in this process: because parts of the community fell outside City authority, it was one of the places in London that offered economic possibilities outside of the strictures of the guilds. Overall, the actual power of the guild varied from company to company, and the degree of enforcement of regulations was highly variable.[40] The power of the London guilds was further undermined by the economic disruption caused by the Great Fire: the building trades in particular had to respond to a massive spike in demand that could not be fulfilled by the guilds, so company restrictions had to be relaxed in order to rebuild the city. But in many of the old cities of England, guild restrictions were a contributing factor to economic decline, as development gravitated toward rural communities and other locations where economic activity was less strictly controlled.

Above the shops of Long Southwark, and clustering in the yards and alleys off the main street, were the residential **The Urban** dwellings. English towns as shaped during the Middle Ages **Home** were generally not segregated by wealth: rather than living in different neighborhoods, wealthier people lived on main streets, and poorer people lived on subsidiary streets, alleys, and yards and toward the tops of the buildings rather than on the ground floor. However, this was changing by 1600, as new housing for the growing cities targeted specific markets.

In the Middle Ages, a significant number of aristocrats and high-ranking churchmen had maintained residences in Southwark for their visits to London. During the sixteenth century, most of these were sold off, and although the upper classes in Stuart England were increasingly maintaining houses in London, they were gravitating toward newly developed neighborhoods at the western end of the city, which offered better access to the institutions of government at Westminster. Many of the poorer newcomers to London settled east of the Tower or in Southwark, where rents were cheaper and labor laws less restrictive than in the City. This meant that Southwark was increasingly populated by petty craftsmen and tradesmen, as well as laborers and the poor. By the 1600s, the overall social geography of modern London was well established, with upper-class residences in the West End, and the less affluent areas of town in the East End and south of the river.

The Boroughside section of St. Saviour's was the most prosperous part of Southwark: there were very few people here of the upper classes, but probably about one-sixth of the householders were sufficiently well-to-do to pay the subsidy, a tax that entitled them to vote in parliamentary elections. Below them, another sixth had some surplus income, enough to be contributing to the poor rate. About one-half had adequate income, enough to make ends meet and perhaps to keep a servant. At the bottom, about a quarter were poor—the unemployed or underemployed or the ill or elderly who were unable to make a living, and were dependent on charity.[41]

The occupant of a building or residence was rarely its owner. During the Middle Ages and early modern era, multiple levels of tenure had evolved in the cities: the owner of a given plot of city land would subdivide it to leaseholders, who themselves would rent to subtenants. Much of the property in Southwark was owned by one of a few large landowners: some of the largest were the local churches and schools, St. Thomas's Hospital, and the City of London. These landowners would lease their property to an entrepreneur, for a period ranging anywhere from a number a years to a lifetime; a lease of 21 years was common. This entrepreneur would in turn sublease to the actual occupants, though in some cases there were further levels of subletting. A typical case is the tenements of the Bell Yard on the west side of St. Margaret's Hill: these were owned by St. Thomas Hospital, but were let during the middle part of the century to Jane Evelyn of Drury Lane (in the City) on a 60-year lease; Evelyn sublet the tenements to their actual occupants. The George Inn in the late seventeenth century was owned by John Sayer, who leased the premises to Mark Weyland, for an annual rent of £50 and a sugar loaf.[42]

At the base of the tenurial chain was the actual occupant of the dwelling. A prosperous townsman might occupy an entire building, but many houses were subdivided into smaller lodgings. The tenements of Ship Yard off the east side of Long Southwark mostly consisted of one or two rooms, and those in Christopher Yard (a bit south of the Tabard Inn) included two or three; the Ship Yard tenements rented for 50–60s. a year. Many people had long-term lodgings in innyards, either as tenants of the inn or as occupants of a separate tenement within the inn complex. Some inns had entirely ceased to function as short-term hostelries and were entirely converted into long-term housing; residents of Bell Yard and Christopher Yard were living in lodgings that had once been rented by the night. A number of former stately residences had similarly been subdivided into cheap tenements: in former centuries, Southwark had been the London residence for a number of important abbots and priors, and their houses had come on the market after the dissolution of the monasteries. Among buildings subdivided in this fashion were Battle Place (once the residence of the abbot of Battle Abbey), Chaingate Churchyard (formerly the grounds of the Priory of St. Mary Overies), and Rochester Place (formerly belonging to the bishop of Rochester).

Those who could not afford a tenement of their own might lodge in someone else's home. As population pressures mounted, especially in the early part of the century, substandard housing was common, with people being crowded into one-room tenements and even cellars.[43] It was also quite common for people to move from house to house in town. Turnover was lower among the more affluent and higher among the poor: a study of housing in St. Saviour's parish in 1631 found 86 percent of poor-rate payers still resident a year later but only 72 percent of non-ratepayers.[44]

The typical urban house of the period was a timber-frame structure two or three stories high, generally with an attic or loft above and often with a cellar. The frontage was usually a mere 8 to 12 feet, but the tenement might extend as much as 80 feet back from the street, including a long garden at the back and a privy at the far end. The front of the ground floor would usually be the householder's shop, with a large window having shutters that opened to form a kind of display stall. Behind the shop might be the kitchen, although not all households had them—prepared meals were relatively cheap, and eating out or bringing prepared food home was very common. Sleeping quarters were on the upper floors. The structure of tenements was sometimes interlocking, with rooms above one tenement belonging to the tenement next door. A typical example of a small urban house in Southwark was the three-story home with a single chamber (bedroom) that was rented by a Widow Slow in the early part of the century, at a rate of £5 a year plus a £35 entry fee, on a 21-year lease—the most typical length for such a lease.[45]

A typical Southwark home housed about four people; numbers tended to be higher for the well-to-do. At the core of the household was the householder, most often a married man with his wife; only about 1 household in 20 was headed by a widower or single man, although 1 in 6 was headed by a widow or (occasionally) a single woman. The other members of the household were the children and servants. Analysis of Boroughside parish records have found a mean household size of 3.8 people in 1631; when lodgers are added to the figure, it becomes 4.2. Servants, apprentices, and lodgers generally occupied the highest floors of the house. A typical prosperous household in Southwark was that of Ralph Babington, a vintner, who in 1622 was living with his wife, a son, and six servants, half of them men, the other half women.[46]

Leadership of a household was not limited to the established independent craftsman or tradesman. Many were of much humbler standing—peddlers, tinkers, sailors, laborers. Some were even servants. In fact, it was common for households engaged in a large-scale enterprise (such as an inn, bakery, or brewery) to have one or more economically dependent households whose heads worked for the principal household but lived in their own homes.

Care of the home garden was in the hands of the housewife, as were domestic livestock—many households kept poultry or swine, and regulations were periodically issued warning householders to keep their pigs out of the streets, where they could be a public menace. Wives might also

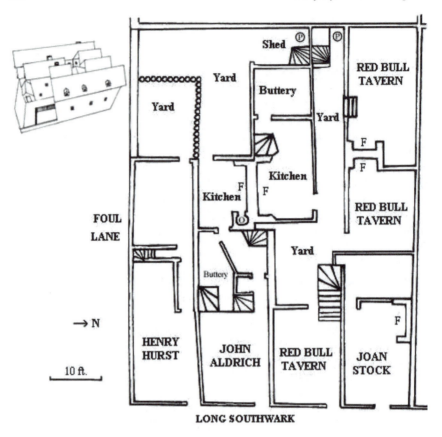

Figure 6.5 Houses at Long Southwark and Foul Lane, located just south of St. Saviour's Church and across from St. Thomas, at the south end of the market. The ground plan is based on an early seventeenth-century survey by Ralph Treswell, with a schematic reconstruction looking north from Foul Lane ("F" designates fireplaces, "O" is an oven, "P" are privies). The shopfront tenements occupied by Henry Hurst and John Aldrich were both rented from George Dalton, a local joiner. Thomas Brackle rented the Red Bull Tavern from Joan Stock, a widow who appears to have lived in the small tenement at the bottom right. The buildings were three stories tall, with a garret above, and in some places a cellar below.

assist in their husbands' work, but many had unrelated jobs of their own: in 1620, a smith named William Keyes was fined 50s. "for that his wife being a common forestaller of the market taketh in butter and such like commodities at her door of the country people as they came to town, before the same be carried into the market, and selleth it again." Other Southwark wives had independent work as bakers, weavers, seamstresses, laundresses, and nurses. Children might also be sent to an employer to bring in extra money.[47]

One of the most important responsibilities of the woman of the house was the domestic water supply. Water and sanitation were perennial problems in Stuart towns, although water was more plentiful in Southwark than in many parts of London. The area was low-lying and swampy, with numerous ponds and bogs. Several streams flowed through Southwark, and there was a network of ditches and embankments to keep the land drained and to minimize damage when the Thames flooded: in 1630, the flooding of the Thames inundated St. Olave's Street. The ditches and streams also tended to function as open sewers, so the water was unsuitable for consumption, as was water from the Thames: such water was chiefly reserved for laundering, cleaning, and manufacturing. Southwark households generally got their consumable water from private wells in their gardens or from public wells in the streets (the latter at a charge to the user); there were several public wells and pumps in Long Southwark and St. Margaret's Hill.[48] Some parts of London were served by water piped into the city through wood or stone conduits, and a few of the very richest households actually had pipes bringing water directly into their homes. Many households purchased their water from professional water bearers, who filled tall conical barrels (called "tankards") at the public wells and pumps and brought them from door to door on their backs. Most households had some sort of cistern to store this water until it was needed.

Refuse was collected by hired "rakers" three times a week, and the householders were expected to put their rubbish out at the appropriate time for it to be carted out of town to designated dumping grounds called "laystalls." Some waste ended up being dumped into the streets, streams, or the Thames, though regulations were periodically issued prohibiting these practices. The rakers were also responsible for removing the animal dung that accumulated in the streets. Privies were built over cesspits (also used for emptying out chamber pots), and these pits were periodically cleaned out by "jakes farmers," sometimes known as "goldfinders," who carted the waste to laystalls—urban bylaws required this work to be done at night.[49]

ST. MARGARET'S HILL: FAIRS AND THOROUGHFARES

A hundred yards south of the Market House, Long Southwark opened out into a very broad street called St. Margaret's Hill. St. Margaret's Hill was the site of the annual Southwark Fair, theoretically held on September 7, 8, and 9, but in practice extending for two weeks, although London's Court of Aldermen periodically issued orders for the bailiff to pull down any booths still standing after September 9. Southwark Fair was considered one of the three most important fairs in England, along with Bartholomew Fair in Smithfield (at the west end of London) and Sturbridge Fair near Cambridge. Southwark Fair was also called Lady Fair (from being held on Lady Day—that is, the Feast of the Nativity of Our Lady on September 8) or St. Margaret's Fair. During the fair, the street would be packed with buyers and sellers from around England and across Europe, although the fair's commercial function gave way to entertainment over the course of the century, as the fair became increasingly a place of performers, pleasure-seekers, and pickpockets.[50] Here in 1660, John Evelyn saw various wonders, including conjoined twins, dancing apes, and an Italian weight lifter,[51] and Samuel Pepys described a day at Southwark Fair in 1668:

I turned back and to Southwark Fair, very dirty, and there saw the puppet-show of Whittington, which was pretty to see; and how that idle thing doth work upon people that see it, and even myself too. And thence to Jacob Hall's dancing on the ropes [acrobatics on ropes], where I saw such action as I never saw before, and mightily worth seeing. And there took acquaintance with a fellow that carried [brought] me to a tavern, whither came the music [musicians] of this booth, and by and by Jacob Hall himself, with whom I had a mind to speak, to hear whether he had ever any mischief by falls in his time; he told me, "Yes, many; but never to the breaking of a limb." He seems a mighty strong man. So giving them a bottle or two of wine, I away with Payne the waterman; he, seeing me at the play, did get a link [torch] to light me, and so lit me to the Bear, where Bland my waterman waited for me with gold and other things he kept for me, to the value of £40 and more, which I had about me, for fear of my pockets being cut. So by link-light through the Bridge, it being mighty dark, but still water; and so home.[52]

Urban Streets   Like other major city streets, Long Southwark and St. Margaret's Hill were paved with cobblestones, arranged to slope toward a channel in the center for drainage; St. Margaret's Hill was so broad that it had two separate channels for drainage.[53] Such well-appointed streets were by no means universal in town: most streets were much narrower, and many remained unpaved, making them difficult to travel in wet weather, though there were ongoing efforts during the century to increase the proportion of paved streets. The streets also tended to accumulate refuse, not only from passers-through, but also from householders and tradesmen dumping the waste from their homes and businesses. Butchers were especially notorious for fouling the public ways: in 1620, Southwark butcher Giles Foster was summoned before the manor court "for sweeping down blood and soil in the way leading to the church to the annoyance of passengers."[54] Urban bylaws prohibited such practices and required householders to maintain the section of street in front of their house, repairing the surface, sweeping before their doors, keeping the central channel clear, and even hanging out candles at night to provide some light for pedestrians. Yet enforcement was uneven. Long Southwark and St. Margaret's Hill were probably reasonably well policed: in 1620, the court of King's Manor fined 25 men 3s. 6d. each for failing to repair their section of street since the last meeting of the court, and it issued warnings to 59 others; Guildable Manor issued fines to another 25 for failing to keep their waste until the rakers' cart was ready to collect it.[55] But the further one went from the main streets, the less the regulations were observed.

The city's traffic problems were exacerbated by a population that had far outgrown the medieval streets. To make matters worse, private and public coaches were becoming increasingly popular, coming into conflict with pedestrians and with commercial carts and wagons. The medieval streets of Stuart towns were too narrow to handle such a large volume of wheeled traffic. London authorities tried to alleviate the problem with measures such as the proclamation of 1636 that forbade the hiring of coaches for journeys of less than three miles, requiring that they be used only for traveling into or out of the city. Increasing traffic problems are reflected in the punishments meted out for violations: in 1624, anyone who parked a cart in Southwark's main street longer than necessary for unloading was subject to a fine of 6d., but by 1667, the rate had jumped to 3s. 4d.[56] Such laws were difficult if not impossible to enforce effectively, and one of the beneficial side effects of the Great Fire of 1666 was that it provided an opportunity for rebuilding the City with broader streets.

ST. GEORGE'S PARISH AND THE LIBERTIES: THE MARGINS OF URBAN LIFE

St. Margaret's Hill continued as far as the parish church of St. George's, where it turned into Blackman Street and headed toward the Surrey village of Newington, and Kent Street branched off east toward Kent. This was one of the poorest areas in Stuart London. Southwark had more than its share of London's paupers, and as in other parts of town, many of them lived toward the edges of the urban settlement. Property here was cheaper than in the heart of town, and a great deal of cheap new housing was being created at the margins of Southwark, in areas like St. Olave's Street, Bermondsey Street (which ran from the eastern end of St. Olave's Street southward to the village of Bermondsey), and the southern end of St. Margaret's Hill, leading into Blackman Street and Kent Street. Kent Street was one of the poorest parts of London: the hearth-tax returns of 1664 show 376 houses in the street and its alleys, of which 324 were too small or poor to be taxed. Kent Street was notoriously the home of tinkers, thieves, prostitutes, and poor people practicing low-paying crafts that involved minimal skills. The craft proverbially associated with Kent Street was broom-making: entrepreneurs laid out plots of land for raising broom-plants and staffs suitable for broom-making; these were harvested and put out to broom-makers to produce brooms for the London market (this is alluded to in the broadside ballad of "The Jolly Broom-Man," described as "A Kent Street soldier's exact relation of all his travels in every nation"—see the songs in chapter 8).[57]

One of the reasons for the rapid expansion of poor hous-
The Liberties   ing in Southwark was that the area was less effectively regulated than the City itself. In principle, the Borough was
under the City's jurisdiction, but this jurisdiction was harder to enforce
the further one went from the City. The situation was greatly complicated by the existence of a number of "liberties"—areas not subject to City
authority—within and around the Borough. This situation reflected the
Stuart town's medieval heritage and was mirrored in other urban communities as well.[58]

Two substantial manors in Southwark fell outside of the Borough's
jurisdiction: the Liberty of the Clink, just west of London Bridge, and the
Manor of Paris Garden, adjoining the Clink to the west. Together they were
known as the Bankside. The Liberty of the Clink was under the lordship
of the bishop of Winchester, whose diocese included Southwark. Since the
Middle Ages, the bishops of Winchester had had their London residence
at Winchester House in the Bankside, although in the seventeenth century
they ceased to use it. With a manor lord who was rarely present, the Clink
was poorly policed, and since the Middle Ages, it had been notorious as a
center for prostitution.[59]

Paris Garden had formerly been a rural manor, but by the 1600s, it was
increasingly being built up. It passed through the hands of multiple investors over the course of the century. During the early part of the century,
the old manor house, no longer occupied by a manor lord, was given over
to gambling and prostitution, and in 1631, the place was the subject of
a notorious "vice squad" raid commemorated in print, ballads (it too is
mentioned in "The Jolly Broom-Man"), and even a stage play.

Like the manors of the Borough, the Clink and Paris Garden had manorial officers of their own as well as their own enforcement system. These
manors were a constant thorn in the City's side because they could not be
controlled by the City, and they were much less rigorously policed than
the Borough.

There were also a few localities within the Borough itself that enjoyed
special privileges. Montague Close consisted of a chain of alleys north of
St. Saviour's church. It had once been the yard of the priory of St. Mary
Overies, and as former church grounds, the Close still retained some of
its old privileges of sanctuary, and the inhabitants claimed various legal
exemptions and liberties. The Close was therefore a haven for debtors,
criminals, and perhaps conspirators. In the sixteenth century, the Close
had come into the possession of the Catholic Montague family, who lived
there until it was converted into tenements in 1612. Lord Montague nar-
rowly escaped implication in the Gunpowder Plot of 1605; Guy Fawkes,
the lead figure in the plot, had in fact been a servant of the family in the
early 1590s. Many of Southwark's Catholics settled here, but overall, Catholics were a tiny minority in Southwark—perhaps 1 percent of the population in 1603, roughly the national average.[60] The area remained a haven

from the law until an act of Parliament abolished the custom of sanctuary in 1697.

The Mint, across from St. George's church, was another independent jurisdiction. This had once been the site of a palace belonging to the Duke of Suffolk. The palace was sold to Henry VIII, who used it for a time as a royal mint. It was pulled down in 1557, but the name stuck to the neighborhood, and the Mint remained royal land, independent of the Borough. It was redivided into a number of smaller tenements and enjoyed privileges and immunities as if it were outside of the Borough. It tended to attract debtors and others who had reason to keep out of reach of the Borough authorities: in 1683, a certain Captain Aubery hid a large quantity of arms in the area, which in the highly charged political climate of the day led to suspicions of treasonous conspiracy. The Act of 1697 also tried to suppress the Mint's privileges, but without success, and it remained dangerous for law enforcement officials into the following century. Daniel Defoe in 1706 described it as a place "where insolent debtors raise war against the laws, bully the magistrates, defy the parliament, stand battle with the posse, drench the officers, debauch their own principles, and damn their creditors."[61]

These areas outside City jurisdiction allowed for the flourishing of activities otherwise suppressed by the Puritan-minded City authorities. There were bowling alleys and gaming houses concentrated in the Bankside and Montague Close, and prostitution was rife in the Bankside. Most notably, the Bankside in the early part of the century was the most important center of the English theater, which had been suppressed in the areas under City authority. In the early seventeenth century, there were three playhouses in the Bankside: the Swan in Paris Garden and the Globe and the Hope in the Clink. However, during the first half of the 1600s, indoor theaters became more fashionable, and the "wooden Os" celebrated by Shakespeare fell out of favor as London's theaters migrated toward the increasingly fashionable West End. The Swan was largely disused after 1620. The Globe was destroyed by fire in 1613, but rebuilt, and it continued in use until the suppression of the playhouses by Parliament in 1642; it was pulled down in 1644. The Hope fell out of use as a theater after 1616, but continued to be used for bearbaiting and fencing displays. Bearbaiting was also suppressed during the Civil Wars, although it survived clandestinely: seven bears associated with the Hope "by the command of Thomas Pride, then High Sheriff of Surrey, were shot to death on Saturday the 9 day of February 1655 by a company of soldiers."[62] The Hope was revived as a site for baiting and fencing after the Restoration, but was finally closed in 1682.

Ironically, law enforcement was made even more difficult by the presence of several prisons on the east side of St. Margaret's **Prisons** Hill, toward St. George's church: the royal prisons of the Marshalsea and King's Bench and the Surrey prison called the White Lion. The Marshalsea was one of the main royal prisons in London, traditionally used for those to be tried by the courts of the King's Marshal, the King's Palace, or the Admiralty, but increasingly it was also occupied by people imprisoned for debt: two centuries later, Charles Dickens's father would be imprisoned as a debtor in the Marshalsea, an experience the author explores in his novel *Little Dorrit*.

The King's Bench and the Marshalsea were independent jurisdictions. Some of the more privileged prisoners of the King's Bench were actually permitted to live in the area outside the prison building, known as the "Rules of the King's Bench Prison," which included most of St. George's parish. Enforcement was lax, the marshal claimed jurisdiction over the area against local authorities, and the presence of impoverished inmates drew their indigent families to the neighborhood as well: the Rules were notorious as a disorderly area of town.[63] All of this made law enforcement difficult in the neighborhood. These prisons could also be flashpoints for civil disturbances originating both inside and outside the walls. There were riots at the King's Bench prison in 1620 and 1640; the prisoners at the Marshalsea rioted in 1639, pulling down a wooden fence, setting it on fire, and throwing stones and firebrands at the constables and watchmen who were called out to suppress them; and in 1628, a party of sailors threatened to set fire to the White Lion if certain prisoners were not

Figure 6.6 Outside a prison (Traill and Mann 1909).

released.[64] Even when the prisons were not causing actual tumult, they brought problems for the neighborhood as incubators of epidemics and as a burden on private charity, since most prisoners were dependent on alms for their sustenance.

There were smaller jails elsewhere in Southwark: in addition to the Borough Compter at the head of St. Margaret's Hill, there was the Clink in the Bankside, a prison that served the Liberty of the Clink as well as the bishop of Winchester; it was often used for religious prisoners. In all of these prisons, long-term prisoners were usually either debtors or those accused of crimes with political overtones. Violent crimes and major thefts tended to be punishable by execution—prisoners sentenced to execution were generally taken to the gallows at St. Thomas Watering, south along Kent Street beyond the boundary of Southwark. Less serious infractions included petty thefts and dishonest business practices, especially fraudulent goods and measures. The typical punishments for these minor crimes included monetary fines, the stocks, and the pillory. Rather more unpleasant punishments were provided by the ducking stool or the whipping post. Each manor had its own set of punishment devices.

BLACKMAN STREET AND ST. GEORGE'S FIELDS: CITY AND COUNTRY

Proceeding south to where St. Margaret's Hill turned into Blackman Street, the traveler would begin to see more greenery. London was encroaching on the countryside over the course of the century, and this was particularly true in Southwark, but even in the center of the City, one was never more than a few minutes' walk from open country. Farming, especially pastoralism, was still a significant part of Southwark's economy at the beginning of the century. Paris Garden, already well on its way toward urban development by 1600, still retained some rural settlement. Winchester Park, belonging to the bishop of Winchester, was largely pasture at the beginning of the century, though by the end, much of it had been divided up and developed. The same was true of Horseleydown, at the eastern end of St. Olave's Street. Bermondsey, which had once been an abbey, was still something of a village at the opening of the century, but by 1700, it also was largely built up and had become an important center for leatherworking.

One of the few areas of Southwark relatively untouched by urbanization during the century was St. George's Fields, about 144 acres on the west side of Blackman Street, which included both pasture and arable land. In addition to farming, the fields were used for a variety of outdoor activities, including country walks, archery, duels, and musters of the trained bands; by mid-century, they were home to an inn called the Dog and Duck, much frequented by those who enjoyed the sport of hunting ducks with spaniels.[65] At the beginning of the century, Londoners looking to rusticate would often go to St. George's Fields and to Newington, the village just south of the fields, but by the latter part of the century, leisure was increasingly commercialized. Samuel Pepys, like many well-to-do Londoners, preferred to resort to the pleasure gardens at Vauxhall, further upriver to the southwest of Southwark: the gardens were laid out after the Restoration, and admission was free, revenue being generated by the sale of food and drink. Among less privileged Londoners, St. George's Fields remained an important destination. On May 6, 1640, the day after the dissolution of the Short Parliament, the glovers and tanners of Southwark and Bermondsey, who had repaired to the fields for traditional May festivities, joined up with other working-class city residents to march west to Lambeth Palace, the London home of the archbishop of Canterbury, in an attempt to seize Archbishop Laud.[66]

The complex interface between city and country manifested itself at the legal level as well. Southwark lay in the county of Surrey: many legal matters were of unclear jurisdiction, and there was ongoing conflict between the City and Surrey over their respective rights in the Borough. Civil matters and petty crimes could be tried by Surrey justices of the peace as well as by the manor courts. Felonies could be tried by the quarter sessions courts of either the City or Surrey, and major crimes were tried at assizes held once a year in Southwark, but could also be tried at the London or Surrey assizes. The Surrey justices of the peace also had some responsibility for overseeing the work of local officers such as constables and overseers of the poor, and authority over the Southwark trained bands bounced back and forth between the City and Surrey over the course of the century.[67]

The Urban Experience Most people in Southwark spent their days within a very limited physical radius. Many worked in the same house where they slept, and the rest did not have far to walk to their place of employment. Shops and markets were close to hand, particularly for the ordinary kinds of wares that were needed on a regular basis. Many goods and services could be purchased without even leaving the home by patronizing the tradesmen who went door-to-door with their tools or wares. Venturing further afield—to another part of town, or out into the country—was more likely to happen on a day of leisure than on an ordinary working day. The level of mobility tended to increase for people further up the social scale: Samuel Pepys wandered a fair bit around the various neighborhoods of London, both for work and for pleasure, although he rarely ventured south of the bridge into Southwark. For most people, the neighborhood was a highly developed and self-contained social community, a fact reflected in Southwark marriage patterns: among marriages in St. Saviour's over the period 1655–1665, 83 percent of the couples were both from within the parish.[68]

The environment within which these city-dwellers lived was one that assaulted the senses. The streets were filled with a constant bustle of people and traffic. Above this resounded the half-sung cries of the various tradesmen announcing the goods or services they offered: rag-and-bone men soliciting for the saleable waste products of the household, peddlers crying their various wares, woodcutters offering their services, food vendors carrying fresh victuals through the streets. This curious cacophony of sound captured the imagination of contemporaries: the criers and their calls are extensively commemorated in both prints and music of the period (see the song "New Walefleet Oysters" in chapter 8).[69]

Not only were the streets crowded with people, but animals were numerous as well. Carts and coaches were drawn by draft horses, travelers and messengers rode on horseback, and in addition to domestic animals such as dogs, pigs, and poultry that inevitably got loose into the streets, large numbers of cattle, sheep, and poultry were daily driven into the city, on their way to urban dining tables. Southwark's manor courts had to mandate fines for those who allowed their dogs to frighten passing cattle, and they issued ordinances against driving into any shop or slaughterhouse oxen, bullocks, or cows "that are so wild, that they will not quietly enter, but run away (as often it happeneth)."[70]

The presence of so many animals in the streets inevitably left plenty of manure on the streets, but the distinctive smell in London was the reek of smoke. By the mid-seventeenth century, coal had replaced wood as the dominant fuel for domestic heating, a position it would retain for centuries, until the pollution reached crisis levels in the mid-1900s. Already in the late 1600s, contemporaries were remarking on the problem. The scholar John Evelyn wrote one of the world's earliest treatises on urban development, recommending that London be rebuilt as a planned community with ample garden space to counteract the "hellish and dismal cloud of sea-coal" by which the city was so engulfed that "catarrhs, phthisics, coughs, and consumptions rage more in this one city than in the whole earth besides."[71]

At night, the street scene changed completely. Depending on the stage of the moon, city streets could get very dark. Householders were supposed to set lights in front of their doors, but even if this had been fully enforced, the candlelight would have had limited effect. Pedestrians on the streets after dark were well advised to carry their own light or to hire someone to do it for them. The nighttime streets could be dangerous, and suspicion inevitably attached to anyone found wandering the town after sundown. A town watch was set every night to man the city gates and patrol the streets, detaining suspicious wanderers. Since there were no walls around Southwark, chains were extended across the streets at night to demarcate the town limits. An armed "bellman" also walked the streets by night: he was charged to keep a weather eye open for untoward activity and to ring out the hours with his hand-bell.[72]

Not all the nighttime dangers were human. In a world dependent on open flames for cooking, heating, and light, fire was an ever-present risk, above all in the city where the dwellings stood cheek-by-jowl. Fire was one of the chief concerns of the night patrols, and every parish in London kept hooks for pulling down burning buildings (to keep the fire from spreading), ladders for rescuing those trapped inside, and leather buckets for bringing water to douse the flames. London also had a number of water-pumping devices to assist in the task. Fire prevention was one of the chief concerns of Southwark's manor courts, which frequently fined owners of houses with thatched roofs or wooden chimneys, with mixed results: in 1620, a Thomas Snelling was fined 20s. for failing to replace thatch with tiles on three tenements in the Mint, as the court had previously ordered, but by 1624, he had still not complied, and the fine was increased to £6 13s. 4d.[73]

Seventeenth-century towns were inevitably struck by fire from time to time. Southwark had two major fires during the century. In 1676, a fire destroyed several major inns (including the George and Chaucer's Tabard) and about five hundred houses along Long Southwark, though it was eventually brought under control with the assistance Southwark's water-pumps.[74] Another fire near King's Bench Prison during Southwark Fair in 1689 destroyed fair booths and about a hundred houses, although the watch spotted the fire early enough to contain the damage. Neither of these compared to the Great Fire that struck London in 1666, which ranks as one of the worst conflagrations in European history. On September 2, a baker's oven had been inadequately extinguished for the night, and over the next few days, almost the entirety of the City within the walls was destroyed. Southwark was untouched by the flames, and many Londoners, among them the diarists Samuel Pepys and John Evelyn, fled south of London Bridge during the night for safety: Pepys watched the fire rage from an alehouse in the Bankside.[75] In the following years, the city was rebuilt almost from scratch, marking a major physical and symbolic break between modern London and its medieval heritage.

NOTES

1. Keith Wrightson, *Earthly Necessities: Economic Lives in Early Modern Britain* (New Haven: Yale University Press, 2000), 172, 235; Julian Hoppit, *A Land of Liberty? England 1689–1727* (Oxford: Clarendon Press, 2000), 54.

2. Eric S. Wood, *Historical Britain* (London: Harvill Press, 1995), 19; Peter Laslett, *The World We Have Lost* (New York: Scribner, 1966), 55–56; Hoppit, *Land,* 419.

3. Hoppit, *Land,* 419–20; Wood, *Britain,* 19; Laslett, *World,* 55–56.

4. Hoppit, *Land,* 331.

5. Important sources on London and Southwark include the following: Jeremy Boulton, *Neighbourhood and Society: A London Suburb in the Seventeenth Century* (Cambridge: Cambridge University Press, 1987); Norman G. Brett-James, *The Growth of Stuart London* (London: George Allen and Unwin, 1935); Thomas De Laune, *Angliae Metropolis, or, The Present State of London* (London: John Harris and Thomas Hawkins, 1690); James Howel, *Londinopolis: An Historical Discourse*

or Perlustration of the City of London (London: Henry Twiford, George Sawbridge, Thomas Dring, and John Place, 1657); David J. Johnson, *Southwark and the City* (London: Oxford University Press for the Corporation of London, 1969); London Borough of Southwark, *The Story of Bankside.* London Borough of Southwark Neighbourhood Histories No. 8 (London: Council of the London Borough of Southwark, 1985); London Borough of Southwark, *The Story of "The Borough."* London Borough of Southwark Neighbourhood Histories No. 7 (London: Council of the London Borough of Southwark, 1982); London Borough of Southwark, *The Story of Bermondsey.* London Borough of Southwark Neighbourhood Histories No. 5, rev. ed. (London: Council of the London Borough of Southwark, 1984); London County Council, *Survey of London. Vol. XXII: Bankside (Parishes of St Saviour and Christchurch, Southwark)* (London: London County Council, 1950); Samuel Pepys, *The Diary of Samuel Pepys,* ed. Robert Latham and William Matthews, 10 vols. (Berkeley and Los Angeles: University of California Press, 1983); Ralph Treswell, *The London Surveys of Ralph Treswell,* ed. John Schofield, London Topographical Society Publication No. 135 (London: London Topographical Society, 1987).

6. Boulton, *Neighbourhood,* 1; Eric S. Wood, *Historical Britain* (London: Harvill Press, 1995), 19.

7. Edward Chamberlayne, *The Second Part of the Present State of England* (London: J. Martyn, 1671), 196.

8. Johnson, *Southwark,* 145.

9. Johnson, *Southwark,* 140ff.

10. Boulton, *Neighbourhood,* 77ff., 264; Johnson, *Southwark,* 174, 273ff., 297.

11. Boulton, *Neighbourhood,* 140–41, 264–65; Johnson, *Southwark,* 302–3.

12. Johnson, *Southwark,* 174, 180ff., 297, 300.

13. Boulton, *Neighbourhood,* 15–19.

14. Boulton, *Neighbourhood,* 286.

15. Boulton, *Neighbourhood,* 146.

16. Boulton, *Neighbourhood,* 147; see also 287.

17. Boulton, *Neighbourhood,* 265–66, 274; Johnson, *Southwark,* 149, 153, 320ff., 330.

18. Johnson, *Southwark,* 105.

19. Boulton, *Neighbourhood,* 161.

20. Boulton, *Neighbourhood,* 92–93, 144, 163.

21. Boulton, *Neighbourhood,* 128.

22. Johnson, *Southwark,* 324–25.

23. Boulton, *Neighbourhood,* 93ff.

24. Boulton, *Neighbourhood,* 273.

25. John Hawkins, *The English School-master Completed* (London: Company of Stationers, 1692). On the schools, see R. C. Carrington, *Two Schools. A History of the St Olave's and St Saviour's Grammar School Foundation* (London: Governors of the St. Olave's and St. Saviour's Grammar School Foundation, 1971).

26. Chamberlayne, *Second Part,* 244.

27. Johnson, *Southwark,* 253.

28. Boulton, *Neighbourhood,* 232.

29. Boulton, *Neighbourhood,* 19, 35–36, 40–41; Wrightson, *Earthly Necessities,* 165.

30. Boulton, *Neighbourhood,* 64; see also R.E.G. Kirk and E. F. Kirk, eds., *Returns of Aliens Dwelling in the City and Suburbs of London from the Reign of Henry VIII to that of James.* Huguenot Society Publications 10. 4 vols. (Aberdeen: printed for the Huguenot Society of London at the University Press, 1900–1907).

31. Boulton, *Neighbourhood*, 74ff.; Johnson, *Southwark*, 298, 305–310.

32. Boulton, *Neighbourhood*, 75.

33. Johnson, *Southwark*, 306.

34. The George, now on Borough High Street, was rebuilt after the fire of 1676; one side of the late seventeenth-century innyard still remains. See Judith Hunter, *George Inn* (London: The National Trust, 1989).

35. Boulton, *Neighbourhood*, 270.

36. John Taylor, *The Carrier's Cosmographie* (London: A. G., 1637), sig. C3 verso.

37. Boulton, *Neighbourhood*, 77.

38. Boulton, *Neighbourhood*, 66, 187–88.

39. Boulton, *Neighbourhood*, 152–53; Johnson, *Southwark*, 314.

40. Johnson, *Southwark*, 311ff.

41. Boulton, *Neighbourhood*, 65, 115.

42. Boulton, *Neighbourhood*, 195–96; Hunter, *George Inn*, 11.

43. Boulton, *Neighbourhood*, 86, 182–83, 193.

44. Boulton, *Neighbourhood*, 212.

45. Boulton, *Neighbourhood*, 83, 194, 205.

46. Boulton, *Neighbourhood*, 16–17, 120–24.

47. Boulton, *Neighbourhood*, 82, 84.

48. Johnson, *Southwark*, 329.

49. Donald Lupton, *London and the Countrey Carbonadoed* (London: N. Okes, 1632), 94–96; Johnson, *Southwark*, 300–301.

50. Johnson, *Southwark*, 210–11.

51. John Evelyn, *The Diary of John Evelyn*, ed. E. S. de Beer (London, New York, and Toronto: Oxford University Press, 1959), 410–11; see also 959.

52. Pepys, *Diary*, 9.313. A seventeenth-century fair is vividly portrayed in Ben Jonson's play *Bartholomew Fair*, and a slightly later glimpse of the fair can be had from William Hogarth's engraving *Southwark Fair* (1733), reproduced in William Hogarth, *Hogarth: Pictur'd Morals* (London: Historical Arts, 1967).

53. Johnson, *Southwark*, 310.

54. Boulton, *Neighbourhood*, 268.

55. Johnson, *Southwark*, 296.

56. Johnson, *Southwark*, 298. On city traffic, see also Joan Parkes, *Travel in England in the Seventeenth Century* (London: Oxford University Press, 1925), 19.

57. Brett-James, *London*, 116, 409.

58. On the liberties, see Johnson, *Southwark*, 330ff.; Brett-James, *London*, 42.

59. Brett-James, *London*, 408; Johnson, *Southwark*, 331.

60. Boulton, *Neighbourhood*, 174–75, 284; Johnson, *Southwark*, 332.

61. Hoppit, *Land of Liberty*, 490. On the Mint, see also Johnson, *Southwark*, 332–33.

62. Brett-James, *London*, 462.

63. Johnson, *Southwark*, 334.

64. Boulton, *Neighbourhood*, 267; Johnson, *Southwark*, 286ff., 336; cf. also Pepys, *Diary*, 3.165.

65. Boulton, *Neighbourhood*, 21–23; Brett-James, *London*, 463.

66. Valerie Pearl, *London and the Outbreak of the Puritan Revolution* (London: Oxford University Press, 1961), 107–8.

67. Johnson, *Southwark*, 151ff., 175–76, 229ff., 234ff., 247, 252.

68. Boulton, *Neighbourhood*, 235.

69. See Lupton, *London*, 92; Boulton, *Neighborhood*, 75; Sean Shesgreen, *The Criers and Hawkers of London* (Stanford: Stanford University Press, 1990); Pierce Tempest et al., *The Cryes of the City of London Drawne after the Life* (London: Pierce Tempest, 1689).

70. Johnson, *Southwark*, 298, 309.

71. Brett-James, *London*, 313.

72. Cf. Pepys, *Diary*, 1.19.

73. Johnson, *Southwark*, 149, 296, 298; Paul Seaver, *Wallington's World: A Puritan Artisan in Seventeenth-Century London* (Stanford: Stanford University Press, 1985), 54.

74. Brett-James, *London*, 407.

75. Pepys, *Diary*, 7.271; Evelyn, *Diary*, 494.

7

FOOD

Food is one of the most basic human needs, and the practices surrounding food are one of the definitive features of any culture. The patterns of food consumption in England at the opening of the 1600s had changed little since the Middle Ages, but over the course of the century, the country began to see portentious changes in its consumption habits that reflected the birth of a truly global market in foodstuffs, as tea from China, coffee from the Middle East, and sugar from the New World became staple features of the new Western diet.

Diet   Humans' single greatest nutritional need is carbohydrates, which in the Stuart diet, as in most societies, came largely from grains.

For the English, this chiefly meant wheat, above all in the form of bread, and secondarily barley, in the form of beer. Other grains were used as well, particularly rye and oats, hardy plants that did well in poorer soils or harsher climates, although neither were grown as universally as wheat. "Corn," which literally means "grain," was (and is) used by the English to mean wheat (in America the term eventually was applied to the ubiquitous grain of the New World, maize).

Proteins in the diet came from a variety of sources. The very poor relied heavily on legumes such as peas and beans. However, even for those of moderate means, poultry (especially ducks, geese, turkeys, and pigeons), eggs, dairy products, pork, mutton, fish, and shellfish were common. Beef was relatively expensive, but still widely consumed by the middling sort; foreigners traveling to England often remarked on the ubiquity of meat in the English diet, even for those of limited incomes:

at the charitable residence of St. Bartholomew's in London in 1687, the residents had cheese three days a week, but beef or mutton four days. Game meats were also consumed, and these included waterfowl, wild-fowl, rabbit, and venison—the last in particular being restricted to the tables of the well-to-do.

Additional nutrients, as well as flavor, were provided by a variety of vegetables. Onions and their relatives, such as garlic and scallions, were found in every garden. Root vegetables such as carrots, turnips, parsnips, and beets were also common. Potatoes from the New World were also finding their way into the diet, though the strains available were equivalent to the modern sweet potato. Leafy vegetables such as lettuce, spinach, and cabbage were not major parts of the diet, but were still widely consumed. Fruits were also important: common domestic ones included apples, pears, grapes, cherries, peaches, plums, strawberries, gooseberries, and currants. Citrus fruits such as oranges and lemons were imported from Spain and other warm climates and were comparatively expensive. Nuts were often incorporated into dishes: important ones included walnuts, chestnuts, and hazelnuts. Important for flavor, though nutritionally less significant, were herbs and spices, the former usually domestic, the latter imported from overseas. Among these, sugar was beginning to play an increasing role: traditionally used in cooking as a spice, sugar production grew substantially through the century with the rise of slave-based plantations in the New World. Prices dropped by 30 percent over the course of the century, and the use of sugar grew correspondingly.[1]

Perishable foodstuffs were generally purchased from markets or came from the household itself, from either the home garden or domestic animals. Bread might be purchased from bakers, if the household lacked a baking oven. Other foodstuffs were normally purchased from grocers.

Overall, levels of nutrition were improving in most sectors of society, though there were major class discrepancies. The wealthy benefited from the ongoing growth of overseas trade, which brought them a greater variety of foods and the nutritional benefits this entailed. For ordinary people, there was less variety in the diet, but basic access to proteins and carbohydrates was improving: as the food supply stabilized and output of both grains and meats increased, prices dropped and famines became increasingly rare: before 1600, there had typically been about 12 years of famine every century, but in the 1600s there were only four.[2]

The actual balance among the dietary components varied with the season. Milk was available when the cows had calves, roughly from spring into summer, although it could be preserved by making it into butter or cheese, which lasted longer because of the reduced water content and could be further preserved by the use of salt. Eggs were likewise dependent on the laying season, which tailed off by wintertime. Vegetables and fruits each had their own seasons, running from summer into fall, although some lasted longer than others. Root vegetables, apples, and pears could be stored in a cool place, packed in straw, to retard spoilage.

Meat and grain were less seasonal. Poultry and fish were available year-round. Fresh meat was more expensive in winter, when the animals had to be supported with hay or grain, but it was always available to those who could afford it. Grain was available year-round, though in a year of scarcity, prices might rise markedly in the summer, when grain reserves were at their lowest prior to the new harvest. Winter fare might be less varied than summer, but when famine came, it was typically a summer phenomenon.

A variety of additional preservative methods were used to make foods available outside of their prime season. Many foods were amenable to drying, including meats, fishes, and fruits. Salt could also be used as a preservative, retarding bacterial growth both as a dessicant and by creating a saline environment hostile to bacteria. Meats were often salted for this reason, and pickling also involved salt as well as vinegar to prevent spoilage. Sugar could similarly be used as a preservative, chiefly for fruit that was candied or made into preserves.

The process of cooking was dependent on the prehistoric technology of fire, yet the sophistication and variety of **Cooking** seventeenth-century cooking techniques was comparable to those of the modern chef, and the repertoire of the late seventeenth-century chef looks quite familiar to the modern eye. At the heart of any meal was some form of meat, typically prepared in one of three ways. Boiled meats were the easiest to prepare, although a skilled cook could introduce a variety of additives to make the stew more interesting. Roast meats were cooked on a spit next to the fire: the meat was basted with sauce to provide flavor and to keep the meat from drying out, while a dripping pan beneath caught the juices that fell from the roast. The task of turning the spit was a tedious one, often assigned to a child or low-ranking servant, although wealthy households sometimes invested in ingenious devices that used the rising hot air from the fire to power a crank system.

The third chief option was baking, which was usually done in the form of a pie: the meat would be cut up, prepared, and sealed inside a heavy pastry shell that kept in the moisture while cooking—the shell often was no more than a cooking container, not intended for eating. Baking required the use of a specialized oven, typically a brick structure with a domed interior lined with daub. A fire was laid in the oven and allowed to burn until the oven reached the required heat; the burning coals were then raked out of the oven, the interior was wiped with a "malkin" (a damp rag mounted on a stick), the food was slipped in, and the oven door was sealed up, leaving the residual heat to bake the food.

Figure 7.1 A London housewife cooking in the 1640s (Unwin 1904).

Randle Holme in 1688 offered a handy overview of the additional ingredients used to add interest to these basic cooking techniques:

Fattenings, as butter, gravy, hogs-grease, suet, marrow, lard.

Liquids, as muscadine, sack, claret, white-wine, cider, verjuice, vinegar, aleger
[vinegar made from ale], cream, milk, salad-oil, pickles of several pickled things,
water, jellies of several sorts, strong-broth.

Thickenings, as eggs, bread or sops, biscuits, onions, leeks, chibols [a kind of
onion], garlic, artichoke bottoms, sweet herbs chopped, asparagus, skirrets [a kind
of parsnip], parsnips, turnips, green peas, cauliflowers, apples, samphire, ancho-
vies, blood, capers, olives, mustard.

Sweetenings, as sugar, cinnamon, cloves, mace, pepper, nutmeg, salt, gooseberries, barberries, grapes, raisins, currants, plums, dates, oranges, and lemons (and
them candied), melocotons [a type of peach].[3]

Only the poorest people relied on grain-based pottages for their carbohydrates: the universal preference was bread, which was **Bread** included in every meal. The wheat was stored as seed because once the grain was milled, it would have a limited life before spoiling. Grinding the grain produced a coarse "grist" that included a good deal of bran (husk) as well as the flour itself. The ground meal was sifted in sieves and cloths to bring it to the desired level of purity. The finest-sifted meal was known as the "flower," the source of the modern term "flour." "Wheaten" or "cheat" bread was made of coarser meal, whereas brown bread was made of the unpurified grist. Further economies were possible by mixing in rye, barley, or oat flour or even dried and ground root vegetables (such as turnips) or legumes (peas or beans).

For leavening, the baker used the equivalent of modern sourdough: a bit of dough from an old batch could be used to start a new one, or it could be started from scratch by leaving a bit of dough sitting out long enough for naturally occurring yeasts to begin fermenting it. The bread was baked in an oven without using a bread pan: fine bread was typically made in small oblong "manchets," while ordinary loaves were dome-shaped. The price of each class of loaf was fixed by law, but the weight was allowed to vary with the fluctuating price of wheat, according to official rates established by the government. Unscrupulous bakers might try to improve their profit margins by adulterating the flour with cheaper ingredients, but they risked severe legal penalties—and implacable public fury—if they were caught. Soldiers were allotted a pound of bread a day, which was probably a fairly typical level of consumption for most people.[4]

A variety of drinks were in use, providing nutrition as well as fluid in the diet. Water was rarely consumed by itself among **Drinks** those who had any alternative: it lacked nutritive substance and was often impure. Other nonalcoholic drinks were available, but were not much more highly regarded. Milk was reserved for dairying. Whey, the watery by-product of cheese-making, and buttermilk, the tart liquid left over after butter-making, might be consumed by the poor, children, and the infirm, but was not popular with healthy adults who could afford better.

The predominant drinks were generally alcoholic: the alcohol content was not necessarily very high, but it served to inhibit bacterial growth, allowing nutritive drinks to be preserved. The most common drinks were ale and beer, both based on barley. The barley was allowed to germinate (which converted a portion of the grain's starches into sugars) and then was roasted and crushed, and hot water was poured through it to absorb its nutrients and flavor. Multiple washings of the grain produced liquids of increasing wateriness, which affected the strength and flavor of the final product. An ale of the first water was more costly, but small beer (from the final washing) was often a good drink for the working man who needed a refreshing drink that would not impair his functionality. Even children drank beer, although John Locke was probably typical in feeling that this should be only small beer.[5]

Prior to fermentation, the liquid was flavored, which was the basis of the distinction between ale and beer. Ale, the more traditional drink, was flavored with various herbs and spices. In beer, the predominant flavoring was hops, which imparted a characteristic bitterness and also had a preservative effect, improving the product's shelf-life. By the 1600s, ale was largely a drink for the more conservative countryside, whereas the more progressive city-dwellers drank beer.

A variety of other fermented drinks were consumed, either domestically produced or imported from overseas. Cider, made from apples, and perry, from pears, were common in the western part of England. Wales and the bordering regions of England were renowned for mead and metheglin, both based on honey. Wine was imported from Continental Europe, as were fortified wines such as sherry, Madeira, and port. Various domestic wines were made from other fruits, including cherries, gooseberries, blackberries, raspberries, and elderberries. Distilled spirits were also coming into use, among them brandy and aqua vitae, distilled from wine; rum, distilled from molasses; and gin, distilled from grain and flavored with juniper berries.

These various brewed drinks were sometimes compounded with other ingredients to produce composite drinks. Wine was mixed with sweeteners and spices to make hippocras, popular as a medicinal drink and sometimes served warm, especially during the Christmas season. Ale might be mixed with roasted apple pulp, sweetenings, and spices to make "lamb's wool," also served warm. It could also be served hot with butter and seasonings; hot buttered ale was especially popular as a medicinal drink. Punch was also coming into use during the period: it was generally prepared from brandy or rum, mixed with sugar, water, lime juice, and spices.

Around the middle part of the century, England was exposed to a variety of stimulant drinks that quickly rose to enormous popularity. Coffee, introduced from the Ottoman Empire, was the first to arrive, making its first appearance in the 1630s and becoming increasingly popular in the 1650s. Tea, originally from China, was first brought to England by Dutch merchants in the 1650s, but it was slower to catch on, in part because it was more expensive. Chocolate from the Americas also rose to popularity in the 1650s: it was not used in cooking, but was enormously popular as a hot drink.[6]

Tobacco The 1600s also saw increasing use of tobacco. Introduced to Europe in the 1500s, tobacco was already quite common by 1600, and its use increased over the course of the century with the growing supply coming from Europe's New World colonies: just in the period from 1622 to 1638, tobacco imports to England increased from

60,000 pounds a year to 2,000,000; its cost at the beginning of the century was around 20s. a pound, but by the end, it cost under a shilling.[7] Seventeenth-century tobacco had a considerably higher level of nicotine than its modern counterpart and was a correspondingly heady intoxicant. It was normally smoked in a pipe, but in the latter part of the century, snuff, inhaled through the nose, was starting to become fashionable.

The hearty English breakfast of today was not a feature of seventeenth-century life. Those who needed a bite in the morn- **Meals** ing might help themselves to some light food and drink, but this was not necessarily a routine meal. The first true meal of the day— and for most people still the principal one—came around noon and was usually called dinner. For most people, the evening meal, supper, was comparatively light: only the well-to-do had substantial evening dinners. For those, like Samuel Pepys, who occasionally wanted a nibble between meals, a snack of bread with cheese or butter was a typical way to stave off hunger.

A glimpse of a full-scale meal is offered in Comenius:

A Feast

When a feast is made ready, the table is covered with a carpet (1) and a table-cloth (2) by the waiters, who besides lay the trenchers (3), spoons (4), knives (5) with little forks (6), table-napkins (7), bread (8), with a salt-cellar (9). Messes are brought in platters (10), a pie (19) on a plate. The guests are brought in by the host (11), wash their hands out of a laver (12) or ewer (14) over a hand-basin (13) or bowl (15), then they sit at the table on chairs (17). The carver (18) breaketh up the good cheer and divideth it. Sauces are set amongst roast-meat in saucers (20). The butler (21) filleth strong wine out of a cruse (25), or wine-pot (26), or flagon (27) into cups (22) or glasses (23), which stand on a cup-board (24) and he reacheth them to the master of the feast (28) who drinketh to his guests.[8]

For those who had to work for their keep, the shared midday meal was one of the few parts of the day not preoccupied with the business of earning a living, so it was an important social occasion, governed by an etiquette that reinforced the familial community while also emphasizing the social hierarchy. The meal was typically served at a permanent table, though some very old-fashioned households still adhered to the older practice of putting out a temporary table on trestles. The table was covered with a linen cloth—in wealthy households, this might lie on top of a carpet that covered the table when it was not being used for food.

At the opening of the century, the cutlery laid on the table consisted of a spoon and perhaps a knife (sometimes the knife was supplied by the diner, a practice dating to the Middle Ages). Much of the food was still eaten with the hands, which is why it was usual to wash them both before and after the meal. By the latter half of the century, households that were keeping up with fashion had added a two-tined fork—an

Figure 7.2 A feast (Comenius 1887).

implement formerly used only in cooking, but introduced to England from Italy as part of a place setting in the early part of the century. At the opening of the 1600s, knives were usually pointed, but by the end, the round-tipped table knife had become the fashion, adding to the need for the fork. Some kind of plate, bowl, and drinking vessel were set out, and linen napkins were also provided: in the early part of the century, women normally laid these on their laps, men on their shoulders, but by the end of the century it was common for both sexes to leave the napkin on their laps.

The quality of one's tableware was an important marker of social status. Poorer households might have plates, bowls, and drinking vessels made of wood or ceramic, and horn spoons. Further up the scale was pewter and glass, and silver was used in the wealthiest households. In the center of the table were laid salt cellars, cruets for oil and vinegar, and mustard pots for the meat. All of these settings were stored in side tables or cupboards in the dining room and might be decoratively displayed to show the family's wealth. A small cistern of water might be laid near the table to keep drinks cool. Some traditional households still observed the medieval custom of serving the food on a "trencher" of old bread, but by the 1600s a trencher was usually a wooden plate, often square, with a shallow indentation in one corner to hold salt.[9]

Seating at the table was also governed by social etiquette. Many people sat on benches or stools, with cushions for added comfort. There might be only one actual chair in the household, reserved for the person of highest status at the meal—usually the householder, but it might be ceded to a guest who was of higher standing. In better-off households, chairs for all the diners were increasingly the norm. Children however might actually stand at the table.

Hands were washed before eating. In a high-status household, a servant would pass among the diners with a pitcher, basin, and towel; in more ordinary homes, this might be a task for the children. Once all had washed, the meal began with a grace.

Meals were served in multiple stages. Bread was available throughout, as were salt and other condiments. The rest of the dishes were served in courses, each of which included a variety of foods organized around a main dish based on meat or fish. For a prosperous household, ordinary meals might be served in two courses, whereas an important meal might consist of six courses or more. The second, and sometimes the first, of a two-course meal often included a sweet dish such as a cake, tart, or custard; only in a very fine dinner would the sweets be served separately as the last course. At the end of the meal came fruits and cheeses.

Hannah Woolley in 1691 offered a month-by-month cycle of sample menus for a prosperous household:

October

1. Roast veal
2. Two brant geese [wild geese] roasted
3. A grand salad
4. Roasted capons

Second course

1. Pheasant, pouts [fish], and pigeons
2. A dish of quails and sparrows
3. A warden [pear] pie, tarts, and custards[10]

At the end of the meal, grace was said again, and the diners washed their hands once more. The period after a meal was an important occasion for conviviality—not only conversation, but also entertainment: books of music might be brought out for the diners to sing and play. Cleaning up

Figure 7.3 Carousing in the later part of the century (Clark 1907).

after the meal was normally the work of servants or children: soap, sand (as an abrasive), and cloths and various other kinds of rubbing devices were used to wash the dishes.

Country people normally ate in their homes, but many city residences lacked cooking facilities, so it was quite common for townspeople to eat out as a matter of routine. A meal could be had at an "ordinary" or "victualing house" (the equivalent of a restaurant) or at an inn. Taverns and alehouses generally served some food as well, but for the most part specialized in drinks—wine in the former, beer and ale in the latter. One could generally get "take-out" meals at all of these establishments as well, and bakers sold pies that could likewise be purchased as take-out meals.[11]

RECIPES

The following pages offer a selection of recipes taken from seventeenth-century sources. In each case, the original text is followed by an interpretation for the modern cook: seventeenth-century recipes rarely offer precise quantities, cooking times, or temperatures (indeed, temperatures were impossible to measure precisely with the technologies available at the time). The interpretations naturally make some allowances for the ingredients and techniques generally available to the modern cook.

In interpreting any period recipe, it helps to have a knowledge of modern cooking techniques: one good references source is Irma S. Rombauer and Marion Rombauer Becker's *The Joy of Cooking*, which has useful information on all kinds of foods and offers recipes for components such as pastry dough, which are not covered here. In many cases, a comparable modern recipe can be used to supply details not covered by the period texts.

Cheat bread

To bake the best cheat bread, which is also simply of wheat only, you shall, after your meal is dressed and bolted thorugh a more coarse bolter than was used for your manchets, and put also into a clean tub, trough, or kimnel, take a sour leaven, that is a piece of such like leaven saved from a former batch, and well filled with salt, and so laid up to sour, and this sour leaven you shall break in small pieces into warm water, and then strain it; which done, make a deep hollow hole, as was before said, in the midst of your flour, and therein pour your strained liquor; then with your hand mix some part of the flour therewith, till the liquor be as thick as pancake batter, then cover it all over with meal, and so let it lie all that night; the next morning stir it, and all the rest of the meal well together, and with a little more warm water, barm, and salt to season it with, bring it to a perfect leaven, stiff, and firm; then knead it, break it, and tread it, as was before said in the manchets, and so mould it up in reasonable big loaves, and then bake it with an indifferent good heat. (Markham, *English Housewife*, 210)

Dissolve **1 tbsp dry yeast, 1 tsp sugar,** and **1 tsp salt** in **1 cup warm water** (alternatively, you can use a sourdough leaven, as described in the recipe). Mix in **1 cup whole wheat flour** and allow to stand for at least 1 hour. Gradually add **2 cups whole wheat flour** (the actual quantity needed can vary: keep adding until the dough is still moist, but no longer sticky) and knead for 10 minutes. Allow to rise for 1 hour, form into a round loaf, set it on a greased baking sheet, and bake at 350° for about 35 minutes (baking time can vary: watch for the surface of the bread to turn golden).

Meat stew

Of boiled meats ordinary: . . . You shall take a rack of mutton cut into pieces, or a leg of mutton cut into pieces; for this meat and these joints are the best, although any other joint, or any fresh beef will likewise make good pottage: and, having washed your meat well, put it into a clean pot with fair water, and set it on the fire; then take violet leaves, endive, succory [a salad herb, closely related to the endive], *strawberry leaves, spinach, langdebeef* [oxtongue], *marigold flowers, scallions, and a little parsley, and chop them very small together; then take half so much oatmeal well beaten as there is herbs, and mix it with the herbs, and chop all very well together: then when the pot is ready to boil, scum it very well, and then put in your herbs, and so let it boil with a quick fire, stirring the meat oft in the pot, till the meat be boiled enough, and then the herbs and water are mixed together without any separation, which will be after the consumption of more than a third part: then season them with salt, and serve them up with the meat either with sippets* [toast] *or without.* (Markham, *English Housewife*, 74)

Cut **1 lb. mutton or beef** into 1" cubes, and brown in a skillet. Put into **1 quart water** and put on the stove on medium high heat. Combine (as available) **1/4 cup violet leaves, 1/4 cup chopped endives, 1/4 cup strawberry leaves, 1/4 cup spinach, 1/4 cup marigold flowers, 1/4 cup scallions,** and **1/4 cup parsley** and chop fine. Add **4 cups oats** to the herbs. When the water is about to boil, remove the scum with a spoon, and add the herb and oat-meal mixture. Boil (scumming as necessary) until the stew is liquid but no longer watery. Add **salt** to taste; you can serve the pottage with **toast**.

Peas porridge

To make pease porridge of old peas: Take 2 quarts of white peas, pick and wash them clean, then set them on in 3 gallons of water. Keep them boiling as the water wastes, fill it up with cold water to break the husks, and as the husks rise, [after] it is filled up with cold water, scum them off into a collander into a dish to save the liquor and peas to put into the pot again. Then t[ake] up all the peas and posh [mash] them with a spoon; then put them in again. And when they have boiled a while, put in 2 cloves of garlic, half an ounce of coriander seeds beaten, some sifted pepper and some salt, an ounce of powder of dried spearmint. All these must be put in at the second boiling. Shred in 2 onions and a handful of parsley very small, and put in half a pound of fresh butter. Then let all boil together for a quarter of an hour. Then serve them up with bread and bits of fresh butter put into them. If you love it, put in a little elder vinegar. (Hess, *Martha Washington*, 68)

Wash and drain **2 cups dried peas.** Put them in **6 cups water** and bring them to a boil. Simmer covered for 1 hour, scumming as necessary. Remove the peas (a slotted spoon can do this), saving the water, and mash them. Return the peas to the water and bring to a boil. After boiling for 15 minutes, scum again, and add **a clove of garlic, 1 tsp crushed coriander seeds, 1/4 tsp pepper, a pinch of salt,** and **2 tsp dried mint.** Chop in **1 onion** and **2 tbsp parsley,** and add **4 oz. butter.** Boil until the peas are still liquid but no longer watery. Serve with bread and butter; one can also add a bit of vinegar (the source specifies vinegar flavored with elderflowers).

Salad

To make a salad of all kind of herbs: Take your herbs and pick them very fine in fair water, and pick your flowers by themselves, and wash them clean, then swing them in a strainer, and when you put them into a dish, mingle them with cucumbers or lemons pared and sliced, also scrape sugar, and put in vinegar and oil, then spread the flowers on the top of the salad, and with every sort of the aforesaid things garnish the dish about, then take eggs boiled hard and lay about the dish and upon the salad. (*A Book of Fruits and Flowers*, 42)

Break or cut up **4 cups mixed vegetables** (such as lettuce, spinach, chives, scallions, radishes, cold boiled carrots, mint, and parsley). Clean **1 cup flowers** (such as violets, nasturtiums, marigolds) and drain. Garnish the salad with the flowers, **1 sliced cucumber or lemon,** and **2 sliced hard boiled eggs.** Sprinkle with **1 tbsp sugar, 2 tbsp vinegar,** and **2 tbsp olive oil.**

Pickled cucumbers

To pickle cucumbers: Take the least [smallest] you can get, and lay a layer of cucumbers, and then a layer of beaten spices, dill, and bay leaves, and so do till you have filled your pot; and let the spices, dill, and bay leaves cover them, then fill up your pot with the best wine vinegar and a little salt, and so keep them. Sliced turnips also very thin, in some vinegar, pepper, and a little salt, do make a very good salad, but they will keep but six weeks. (Hannah Woolley, *The Queen-Like Closet*, 30–31)

In a glass jar, place a layer of **small (or sliced) cucumbers** about 2" deep; sprinkle on top **1 tsp ground mace, 1/4 tsp ground pepper, 1 tsp fennel seeds, 1 tbsp fresh dill,** and **2 bay leaves.** Repeat the layering until the jar is full. Mix **1 cup water** and **1 cup white vinegar**, and dissolve **1 tbsp salt** into the liquid. Pour the vinegar mix into the jar and seal. After a week, the cucumbers will be ready to eat.

Spinach tart

Take good store of spinach, and boil it in a pipkin with white wine till it be very soft as pap; then take it, and strain it well into a pewter dish, not leaving any part unstrained. Then put to it rose-water, great store of sugar and cinnamon, and boil it till it be as thick as marmalade; then let it cool, and after fill your coffin, and adorn it, and serve it in all points as you did your prune tart; and this carrieth the color green. (Markham, *English Housewife*, 108)

Boil **8 cups spinach** in **1 cup white wine** for 5 minutes, or until fully soft, stirring so that the spinach settles into the liquid. Strain out the liquid, add **1/4 cup rose-water, 1 cup sugar,** and **1 tsp. ground cinnamon,** and boil until the liquidity is almost gone. Allow to cool and then pour into a **pie crust,** and bake at 350° for 20 minutes.

Markham's instructions for the prune tart call for "patterns of paper cut in diverse proportions, as beasts, birds, arms, knots, flowers, and such like" to be cut out in pastry dough and laid upon the tart.

Fruit tart

To make all manner of fruit tarts: You must boil your fruit, whether it be apple, cherry, peach, pear, mulberry, or codling, in fair water; and when they be boiled enough, put them into a bowl and bruise them with a ladle; and when they be cold, strain them, and put in red wine or claret wine, and so season it with sugar, cinnamon, and ginger. (*A Book of Fruits and Flowers*, 35)

Boil **4 cups sliced apples, cherries, peaches, or pears** in **1 quart water** until soft (the exact time will depend on the fruit and its ripeness). Remove and crush the fruit. Strain out the water, and add **1/4 cup red wine, 1/4 cup sugar, 1/2 tsp ground cinnamon,** and **1/2 tsp ground ginger.** Bake in a **pie crust** at 350° for 40 minutes.

Pancakes

To make the best pancake, take two or three eggs, and break them into a dish, and beat them well; then add unto them a pretty quantity of fair running water, and beat all well together; then put in cloves, mace, cinnamon, and nutmeg, and season it with salt; which done, make it thick as you think good with fine wheat flour; then fry the cakes as thin as may be with sweet butter, or sweet seam, and make them brown, and so serve them up with sugar strewed upon them. There be some which mix pancakes with new milk or cream, but that makes them tough, cloying, and not crisp, pleasant, and savory as running water. (Markham, *English Housewife*, 69)

Beat **2 eggs;** beat in **1/3 cup water.** Add a pinch each of **ground cloves, ground mace, ground nutmeg,** and **salt** and **1/4 tsp ground cinnamon.** Add **2 tbsp white flour** and stir together. Fry thin in the manner of crêpes, in a buttered pan on medium-high heat, until the batter loses its liquidity. Serve garnished with **sugar.**

Banbury cake (currant cake)

To make a very good Banbury cake, take four pounds of currants and wash and pick them clean, and dry them in a cloth. Then take three eggs, and put away one yolk, and beat them, and strain them with good barm, putting thereto cloves, mace, cinnamon, and nutmegs. Then take a pint of cream, and as much morning's milk, and set it on the fire till the cold be taken away. Then take flour and put in good store of cold butter and sugar, then put in your eggs, barm and meal and work them all together an hour or more. Then save a part of the paste, and the rest break in pieces, and work in your currants. When done, mould your cake of whatever quantity you please, and then with that paste which hath not any currants cover it very thin, both underneath and aloft, and so bake it according to the bigness. (Markham, *English Housewife*, 115–16)

Beat **1 egg** in a large bowl. Stir in **2 tsp yeast, 1/8 tsp ground cloves, 1/8 tsp ground mace, 1/4 tsp ground cinnamon,** and **1/8 tsp ground nutmeg.** Mix the egg mixture into **1 cup half-and-half,** stir, and set aside. Cream together **1/2 cup butter, 1/2 cup sugar,** and **1 cup unbleached flour.** Mix in the egg and cream mixture, and allow to rise for 1 hour. Set aside 1 cup of the dough, and fold **2 lbs. cleaned currants** into the remainder. Spread half the set-aside dough in a thin layer at the bottom and sides of a greased pan; lay the dough with currants inside this and then cover with the remainder of the plain dough (this will keep the currants from drying out). Bake at 275° for about an hour—until a knife stuck into the cake comes out dry.

Modern cakes are make with baking powder, but the universal leavening agent in the 1600s was yeast.

Hippocras (spiced wine)

To make hippocras: Take a gallon of claret or white wine, and put therein four ounces of ginger, an ounce and a half of nutmegs, of cloves one quarter, of sugar four pound; let all this stand together in a pot at least twelve hours, then take it, and put it into a clean bag made for the purpose, so that the wine may come with good leisure from the spices. (Markham, *English Housewife*, 118)

Mix **1 bottle red wine** with **2 tbsp ground ginger, 2 tsp ground nutmeg, 1/4 tsp ground cloves,** and **1 cup sugar.** Allow to stand overnight and then strain through a cloth.

NOTES

1. On the price of sugar, see James E. Thorold Rogers, *A History of Agriculture and Prices in England* (Oxford: Clarendon Press, 1882), 6.426ff. On vegetables and herbs, see Gervase Markham, *The English Housewife*, ed. Michael R. Best (Kingston-Montreal: McGill-Queen's University Press, 1986), 60ff.; John Evelyn, *Acetaria: A Discourse of Sallets* (Brooklyn: published by a Women's Auxiliary, Brooklyn Botanic Garden, 1937); Turloch McSween, *Seventeenth-Century Vegetable Uses* (Bristol: Stuart Press, 1992).

2. Eric S. Wood, *Historical Britain* (London: Harvill Press, 1995), 56b.

3. Randle Holme, *Living and Working in Seventeenth-Century England: An Encyclopedia of Drawings and Descriptions from Randle Holme's Original Manuscripts for The Academy of Armory (1688)* [CD-ROM], ed. N. W. Alcock and Nancy Cox (London: British Library, 2001), Bk. 3, no. 29. This section of Holme is a particularly valuable source on cooking in general; see also Stuart Peachey, *Cooking Techniques and Equipment 1580–1660* (Bristol: Stuart Press, 1994).

4. On bread, see Holme, *Academy*, Bk. 3, no. 30; Gervase Markham, *The English Housewife*, ed. Michael R. Best (Kingston-Montreal: McGill-Queen's University Press, 1986), 209–11; Karen Hess, *Martha Washington's Booke of Cookery* (New York: Columbia University Press, 1981), 17ff., 117ff.; Stuart Peachey, *The Book of Bread 1580–1660* (Bristol: Stuart Press, 1996).

5. John Locke, *Some Thoughts Concerning Education*, ed. John W. and Jean S. Yolton (Oxford: Clarendon Press, 1989), 94.

6. On drinks, see Holme, *Academy of Armory*, Bk. 3, no. 44; Karen Hess, *Martha Washington's Booke of Cookery* (New York: Columbia University Press, 1981), 378ff.; Sir Kenelm Digby, *The Closet of Sir Kenelme Digby, Knight, Opened* (London: printed for H. Brome, 1677); Thomas Tryon, *A New Art of Brewing Beer, Ale, and Other Sorts of Liquors* (London: printed for Thomas Salisbury, 1690); Gervase Markham, *The English Housewife*, ed. Michael R. Best (Kingston-Montreal: McGill-Queen's University Press, 1986), 137ff., 180ff., 204ff.; Peter Clark, *The English Alehouse: A Social History 1200–1830* (London and New York: Longman, 1983), 94ff.; Stuart Peachey, *The Tipler's Guide to Drink and Drinking in the Early Seventeenth Century* (Bristol: Stuart Press, 1992).

7. Roger Lockyer, *Tudor and Stuart Britain 1471–1714* (London: Longman, 1964), 433; Keith Wrightson, *Earthly Necessities: Economic Lives in Early Modern Britain* (New Haven: Yale University Press, 2000), 180.

8. Comenius, *Orbis*, 118–19.

9. On setting, see Holme, *Academy of Armory*, Bk. 3, no. 1ff., 79ff; John Murrell, *Murrels Two Bookes of Cookerie and Carving* (London: for John Marriot, 1641), 152.

10. Hannah Woolley, *The Compleat Servant Maid* (London: T. Passinger, 1683), 133.

11. On eating and drinking establishments, see A. Everitt, "The English Urban Inn 1560–1760," in A. Everitt, ed., *Perspectives in English Urban History* (London: Macmillan, 1973), 91–137; Peter Clark, *The English Alehouse. A Social History 1200–1830* (London and New York: Longman, 1983); R. F. Bretherton, "Country Inns and Alehouses," in *Englishmen at Rest and Play: Some Phases of English Leisure 1558–1714* (Oxford: Clarendon Press, 1931), 145–202.

8

ENTERTAINMENTS

The seventeenth century marked a turning point in the history of entertainments in England. Leisure activities are one of the chief ways in which human beings express and explore their individual and communal identities—witness the role of professional sports in the lives of people today—and the cultural transformations and conflicts of the 1600s played themselves out very dramatically in this sphere. Traditionalists and reformists vied to use leisure time as a means to realize their respective visions for English society. This conflict came to a head during the Civil Wars and Interregnum, and although it receded after the Restoration, a deeper transformation continued, as the English moved away from traditional communal entertainments toward highly class-structured pastimes and away from grassroots folk culture toward commercially based popular culture. As in many societies, the entertainments of Stuart England offer a case study in the dynamics of the culture as a whole.

Then as now, a person's choice of pastimes had much to do with his or her social and personal identity: some pastimes were specifically for men, for mixed company, for children, for the upper classes, for commoners, or for country folk. Edward Chamberlayne in 1669 surveyed English pastimes, emphasizing their social implications:

The King hath his forests, chases, and parks, full of variety of game, for hunting red and fallow deer, foxes, otters, hawking; his paddock courses, horse-races, &c. abroad and at home; tennis, balloon, billiards, interludes, balls, masks, &c. The nobility and chief gentry have their parks, warrens, decoys, paddock courses, horse-races, hunting, coursing, fishing, fowling, hawking, setting dogs, tumblers, lurchers, duck-hunting, cock-fighting, tennis, bowling, billiards, tables, chess, draughts, cards, dice, catches, Questions, Purposes, stage-plays, dancing, singing, all sorts of musical instruments, &c. The citizens and peasants have hand-ball, foot-ball, skittles or nine-pins, shovelboard, stow-ball, golf, troll-madam, cudgels, bearbaiting, bull-baiting, bow and arrow, throwing at cocks, shuttlecock, bowling, quoits, leaping, wrestling, pitching the bar, and ringing of bells (a recreation used in no other country of the world). Amongst these, cock-fighting seems to all foreigners too childish and unsuitable for the gentry, and for the common people bull-baiting and bear-baiting seem too cruel, and for the citizens foot-ball very uncivil, rude, and barbarous within the city.[1]

Sports   Then as now, some of the simplest entertainments were exercises of pure physical prowess. Boys developed their strength and stamina with footraces, and races between adult men were sometimes enjoyed as spectator sports. Samuel Pepys's diary makes reference to several footraces in London and nearby; the participants were often footmen, whose work in delivering messages for their employers required them to be good runners. An equally simple running sport was the children's game of tag, generally known in the period as tick. Prison Bars, also known as "base," was a more complex variant of this and a game with a long history that extends to the present—each team would have a base and a prison and would seek to capture their opponents by tagging them. Prison Bars was played especially by children and was seen as a rural sport; it was also one of the few running sports in which girls were known to take part.[2]

Another rural running game enjoyed by both sexes was Barley Breaks, a traditional game that was starting to decline by the latter part of the century. In Barley Breaks, a pair of players at each end of the field would split to meet their opposites at the far end and were chased by a third pair in the center; if one person in a pair was caught before finding his or her counterpart, that pair would go into the center. This game, with its chasing, grabbing, and mixing of couples, was particularly popular with single young men and women, and it was proverbially an occasion for rustic flirtation, but references to it died out by about 1700. Conceptually similar was the game of Fire and No Smoke, in which six players would stand at the three points of a triangle, two players at each point, one in front of the other; a seventh player (Fire) stood at one of the points and was chased by an eighth. The Fire would run to the next point, standing in front of the other two players, and the player in the back of that line would become Fire. If the eighth player could catch the Fire before he reached the next point, they would trade places.

Feats of athleticism were generally regarded as pastimes for rural folk and others lower on the social scale. Throwing large stones, sledgehammers, iron bars, and pikes (long spears) were popular country sports as well; lifting heavy weights was also practiced. Pulling contests were another demonstration of strength; the game known today as tug-of-war was played under the name England and Ireland. Jumping contests might be practiced for distance or height; one version involved the assistance of a pole, as in modern pole-vaulting. Feats of vaulting were one of the few games of pure athleticism that still had any currency with the upper classes: the sport had once been used by knights as a means of training in horsemanship, and vaulting onto a horse still had something of its old air of chivalric prowess; the sport was also practiced with tables and with inanimate "vaulting-horses" comparable to the ones used by Olympic athletes today. Swimming too was practiced in rural areas, although it was far from widespread.

Ball games are one of the most universal forms of pastimes; a variety of them existed in Stuart England, played **Ball Games** with a range of different types of balls. Solid balls of wood or ivory were used in such games as bowls, billiards, and skittles. Other games involved a ball made from several pieces of leather stitched together into a sphere and stuffed: the stuffing might be feathers, as in stowball, or wool scraps, as in the ordinary playing ball used by children. For tennis, the ball was given extra spring by wrapping the wool scraps very tight with twine. The lightest balls were made of an animal's bladder, tied up at the opening and inflated with a straw or a pump (resembling a simple bicycle pump); such bladders were used on their own as children's toys or were encased in leather to make a sturdier ball for games like football.

Figure 8.1 Tennis and balloon (Comenius 1887).

Football was the stereotypical ball sport of the lower classes, both in town and in the country. It could be played in a number of variants: the basic setup had some kind of goal at each end of the playing area, with each team vying to drive the ball into the other's goal, but the specifics could vary. Some versions allowed for the ball to be carried; others required that it be manipulated only with the feet. The game could be played on a street, in a field, or across open country. Some remoter parts of the country, such as Cornwall and Wales, had especially vigorous versions that pitted one village against another across the territory between them; the Cornish version, known as hurling, involved rules that embedded miniature wrestling matches into the game. From these multiple variants are derived the variety of games known under the rubric of football today. Similar games had once been common in Continental Europe, but by the seventeenth century, they were becoming rare enough that visitors to England found the game unfamiliar and distinctively English.

Similar to football in concept was hockey, usually called bandy or bandy-ball in the seventeenth century. In England, where winters are normally relatively mild, this was played on a field rather than on ice, and the equipment was very similar to that of modern field hockey. In fact, skates were occasionally seen in England during the seventeenth century, the idea having been imported from the Netherlands, but the unusually cold climate of the 1600s (sometimes called the Little Ice Age) did not last long enough for the practice to take deep roots.[3]

Assorted other ball sports were played as well, with a fair bit of local variation. References to cricket become common over the course of the century, chiefly in the southeast part of the country: the game involved one player after another on the team that is "up" using a crooked bat vaguely reminiscent a hockey stick to defend a target, while a player of the opposing team tried to hit the target with the ball.[4] Some versions of the game of stoolball may have had a similar structure, with a stool used for the target, although the only recorded rules for stoolball have no bat and no attempt to defend the stool (see the rules at the end of this chapter). Stoolball was another sport that was occasionally played by women, and it was often associated with Easter festivities.

The game of Horn Billets was analogous to modern cricket, except that the "ball" (called a "cat") was actually a small piece of wood tapered at each end: the cat could be placed on the ground and one end struck with the bat, making the cat fly into the air, and allowing the player to hit it. This manner of hitting the cat was used for the game of Kit Cat, in which the players scored points based on how far they were able to drive the cat in three strokes.

A distinctively regional sport was Stowball, a kind of vigorous cousin of croquet played only in Wiltshire and Gloucestershire: one team used a stick to drive a ball from one stake down the field, around another stake at the far end of the field, and back to the first stake in as few strokes as possible, while the other team tried to strike it back each time it was hit. An upper-class relative of Stowball was Pall Mall, a game comparable to croquet in which balls were struck around a course of targets using wooden mallets. The game came to England from the Continent early in the century, which gave it a certain social cachet, and to be played properly, it required a specialized and well-maintained playing surface that was flat and rectangular: there was one in London, in an area still known today as Pall Mall, or just the Mall—the ultimate origin of the modern shopping mall. Another game in this family imported to England during this century was golf, well established in Scotland before 1500 and increasingly familiar in England after the accession of James I, who was an aficionado of the sport.[5]

Some games involved throwing or hitting a ball back and forth, trying to keep it in the air. A simple version played by boys was sometimes known as I Call and I Call: one boy would throw the ball against a wall or roof and call out the name of another who had to catch it. In the game known as Handball or Fives, the boys took turns striking a ball against a stone wall; the game was similar to modern racquetball, but the ball was struck with the bare hand. Players who needed a stone wall for a game of handball often chose the exterior walls of churches, a practice that predictably led to broken windows and did not endear the game to Puritan-minded local authorities.[6]

During the Middle Ages, a game of this sort had given rise to tennis, which was the ball sport of choice for fashionable young men in the Stuart age. The usual form of the game was not like the customary modern "lawn tennis," but a variant seen only occasionally today, under the name "real tennis." It was played on an indoor court with an asymmetric shape that could vary somewhat from court to court, with complex rules and a number of variants. Courtiers in London frequented commercial tennis courts, and the very wealthy sometimes had courts of their own, as did the king at the royal palace of Whitehall. Pepys recorded one royal match in 1667: "The King, playing at tennis, had a steelyard carried to him, and I was told it was to weigh him after he had done playing; and at noon Mr. Ashburnham told me that it is only the King's curiosity, which he usually hath, of weighing himself before and after his play, to see how much he loses in weight by playing; and this day he lost 4 1/2 lb."[7]

Games akin to lawn tennis were played on the Continent, sometimes with rackets and sometimes with the bare hands, but such games appear to have been less common in England. A distantly related game was Balloon, similar to modern volleyball, in which players batted a large inflated ball back and forth—this game was popular on the Continent, but again, it seems to have had limited currency in England.

Similar to tennis but much less formal was Shuttlecocks. This was akin to modern badminton, but the racket—called a "battledore"—was generally made from a solid piece of wood; the shuttlecock was made of cork or wood with feathers stuck in it. This game could be played indoors as well as outdoors and was enjoyed by women as well as men.

Some physical games relied on finesse rather than strength or stamina. Bowls, played by both men and women of all classes, involved casting fist-sized balls at a smaller target ball, trying to end up as close to it as possible. This was an extremely popular game, played at home, in public bowling greens, and at commercial bowling alleys—Samuel Pepys mentioned playing it on shipboard, which must have been rather challenging,[8] and a variant was played with smaller balls on a tabletop. The Restoration games pundit Charles Cotton described it as "a game or recreation which, if moderately used, is very healthy for the body, and would be much more commendable than it is, were it not for those swarms of rooks, which so pester bowling-greens, bares [i.e., bare areas for bowling], and bowling-alleys . . . where three things are thrown away besides the bowls, viz. time, money, and curses, and the last ten for one."[9]

Similar to Bowls was Quoits, a game played by essentially the same rules, but with flat stones in place of balls; quoits was seen as a country cousin of bowls. Another related game was Skittles, which existed in variant versions known as ninepins and tenpins: the game involved casting a ball at an array of target pins to knock them over. The game could also be played with a casting-stick rather than a ball, in which case it was known as Loggats; this game was considered a country pastime and is alluded to in the final act of *Hamlet,* where the prince muses at the way the callous gravediggers "play at loggats" with the bones of those long dead.

Some of these less vigorous games could be played indoors as well as outside, and there were related games that were purely indoor activities. In Troll Madam, sometimes called "trunks," the players tried to roll small balls through a row of arches, scoring points depending on which arch they passed through. In Shovelboard—known also as shove-board, shove-groat, or slide-groat—they slid coins across a table, trying to get them as far as possible without actually falling off, and scoring points depending on the final position of the coins (see the rules at the end of this chapter).

A purely upper-class game of this type was billiards, played indoors on a purpose-built table with highly specialized equipment. The balls were sent around the table with broad-ended cues, with rules vaguely reminiscent of croquet—in fact, the game derived from a version that was played outdoors on a croquet-like course. A similar game was Trucks, played with very similar equipment and rules, but the table and cues were larger; Trucks was of Italian origin, and billiards had come from France.

Martial Sports   Martial sports were popular across the social spectrum, although the choice of weapons was often a mark of one's social standing. Characteristic weapons for men of the lower classes included the quarterstaff, the backsword (a broad-bladed sword, often with only a single cutting edge), and the sword in combination with a buckler (a small round shield). Country folk also used "cudgels"—wooden swords with hilts of basketwork, generally used in pairs, one in each hand. Boxing starts to appear in records from the latter half of this century, although it is not much attested in England before 1700. Wrestling was a popular sport, mostly restricted to the lower classes and especially associated with northern and southwestern England. Archery, on the other hand, was rapidly losing its popularity: at the beginning of the century, it still enjoyed some currency because bows were still part of the military technology of the late 1500s, but only a few optimistic military theorists of the early 1600s still believed in archery's practical value. The sport was still practiced by some, but even ordinary folk rarely indulged in it, and by 1700, archery was becoming an antiquarian pastime.

Men of the upper classes were more likely to study the arts of the rapier, the rapier and dagger, and, toward the end of the century, the smallsword— a shorter and lighter version of the rapier that had supplanted the older weapon by 1700. The techniques and vocabulary of these weapons were complex and largely imported from abroad—Italy in the case of the rapier, France for the smallsword. It was very common for a gentleman—or one who aspired to be thought a gentleman—to study the use of these weapons under a professional fencing master.

In addition to the arts of personal combat, military training was also practiced as a pastime. The most famous volunteer military organization was the Honorable Artillery Company of London, which met to learn and practice military drill. The musters of the militia, or trained bands, were sometimes treated as a form of public entertainment, and in general, although martial recreations were largely the preserve of men as practitioners, both men and women enjoyed them as spectator sports.[10]

In addition to these physical pastimes, there was a host of non-physical games, most of them still known today to a greater or lesser degree and most of them involving gambling. Dice games had been around since ancient times and were preeminently **Indoor Games** gambling games. This made them common fare in gambling houses and notorious as pastimes for sharping gamesters. The dice were rolled from a small container, and cheating players sometimes used subtle techniques to get the desired roll or even secretly substituted false dice when it was their turn to throw.

In dice games, the players would stake money into the pot to participate, and then each would roll the dice in turn; certain rolls might win or lose, or players might wager on specific outcomes of the rolls. The details varied from game to game: a simple example was Passage, in which the caster threw three dice until he got "doublets" (two dice the same). If the total of the three dice was under 10, he was "out" and lost; if over 10, he "passed" and won. If the roll was 10, the dice passed to the next player, but the pot was not collected.[11]

Cards had not made their appearance until the late Middle Ages, but they were well established in England by 1600, and they too normally involved gambling.[12] The cards had no letters or numbers on them—only the literate minority would have been able to read them. Nor were there patterns printed on the backs, which made them susceptible to marking: by tradition, packs were replaced every year at Christmas time, and the old cards were cut up and dipped in molten sulfur to make matches. The cards used in England were essentially equivalent to the 52-card deck current in the English-speaking world today (there was no Joker card). In fact, like today, one could purchase novelty decks, usually with educational themes: during the century, there were cards displaying maps of English shires, cards showing the events of the Spanish Armada of 1588, and cards depicting the events of the Gunpowder Plot of 1605.

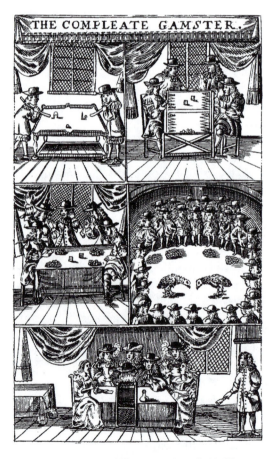

Figure 8.2 Aristocratic pastimes in the 1670s: billiards, tables, dice, cockfighting, and cards (Cotton 1674).

The most fashionable card games tended to involve fairly complex rules. One of the oldest of these was Ruff and Trump (known under various names), in which a card-exchange stage was followed by a trick-taking stage; the game was the origin of Whist. Picket, imported from France during this century, involved scoring points based on having certain card combinations, plus trick-taking; Gleek combined these with a bidding stage. Noddy involved scoring points for certain combinations and then playing tricks to make additional combinations; the results were scored on a board like a cribbage board, and indeed, cribbage was developed during this century as a variant on Noddy—it was thought to have been invented by the poet Sir John Suckling (1609–1642), and Pepys mentioned learning the game in 1660.[13]

Simpler games included One-and-Thirty (similar to modern blackjack, but counting to 31), Laugh and Lie Down (a matching game akin to Go Fish), and Put, which simply involved trick-taking. Perhaps the simplest game recorded from the period is Wheehee, a card-trading game in which the players tried to garner three cards of a single suit (see the rules at the end of this chapter).

A variety of games were played on a backgammon board; these were known as games at "tables." Backgammon itself was developed during the century as a variant of a game called Irish (see the rules at the end of this chapter). The most common game at tables was Ticktack, a game considerably more complex than backgammon: it could be won by getting all of one's pieces off the board, as in backgammon, but there were a number of other situations that ended the game, making the strategies rather complex. All games at tables had gambling built into the rules.

Chess was one of the few games of this type that did not involve gambling; the rules were essentially the same as the ones used today. Draughts (known today in America as checkers) was also known, although it seems to have been less popular than games at tables or chess. Another board game was Fox and Geese, in which 15 pieces called "geese" would try to trap a single "fox" on a cross-shaped board; the fox could take the geese by jumping over them. In the games of Nine Men's Morris and Three Men's Morris, the object was to get three pieces in a row; the latter was essentially equivalent to modern Tic-Tac-Toe, except that the pieces could be moved after they were placed (see the rules at the end of this chapter). A strikingly modern style of board game was Goose, imported from the Continent during the sixteenth century: in this game, played on a commercially printed board, players rolled dice to race along squares on a track and would have various events happen if they landed on certain squares.[14]

Word games were also popular and overlapped with many of those that remain familiar today. Riddles had been popular in England since the Middle Ages, and tongue-twisters appear in the records beginning in the seventeenth century, under the name of Gliffs. A range of other word games were popular as parlor entertainments for socially aspirant people: a typical example, mentioned by Pepys in 1669, was "I Love My Love with an A" (see the rules at the end of this chapter). Educational reformers were also beginning to advocate the use of word games to facilitate the learning process: one well-established schoolboys' game, called Capping Verses, involved using the last letter of a verse of classical Latin poetry for the first letter of another verse, continuing until one player could not think of a line from the classics that began with the letter in question.

Children's Games
Many of the games in the Stuart repertoire were exclusively or predominantly the preserve of children. Quite a few of them still exist today: examples include hide and seek, leapfrog, hopscotch (known in the period as Scotch Hoppers), checkstones (equivalent to the modern game of jacks), and marbles. Blindman's Buff was a popular game, although not exclusively for children; in particular, adults were known to play it at Christmas time. Another children's game often played by adults during the Christmas season was Hot Cockles: one player hid his eyes in the lap of another while the others took turns striking him on the backside—if he could guess who struck him, the two would change places. The game of Hunting a Deer in My Lord's Park was very similar to the modern Duck, Duck, Goose (see the rules at the end of this chapter). Somewhat less familiar today, though it survived to the modern period, is Span Counter, a boys' game in which the players bounced coins off a wall, trying to end as close as possible to a target counter. A simple children's game, often used by adults as well, was the coin game known as "cross and pile"—the same as the modern "heads or tails."

Then as now, many children's games made use of small and plentiful objects that could be acquired without cost. Cherry Pit involved casting cherry pits into small holes in the ground; in Cob Castle, four nuts or cherry pits were arranged in a pyramid, and the children cast a nut or other projectile at it to knock it over. In Cobnut, a string was run through a nut, and two contestants swung the nuts against each other, each trying to break the nut of the other.

As with adults' games, children's games often involved some sort of gambling, though the stakes were typically items of small value such as pins or points (the laces used in fastening clothes). Many boys' games tended to be somewhat violent: in Buying Bees, one player stood between two others with his hat upside-down on the ground before him, holding his hands before his mouth and making a buzzing sound; then he would suddenly strike his companions, and plunge his hands into his hat: they could strike him back, but not after he got his hands into the hat. In Cropping Oaks, two boys sat facing each other on a bench, each with his left hand over his left ear; with their right hands they would take turns striking each other's left ear; the first to knock his opponent off the bench was the winner.

Figure 8.3 Boys at their games, including ninepins, bowling, whipping the top, and pall mall (Comenius 1887).

Toys were very much a part of children's lives then as today. These included tops, hobby horses, pop-guns, drums, stilts, kites, swings, see-saws, and dolls. John Locke decried the growing consumerism in the world of children's toys and its detrimental effect on young attention-spans:

They should have of several sorts [of playthings], yet I think they should have none bought for them. This will hinder that great variety they are often overcharged with, which serves only to teach the mind to wander after change.... I have known a young child so distracted with the number and variety of his play-games, that he tired his maid every day to look them over; and was so accustomed to abundance, that he never thought he had enough, but was always asking, "What more?" ... They should make them themselves, or at least endeavor it.... A smooth pebble, a piece of paper, the mother's bunch of keys, or anything they cannot hurt themselves with, serves as much to divert little children, as those more chargeable [expensive] and curious toys from the shops, which are presently put out of order and broken.[15]

Music and dance were also a part of seventeenth-century life and very much an area in which people demonstrated their place in society. As had been the case for some time, the most fashionable forms were imported from the Continent: the coranto came from Italy, the bransle (pronounced "brawl") from France. These Continental dances were typically for couples and involved intricate steps, highly formalized posture, and complex floor patterns.

Music and Dance

Dances in the native English tradition were known as country dances, most often danced by "sets" of two to four couples in a square or rectangular formation—some country dances were done by couples in rings or in long lines of couples, men facing women down the line.

In both music and dance, there was something of a "folk revival" in the period, with people of the upper classes taking an interest in traditional popular song and dance and adopting them for their own uses: quite a number of anthologies of country dances and popular songs were published during the century, and country dances were danced at the royal court as well as in the villages. Pepys described one such dance in 1662:

Mr. Povey ... brought me ... into the room where the ball was to be, crammed with fine ladies, the greatest of the court. By and by comes the King and Queen, the Duke and Duchess, and all the great ones; and after seating themselves, the King takes out the Duchess of York, and the Duke the Duchess of Buckingham, the Duke of Monmouth my Lady Castlemaine, and so other lords other ladies; and they danced the bransle. After that, the King led a lady a single coranto; and then the rest of the lords, one after another, other ladies. Very noble it was, and great pleasure to see. Then to country dances; the King leading the first which he called for; which was, says he, "Cuckolds all a-row," the old dance of England.[16]

Across society, musical proficiency was a common social skill. Only the privileged classes could afford to hire professional musicians on a regular basis: most people who wanted music had to make it themselves. Educated men and women were expected to be able to read music, and after a meal, it was quite common for the company to bring out printed music to sing or play. Samuel Pepys was probably more than ordinarily musical: he read music reasonably well, and in addition to singing, he played the flageolet (recorder), viol (viola), virginals (small harpsichord), and lute, and he practiced quite regularly, occasionally playing music with his wife.[17] For ordinary people, musical literacy was less common, but musical competence was still widespread: vocal and instrumental music was a common feature of social occasions, and most people would at least be able to join in on a chorus, a round, or the melody-line of a part-song. Popular rural instruments included the fiddle, bagpipes, and pipe and tabor (a drum played in conjunction with a one-handed whistle akin to a recorder). Even barber shops commonly kept musical instruments on hand for the patrons to entertain themselves while they waited.

Although recorded music was still far in the future, there was still a significant music industry, based on the broadside ballad. These were lyrics set to familiar melodies, generally printed on a single sheet of paper with one or more woodcut images; the themes included folktales, current events, satire, and biblical stories. Broadsides were churned out by the presses in substantial numbers every year and could be found in alehouses, private homes, and other places where people gathered socially, providing material for the traditional sing-along. In addition to ballads, popular forms of song included part-songs and rounds. Religious-themed music was also very much a part of the popular musical tradition; everyone was familiar with at least the psalms from Sunday services, and psalms enjoyed some currency as music for pastime as well as for worship.[18]

Other forms of popular musical entertainment were oriented toward performance rather than participation. The patterned ringing of church bells, mentioned by Chamberlayne at the head of this chapter, was a characteristic country pastime of the age, as was morris dancing, a performance dance of the summer season in which the dancers wore bells and outlandish costumes and were often accompanied by the figures of a fool, a "Maid Marian" (played by a man), and a hobby-horse. Folk drama was rapidly waning by this period, although some versions did survive, most particularly in the form of mumming plays performed during the Christmas season. Traditional public festivals had been at their height in the 1400s and 1500s, but by 1600, they were in decline, partly because of social and economic transformations and partly because of active suppression on the part of Puritan-minded authorities. Nonetheless, some traditional festivities did survive, and there were some efforts to revive them in the late 1600s with the restoration of the monarchy.[19]

Theater and Spectacle

Overall, the trend in seventeenth-century England was away from these folk entertainments and toward entertainments provided by professionals. Standing professional theaters were still a relatively new phenomenon in 1600—the first one in England had only been built in 1576—but professional drama had already taken deep root in the country. Within the first two decades of the century, the open-air theaters associated with Shakespeare were fast losing ground to the newer indoor theaters. London's theaters were closed by Parliament in 1642, and by the time they were officially reopened at the Restoration, the indoor theaters had entirely won the field. Each theater was associated with a professional acting company that performed both in the city and on tour. The indoor theaters were significantly more expensive to attend: whereas Shakespeare's audiences could get into the Globe for as little as 1d., the indoor seats of the Restoration ranged from 1s. to 4s.

The repertoire that developed over the course of the century included both established old plays—the works of Shakespeare being prominent among them—and works by current writers. One innovation was the development of opera: stage plays were prohibited during the Civil Wars and Interregnum, but musical performances were not, and people exploited this loophole in the 1650s by performing dramas in song; the genre remained popular after the Restoration. Another seventeenth-century innovation was the introduction of actresses: in Shakespeare's time, women's roles were played by boys, but after the Restoration, it became legal for women to perform in the theaters.[20]

Animal Sports   A range of sports and spectacles involved animals in various ways. Riding was one of the distinctive pastimes of the upper classes: it was to some degree practiced by ordinary people for practical purposes, but only the well-to-do could afford to keep horses for pleasure and to spend time learning the niceties of advanced equestrianism. Among traditional equestrian sports, the tournament was already fast declining in England during the early part of the century. However, horse racing was rapidly growing in popularity at the same time, and by the Restoration, it had been firmly established as one of the distinctive spectator sports of the English upper classes, with permanent racing courses at places like Newmarket and Banstead Downs.

Another distinctive pastime of the privileged classes was hunting. This took a number of forms depending on the quarry: by the 1600s, most large game had vanished from England, the sole exception being deer, who could still be found because they were deliberately stocked in private hunting parks and in royal forests. Because large game was lacking, the fox was well on his way to becoming the characteristic prey of the English gentleman. This form of hunting was an equestrian sport, with the quarry being chased on horseback with the assistance of a pack of hounds. Firearms were also used in hunting, particularly for taking down birds, although there were some who still practiced the medieval sport of falconry, also chiefly used for fowling. Fishing was another popular pastime—Izaac Walton's classic *The Compleat Angler* was first published in 1653. Coursing, the predecessor of modern greyhound racing, involved letting slip two greyhounds after a hare; the first dog to come close enough to the quarry to make it suddenly change direction was considered the winner. Only landowners were legally permitted to engage in most of these hunting sports: poaching was widespread, but its purpose was more practical than recreational.[21] In addition to the animals involved in various types of sports, people of the privileged classes often kept pets, including lapdogs, parrots, and monkeys. Ordinary households kept dogs and cats, but again, these were largely for practical purposes, the one serving as watchdogs, the other preying on domestic rats and mice.

Many of the sports involving animals had a strong element of cruelty. One highly popular sport was bearbaiting, in which a pack of dogs were loosed against a chained bear; the contest might take place in a marketplace or in a theater-like arena, and the audience would lay wagers on the outcome of the fight. Another version pitted the dogs against a bull. Cockfighting set two fighting cocks against one another and was somewhat more participatory, since spectators might bring their own birds to the contest. Only somewhat less cruel was the sport of cockshies, a common feature of Shrove Tuesday celebrations: a cock was tied to a peg, and participants would throw sticks at him, paying the owner for a certain number of throws; if the cock was knocked from his feet, and the thrower could pick him up before he got up again, he became property of the player.

Although these sports had a wide following, many people abhorred their brutality: Samuel Pepys, who witnessed a bullbaiting in 1666, admitted that he "saw some good sport of the bull's tossing of the dogs" but also found it "a very rude and nasty pleasure."[22] Reform-minded Protestants in particular were largely opposed to them.

Animal baiting, like many of the pastimes of the English in this period, often involved gambling, a form of entertainment **Gambling** deeply embedded in seventeenth-century culture. As we have seen, not only did adults gamble at the kinds of games found in modern casinos, but children also gambled at their own pastimes. Even day-to-day events could become the subject of a wager: Samuel Pepys recorded an instance when he was dining with friends at a tavern and won "a quart of sack of Shaw, that one trencherful that was sent us was all lamb, and he [said] that it was veal."[23] Gambling was particularly rife in the upper classes and above all at the royal court under Charles II, where the ability to play fashionable games for high stakes was considered essential for anyone of social aspirations. John Evelyn remarked on the cult of games at the royal court:

This evening (according to custom) his Majesty opened the revels of that night, by throwing the dice himself, in the Privy Chamber, where was a table set on purpose, and lost his 100 pounds; the year before he won 150 pounds. The ladies also played very deep. I came away when the duke of Ormond had won about 1000 pounds and left them still at Passage, cards, &c, at other tables, both there and at the Groom Porter's, observing the wicked folly, vanity, and monstrous excess of passion amongst some losers; and sorry I am that such a wretched custom as play to that excess should be countenanced in a court, which ought to be an example of virtue to the rest of the kingdom.[24]

At a less exalted level, commercial gaming houses were numerous in the cities, and even ordinary eating and drinking establishments often served as venues for gambling.

Also worthy of mention are a range of more quiet and solitary pastimes. In an age when literacy was rapidly spreading, **Solitary and** reading was becoming increasingly prominent as a leisure **Intellectual** activity, and the century witnessed a massive increase in the **Pastimes** output of the presses. As had been the case since the first appearance of printing two centuries earlier, the single largest component of this output was religious material, but other genres were accounting for a growing share: important domains included literature (especially drama and poetry), technical writings, science, and philosophical works. The output of the presses increased markedly in the 1640s and 1650s with the collapse of the traditional apparatus for censorship: according to Edward Chamberlayne, "There have been during our late troubles more good and more bad books printed and published in the English Tongue, than in all the vulgar languages of Europe."[25] Among new genres that took off during the Civil Wars were the news sheets: Englishmen eager for news of the war could purchase journals (usually affiliated with either the Royalist or Parliamentarian cause) with accounts of the latest battles and political developments. Similar journals, known as "corrantoes," had already existed in England before the war, mostly focusing on the news of the Thirty Years' War, but it was the domestic conflict that brought the newspapers into a prominence that they have continued to enjoy to the present day.[26] Censorship of the press was revived with the Restoration, but never with the same effectiveness, and in 1695, the Licensing Act, which had established the governmental apparatus for censorship, was finally allowed to lapse.

Connected to this increase in reading was the rise of amateur science and scholarship: a large number of people of the leisured classes were devoting time and energy to studying the natural and human worlds. Samuel Pepys is a good example of amateur interest in the sciences: he visited the Royal Menagerie at the Tower of London,[27] attended public anatomies (dissections of the corpses of executed criminals, used to teach human physiology),[28] and purchased a microscope as well as a book explaining how to use it.[29] Self-improvement did not stop with the sciences: a well-rounded gentleman of the period was expected to have some facility with a wide range of scientific, technological, humanistic, and artistic disciplines: this was the age of the "Renaissance man," known to contemporaries as the "virtuoso." Pepys's description of a visit with John Evelyn offers an exceptional example of this ideal:

Mr. Evelyn . . . showed me most excellent painting in little—in distemper, Indian Ink—water colors—graving; and above all, the whole secret of mezzo tinto and the manner of it, which is very pretty, and good things done with it. He read to me very much also of his discourse he hath been many years and now is about, about gardenage [gardening], which will be a noble and pleasant piece. He read me part of a play or two of his making, very good, but not as he conceits them, I think, to be. He showed me his *Hortus hyemalis*—leaves, laid up in a book, of several plants, kept dry, which preserve color however, and look very finely, better than any herbal. In fine, a most excellent person he is, and must be allowed a little for a little conceitedness; but he may well be so, being a man so much above others. He read me, though with too much gusto, some little poems of his own, that were not transcendent, yet one or two very pretty epigrams.[30]

Some of the more scientific pursuits were largely the domain of men, but leisured women were also studying to improve their intellectual and artistic skills: Pepys's wife Elizabeth took lessons in music and drawing, and John Evelyn took great pride in his daughter Mary's extensive reading in religion, history, geography, and the Classical poets; her facility with French and Italian; and her skill in singing, playing the harpsichord, and dancing.[31]

Among the quieter entertainments was a trend toward "taking the air" as a form of recreation. The stresses of living in an increasingly modernized environment seem to have been felt by seventeenth-century Englishmen, who increasingly took an interest in getting out of the urban environment to rural settings and commercial gardens to refresh themselves. Early in the century, Robert Burton mentioned walking "amongst orchards, bowers, and arbors, artificial wildernesses, and green thickets" as a healthful pastime,[32] and by the latter part of the 1600s, commercially based gardens were being founded at places such as Vauxhall, near London, as resorts for city-dwellers to escape the urban environment.

For most people, leisure was something that happened when work was ruled out, either because of darkness or because it was a day when work was neither expected nor permitted. This meant that Sundays and other religious **The Settings of Recreation** holidays were the chief occasions for leisure activities, "for," as James I observed, "when shall the common people have leave to exercise, if not upon the Sundays and holy days, seeing they must apply their labor, and win their living in all working days?"[33] Everyone was theoretically expected to attend religious services on Sunday morning, but on Sunday afternoons, more people were inclined to engage in leisure activities than to attend the afternoon service. The same applied to the three dozen church holidays in the annual cycle; these holidays gave leisure a kind of seasonal rhythm, and many pastimes were strongly associated with particular seasons or days in the year. Many communities traditionally held annual fairs or parish festivals during the summer, when the weather was amenable to outdoor activities. The Christmas season, particularly the two weeks from Christmas Eve to January 6, was a prime occasion for indoor entertainments involving friends and family. Shrove Tuesday was the setting for a number of traditional entertainments, including football and cockshies; Easter was often associated with games of stoolball.

The social and religious ramifications of leisure activities were the source of intense conflict in the first half of the 1600s. Since the Middle Ages, the state had sought to regulate recreation. By law, the upper classes had the greatest freedom in choosing their entertainments, whereas commoners were officially forbidden to engage in gambling, although gambling remained an integral part of their lives, official disapproval notwithstanding. From the late thirteenth century onward, the crown also sought to promote English military might by encouraging archery, a policy that involved an ongoing effort to suppress other forms of recreation among the commonality. Such efforts were doomed to failure, yet the laws suppressing sports like football in favor of archery remained on the books in the seventeenth century, even if they were rarely enforced.[34]

With the rise of gunpowder small arms in the 1500s, battlefield archery waned in significance. Governmental interest in regulating games and sports lost its urgency, and the initiative in this direction passed into the hands of Protestant reformers. These reformers often had strong objections to many traditional entertainments. Sports like football tended toward violence; indoor games such as cards and tables were occasions for gambling; and dramatic performances were seen as fostering sloth and lechery. Aside from any faults within the entertainments themselves, the realities of their place in the workweek entailed conflict with the reformers. For most people, Sundays and church holidays were the chief opportunity for leisure activities, but for the reformists, the sanctity of the Sabbath outweighed any need for recreation, and they also looked askance on the yearly cycle of religious holidays because they had no basis in Scripture.

By the early seventeenth century, games had become an explosive political issue. Reformist local authorities in the first half of the century sought to suppress activities such as gaming, sports, and dancing on Sundays. In 1616, the quarter-sessions justices of the peace in Lancashire issued orders completely banning piping, dancing, and any other "profanation" on Sundays. James I visited Lancashire the following summer and was disturbed by the fractiousness that these orders had fostered, on the one hand encouraging the dangerous zeal of the more extreme Protestants and on the other, prompting his traditionalistic subjects to turn toward Catholicism. In response, James issued his "Declaration of Sports," first just for Lancashire and then in 1618 in an amended version to cover the nation as a whole. The declaration decreed that, despite the disapproval of "Puritans and precise people," the citizenry of England should not be "disturbed, letted, or discouraged from any lawful recreation, such as dancing, either men or women, archery for men, leaping, vaulting, or any other such harmless recreation … so as the same be had in due and convenient time, without impediment or neglect of divine service."

James's actual attitude toward games was not fundamentally different from that espoused by centuries of English monarchs. He adhered to the traditional double standard of his predecessors, countenancing gambling among the aristocracy, but disapproving of such "unlawful" pastimes among the commons: in fact, the Lancashire justices had based their ruling on one of James's earliest royal decrees, forbidding "disordered or unlawful exercises" on Sundays. The shift was one of tone and emphasis, but it proved highly controversial nonetheless, as reformists were outraged by what they saw as an assault on the Sabbath. James felt compelled to issue a further defense of his declaration in 1624, and Charles I issued his own version in 1633. Responsibility for Charles's Declaration of Sports was one of the charges levied against Archbishop Laud by the Long Parliament, and there were those who believed that the declaration was one of the principal causes of the Civil War.[35]

With the triumph of Parliament in the 1640s and 1650s, reformists had the opportunity to implement policies enforcing observance of the Sabbath and suppressing traditional holy days. In 1641, the House of Commons issued a prohibition of all Sunday dancing and sports. In 1644, a parliamentary ordinance forbade "any wrestlings, shooting, bowling … games, sport, or pastime whatsoever" on Sundays and decreed that Charles's Declaration of Sports was to be publicly burned. Games were also forbidden on the monthly fast days instituted by Parliament, although

Parliament also established a monthly day of rest and recreation to replace the traditional holy days. As with previous efforts to suppress unlawful gaming, such measures met with only limited success.[36]

With the Restoration, these political issues were resolved in favor of the traditionalists, and games were once more restored to governmental favor. As the Duke of Newcastle advised Charles II, traditional games "will amuse the people's thoughts, and keep them in harmless action, which will free your majesty from faction and rebellion." Charles himself actively cultivated gaming, and high society followed his lead.[37]

Yet the traditional contexts of leisure were undergoing transformations that ran deeper than political divisions over Sabbath observance. The cult of games at Charles's court coincided with a growing interest among the privileged classes in refining and elaborating the distinctions that set them apart from the rest of society. Because they were the leisured class *par excellence*, games were an important part of their self-definition, and the ability to pursue the right sorts of games according to the most current fashions, and especially to gamble freely, was seen by many as the mark of a gentleman. At the same time, the upper classes were increasingly withdrawing from involvement in traditional and communal entertainments, which were coming to be seen as activities for those of lower standing.

These developments coincided with the gradual relocation of leisure activities away from the sphere of traditional folk culture and into the domain of the cash economy. A telling case is the Cotswold Games organized by the lawyer Robert Dover in 1612. There had traditionally been summer festivals near Chipping Camden, Gloucestershire, in the Cotswolds, but by the early 1600s, these were rapidly declining. With the encouragement of the crown, Dover secured space for a revived festival featuring traditional country pastimes such as races, leaping, sports, dancing, coursing, cudgels, and throwing the sledge, bar, and pike; Dover added some spectacular flourishes, notably a castle made of canvas from which cannons could be discharged, and he imparted to the whole a certain classicizing and gentrifying flavor.[38]

Although Dover's enterprise was in part inspired by an interest in reviving an idealized vision of "merry England," Dover was an entrepreneur, and his games were an artificial creation, with money charged at the entrance. Dover succeeded in transforming this local celebration into a major event with national visibility, and although his games fell casualty to the Civil Wars, his entrepreneurial approach to entertainments was the way of the future. After the Restoration, other entrepreneurs similarly developed commercially based festivals and pleasure sites: examples include the pleasure gardens at Vauxhall and the racing track at Newmarket, both close to the lucrative London market. Traditional folk culture had not died out by 1700, but it was fast losing ground to commercial popular culture, and it is a telling case that folklorists collecting oral ballads in the nineteenth century often found that the lyrics derived from printed broadsides of the seventeenth century.

Yet if the broad contexts of entertainments were undergoing radical change, some of the traditional interpersonal dimensions remained firmly in place. Leisure activities were one of the chief contexts in which people gave their lives meaning and cultivated the network of social relationships on which all were dependent. People took advantage of leisured moments—meal times and drinking times, in particular—to seek out personal friends and professional associates to share news, gossip, and perspectives, to affirm their relationships, and to enjoy some leisure time together. Pepys's account of an evening spent with friends in September 1665 offers insight into the importance of time spent in company:

I never met with so merry a two hours as our company this night was. Among other humors, Mr. Evelyn's repeating of some verses made up of nothing but the various acceptations of "may" and "can," and doing it so aptly, upon occasion of something of that nature, and so fast, did make us all die almost with laughing, and did so stop the mouth of Sir J. Mennes in the middle of all his mirth (and in a thing agreeing with his own manner of genius) that I never saw any man so outdone in all my life; and Sir J. Mennes's mirth too, to see himself outdone, was the crown of all our mirth. In this humor we sat till about 10 at night; and so my Lord and his mistress home, and we to bed—it being one of the times of my life wherein I was the fullest of true sense of joy.[39]

RULES FOR SEVENTEENTH-CENTURY GAMES

In the seventeenth century as today, many games began by tossing a coin to determine priority of play. In dice games, the players rolled a die for this purpose, the highest roller going first. Card games began with players lifting to see who would be the dealer: each player would lift a random number of cards from the deck, looking to see which was underneath; the player with the lowest card was the dealer. The dealing normally went counterclockwise, and the first player to receive a card was called the "eldest," the last was the "youngest."

Stoolball

PLAYERS: Any number

Equipment:

—1 ball (preferably about the size of a softball)

—1 stool

Stoolball was a game with rustic connotations, played by both men and women and often associated with Easter. One version of the game may have resembled cricket, but the sole surviving rules of the period are quite different. The stool is placed on its side at the high end of the playing field, with the seat facing toward the low end. Team A is in the field, and Team B stands by the stool. The first player on Team B "posts" the ball into the

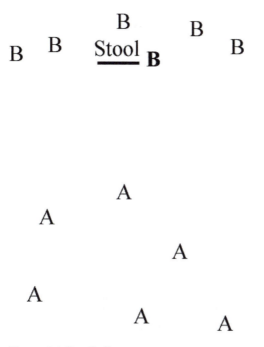

Figure 8.4 Stoolball.

field—that is, serves it tennis-style—tossing it up with one hand and hitting it with the other, either overhand or underhand.

Team A tries to catch the posted ball. If they miss, one of them must retrieve the ball and throw it at the stool. If he hits the stool, the player who posted is out, and the next player on Team B posts; if he misses, Team B scores 1 point, and the first player posts again.

If someone on Team A catches the ball on the first post, Team A and Team B begin posting it back and forth. If Team B is the first to miss the ball, the first player is out. If Team A is the first to miss the ball, one of them must again retrieve it and throw it at the stool, putting the first player out if he hits and scoring 2 points for Team B if he misses.

Once all the players on Team B have posted, the teams change sides. Play is to 31 points.[40]

Hunting a Deer in My Lord's Park

PLAYERS: Any number

This was a children's game. One player is "it," and the rest join hands in a circle. The player who is "it" goes around the outside of the circle and taps one of the players, drops a glove behind the player, or uses some other predetermined signal. The chosen player leaves the circle and chases the first player, who can weave under the others' arms in and out of the circle at will; the chasing player has to follow exactly. If the first player is caught, he goes into the circle, and the chasing player is "it"; but if the chasing player fails to follow exactly or cannot catch the first player before he gets all the way around the circle, he goes into the circle instead. Play continues until the circle is full.[41]

Bowls

PLAYERS: Normally 2 to 4

Equipment:

—2 wooden balls for each player, about the size of an apple (each pair of balls should be color-coded to tell them apart from other pairs)

—1 "mistress" (a stake set upright in the ground) or 1 "jack" (a ball smaller than the others and preferably of a bright contrasting color)

Bowls was one of the most common games of the period, enjoyed by men, women, and children at all levels of society. A point is designated as the casting spot. If using a mistress, it is set up on the pitch some distance away (two mistresses can be set up, each serving as the other's casting spot, which will save walking back and forth). If using a jack, the first player casts it out onto the pitch. Each player in turn casts one ball onto the pitch, trying to get it as close to the jack or mistress as possible; then each in turn casts a second ball. The player whose ball is closest at the end scores 1 point—2 points if he has the two closest balls. A ball that is touching the target counts double. Balls can be knocked about by other balls, and the jack can also be repositioned in this way. Play is normally to 5 or 7. Quoits is played the same way, except with stones or pieces of metal replacing the balls; this version was considered a rustic sport.[42]

Shovelboard

PLAYERS: Normally 2 or 4

Equipment:

—1 smooth playing surface (a table or a table-sized board)

—2 counters (e.g., a large coin, preferably 1–1 1/2" across) for each player or team of 2 players

Shovelboard was a highly popular indoor sport and often appears in legal records as a pastime enjoyed in alehouses. The table is marked as in the diagram in Figure 8.5 (this can be done with chalk), with the players standing at GH to play their counters. Tables made for the purpose would have a box at the far end to catch any counters that fell off. Each player or

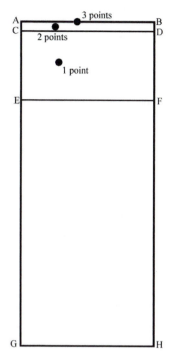

Figure 8.5 Shovelboard.

side in turn slides one of their counters from GH toward the far end. Once all pieces are played, the side that has the counter closest to the far edge scores; if that side has the two closest counters, it scores for both counters; if both sides' closest counters are an equal distance from the edge, neither scores. A counter that stops short of EF (which Willughby describes as "towards the further end of the table") scores nothing. A counter between EF and CD scores 1 point. A counter between GH and the edge of the table scores 2. A counter that projects over the edge is called a "looker" and scores 3. If one side gets 2 lookers, it scores 3 for each, but if both sides have lookers, neither scores. Play is normally to 5 or 7 points.

Counters may be knocked into new positions by subsequent players. A counter that goes off the edge is worth nothing. To identify a looker, a straight edge can be run along the edge of the table—if the coin moves, it is a looker.[43]

Irish

Players: 2

Equipment:

    —1 backgammon set

Irish was one of the most common "games at tables" (i.e., games played on a backgammon board). The rules are exactly the same as for modern backgammon, save that backgammon's special rules for doubles do not apply. The 15 "men" are placed as indicated by the numbers on the diagram in Figure 8.6, the upright numbers belonging to Player 1, the upside-down ones to Player 2. Player 1 moves his men clockwise around the board from **z** toward **a** (his "home point"), and Player 2 moves counterclockwise from **a** toward **z** (his home point). The 6 points from **a** to **f** are Player 1's home points; the 6 from **z** to **t** are Player 2's home points.

The players each roll 1 die, and the higher roll moves first (if the rolls are equal, roll again). The first player rolls 2 dice and may move one man for the number on each die (the same man may move for both). Once touched, a man must be played. After the first player has moved, it is the second player's turn.

A man cannot be moved onto a point already occupied by 2 or more opponents. If a man is left alone on a point, and an opponent's man lands on it at the end of 1 die's move, that first man is removed from the board and must be played again from the far end.

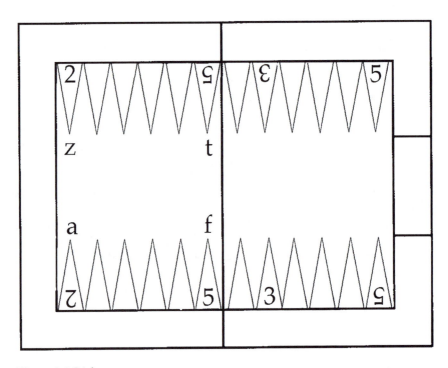

Figure 8.6 Irish.

Any player who has a man off the board must play it before he can move any other men. This means that if the roll would require placing the entering man onto a point already occupied by 2 or more opponents, he must forfeit his turn. If a player has 2 or more men on all of his 6 home points, and his opponent has a man to enter, one of those points must be "broken": both players roll 2 dice, and the higher chooses a point from which all but one of the men are removed. The removed men must reenter the board again.

The player who plays all his men off the board first wins. No man may be played off the board until all of the player's men are in the 6 home points. It does not require an exact roll to play a man off the board.[44]

Nine Men's Morris/Three Men's Morris

Players: 2

Equipment:

—Morris board

—9 or 3 pieces for each player

> These were widely familiar games and could easily be played on a board incised onto a barrelhead or scratched into the dirt. In Nine Men's Morris, each player has 9 pieces. Players draw lots to start and then take turns placing their men on the board, one man on each corner or intersection. After all men are placed, the players take turns moving them. A man can be moved to any adjacent corner or intersection, provided it is connected to the man's current location by a line. A player who manages to place or move such that
>
> three of his men come to be in a row removes one of his .opponent's men; and a player whose pieces are so hedged in that they cannot move also has a man removed by his opponent. To be in a row, the three men must be connected by a single straight line. The last player on the board wins.

A simpler version of the game is Three Men's Morris, played on the smaller board depicted in Figure 8.8. In this version, each player has three men. Men are positioned and moved as in Nine Men's Morris, and the first player to get his three men into a row wins.[45]

In and In

PLAYERS: Normally 2 or 3

Equipment:

—4 dice

This dice game is played for a standard stake, which each person puts in the pot at the beginning and stakes again when called to do so. The first player rolls 4 dice. If the player rolls Out (no doublets—i.e., no two dice

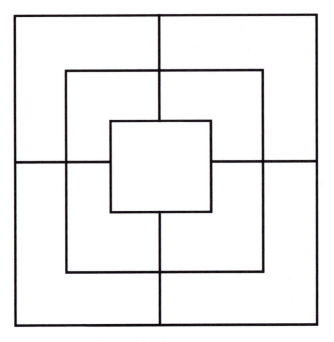

Figure 8.7 Nine Men's Morris.

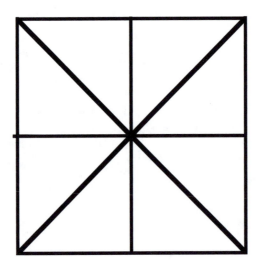

Figure 8.8 Three Men's Morris.

the same), that player is out of play, and the opponent collects the pot (if there is more than one other player, they can divide the pot or continue to play for the whole pot between them). If the player rolls In (one doublet), they stake again and pass the dice to the next player. If the player rolls In and In (all four dice the same), that player collects the entire pot, and all the players stake again. Play is normally up to an agreed maximum total of stakes.[46]

Loadum

PLAYERS: Any number

Equipment:

—52-card deck

—3 counters for each player

This is a trick-taking card game in which taking a trick is disadvantageous. Each player stakes the agreed-on amount and is given 3 counters. The cards are all dealt out for as many rounds as possible, provided at least one card is left over to determine the trump—this card is left face down. The eldest hand leads the first trick. The other players must follow suit; if they cannot, they may play another suit. If another suit is played, the top remaining card is turned up to reveal the trump suit and then turned back down again. The highest trump—or the highest card in the suit led, if no trumps are played—takes the trick,. The player who takes the trick leads the next.

Players amass points when they take "loaders" in a trick. These are the Ace (worth 11 points), the ten (10), the knave (1), the queen (2), and the king (3). The rest of the cards have no effect. Players are "out" when they have amassed 31 or more points in the tricks they have taken. When a player is out, the player loses one of his or her counters—and loses another upon getting out again, and so on; when a player has lost all of his or her counters, he or she is out of the game. If no one has 31 points when all tricks have been played, the player with the highest number of loaders is out. The game is over when only one player is left—this player wins all the stakes.

Players may "challenge" when they believe another has reached 31. The player challenges the other to show his or her tricks. If the one challenged does not have 31, the challenger is out.

When there is a trump in the trick, and the player with the highest card in the suit led does not notice it and takes the trick, this is called "swallowing."

At any point, players may exchange loaders with each other by mutual consent. They do not have to specify what their cards are, but only offer to exchange "a court for a court" (i.e., a court card for another court card) or "a card for a card" (an ace or ten for an ace or ten). If the cards turn out to be of the same suit, the exchange is automatically canceled.

The players may vary the number of counters issued at the beginning by mutual consent.[47]

Wheehee

PLAYERS: Any number

Equipment:

—52-card deck

Each player is dealt 3 cards, and the eldest hand to have all 3 of the same suit wins. If no player wins on the deal, the eldest trades a card with the second. If neither has won after this exchange, the second exchanges a card with the third, and then the third with the fourth, and so on. If no one has won by the time they have gone once around, they may exchange cards with each other at will. If no one wins after this, the cards are turned in to a new dealer. Wheehee appears to have been a children's game, although the diary of one Oxford student of the period mentions playing a version of it.[48]

The Lover's Alphabet ("I Love My Love with an A")

PLAYERS: Any number

The first player must fill in a series of sentences with words beginning with an *A*, for example:

I love my love with an *A*, because she is *Amiable*. I hate her with an *A* because she is *Apish*. Her name is *Alcinda*, and the best part about her is her *Arm*. I invited her to the sign of the *Artichoke*, and I gave her a dish of *Asparagus*.[49]

The next player replaces the A-words with B-words, and so on through the alphabet (the "sign of the Artichoke" refers to the signs that hung outside of eating and drinking establishments). Pepys mentioned an instance of this game at the royal court: "I did find the Duke of York and Duchess [the future James II and his wife] with all the great ladies, sitting upon a carpet on the ground, there being no chairs, playing at 'I love my love with an A because he is so and so; and I hate him with an A because of this and that'; and some of them, but particularly the Duchess herself and my Lady Castlemaine [Charles II's mistress], were very witty."[50] The game was still popular in the nineteenth century: Lewis Carroll mentioned it in *Alice's Adventures through the Looking-Glass*.

SONGS

A Round of Three Country Dances in One

SOURCE: Thomas Ravenscroft, *Pammelia* (London: printed by William Barley for R. B. and H. V., 1609), #74.

Figure 8.9 A Round of Three Country Dances in One.

This song seems to have been assembled from previously existing songs or dance tunes: "The Cramp" appears in 1569–1570 as the name of a ballad tune, and "Robin Hood" appears in a seventeenth-century manuscript of lute tunes; it is a melody used for many of the Robin Hood broadside ballads of the period. The four parts are painted on the ceiling of the music room in Bolsover Castle, Derbyshire, built during the reign of Charles I.

> *toy:* entertainment
>
> *bide:* remain
>
> *ween:* suppose
>
> *petticoat:* jacket

Hey Ho What Shall I Say

Sources: Thomas Ravenscroft, *Pammelia* (London: printed by William Barley for R. B. and H. V., 1609), #99; *The Melvill Book of Roundels,* ed. Granville Bantock and H. Orsmund Anderton (London: Roxburghe Club, 1916 [1612]), #67.

This round is simple, but dramatic when sung in its full eight parts. Each new part begins at the asterisks.

> *ere I wist:* before I knew it
>
> *when she list:* when she pleases.

Both of these expressions were already rather old-fashioned by 1600.

Figure 8.10 Hey Ho What Shall I Say.

New Walefleet Oysters

Sources: Thomas Ravenscroft, *Pammelia* (London: printed by William Barley for R. B. and H. V., 1609), #11; *The Melvill Book of Roundels,* ed. Granville Bantock and H. Orsmund Anderton (London: Roxburghe Club, 1916 [1612]), #13.

This is round one of a large body of songs based on tradesmen's cries as heard on London streets; Walefleet was a stream that flowed into the Thames.

Figure 8.11 New Walefleet Oysters.

The Jovial Broom Man

SOURCES: Words by Richard Climsell, printed 1640 (*The Roxburghe Ballads*, ed. William Chappell [Hertford: Ballad Society, 1871–1899]); tune: "The Slow Men of London" aka "Jamaica" (John Playford, *The Dancing Master* [London: John Playford, 1675], 142).

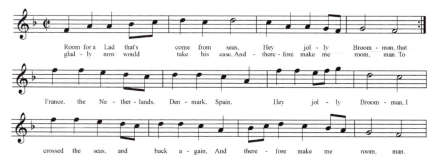

Figure 8.12 The Jovial Broom Man.

The subtitle of this broadside calls it "A Kent Street Soldiers exact relation / Of all his Travels in Every Nation." Broom-men made brooms for a living—they were proverbially representative of the marginal underclass, and Kent Street, a poor area in Southwark, was full of them. "Tilbury Camp" is an allusion to the mustering of the English militia against the invasion of the Spanish Armada in 1588. "Holland's Leaguer" refers to a raid on a notorious Southwark brothel in 1631. The version here is somewhat shortened; several verses omitted after the middle of the third verse are included in the endnotes.[51]

> Room for a Lad that's come from seas,
> *Hey jolly Broom-man,*
> That gladly now would take his ease,
> And therefore make me room, man.
> To France, the Netherlands, Denmark, Spain,
> Hey jolly Broom-man,
> I crossed the seas, and back again,
> And therefore make me room, man.
> Yet in these Countries livèd I
> And seen many a valiant soldier die,
> An hundred gallants there I killed,
> And beside a world of blood I spilled.
> In Germany I took a town,
> I threw the walls there upside down,
> At Tilbury Camp with Captain Drake,
> I made the Spanish Fleet to quake.
> At Holland's Leaguer there I fought,
> But there the service proved too hot.
> Then from the League returned I,
> Naked, hungry, cold, and dry.
> But here I have now compassed the Globe,
> I am back returned, as poor as Job.
> And now I am safe returnèd back
> Here's to you in a cup of Canary Sack.
> And now I am safe returnèd here,
> Here's to you in a cup of English Beer.
> And if my travels you desire to see,
> You may buy it for a penny here of me.

DANCES

[A], [B], and so on designate sections of the music. [A1] and [A2] are two iterations of the same music.

"Up" means the "top" of the hall, normally where the musicians are. All dances begin on the left foot. The man normally stands on the lady's left. All dances begin with a bow or curtsy to one's partner.

The numbers on the left of each step description are beats of the **Steps** music (*"and"* is a half-beat).

Double/Turn Single

1 Step onto the left foot

2 Step onto the right foot

3 Step onto the left foot
and Rise on the toes of the left foot

4 Close the right foot to the left foot as you lower your heels.

The next double starts on the right foot. A double can be done in any direction; a "turn single" is a double step done while turning once around in place.

Single/Set

1 Step onto the left foot

and Rise on the toes of the left foot

2 Close the right foot to the left foot as you lower your heels.

The next single starts on the right foot. A single can be done in any direction: a "set" is a single to the left followed by a single to the right.

Slip-Step

1 Step left foot to the left

and Move the right foot next to the left as you hop onto it.

The next slip-steps will be onto the left foot again—they do not alternate.

The Black Almain

SOURCES: James P. Cunningham, *Dancing in the Inns of Court* (London: Jordan and Sons, 1965), 27, 33, 36; Peter and Janelle Durham, *Dances from the Inns of Court 1570–1675* (Bellevue, WA: privately published, 1997); Peggy Dixon, *Nonsuch Early Dance. Vols. III and IV: Elizabethan Dances Including Playford Country Dances* (London: privately published, 1986), 71–72.

This dance is done by couples processing around the room in a circle or oval.

[A] All dance forward 4 doubles.

[B1] Turn to face partner and drop hands: double back and then double forward.

Figure 8.13 Black Almain.

[B2] All make a quarter-turn left: double forward. All make a half-turn right: double forward.

[C] All turn to face partner. Men set and turn single. Women do likewise on the repeat.

[D] All take both hands: double clockwise to partner's place. All do 4 slip-steps up the hall. All double clockwise back to own place and do 4 slip-steps down the hall. All drop hands: double backward and then double to meet again.

The second time through the dance, the women set first and then the men.

Grimstock

SOURCE: John Playford, *The Dancing Master* (London: John Playford, 1675), 43

This dance is done in a longways set of 3 couples, the men facing the women (men are on the left side when facing toward the music, which is at the head of the set).

M   W

M   W

M   W

Figure 8.14 Grimstock.

1st Verse

[A] All couples lead up toward the music a double step and then go backward a double step. Then they set and turn single. Repeat.

[B] "Mirror hey": First couple go down between the 2nd couple, who come up; then the 3rd couple similarly come up between the 1st couple, who go down. The 2nd couple turn around and go down between the 3rd couple, and then the 1st couple come up between the 2nd couple. The 3rd couple turn around and go down between 1st couple. Then the 2nd couple come up between the 3rd couple.

2nd Verse

[A] "Siding": All couples advance a double step toward their partners to come right shoulder to right shoulder and then go back a double to place and set and turn single. Repeat going left shoulder to left shoulder.

[B] Repeat the mirror hey, but this time as the couples pass each other, the couple on the inside join hands to go under the arms of the outside couple, who link hands to form an arch.

3rd Verse

[A] "Arming": All couples link right arms and turn around their partners in 8 steps, to come all the way back to place; set and turn single. Repeat linking left arms.

[B] First couple cross over, passing right shoulders, passing between the second couple to begin a mirror hey (without arching) on the opposite side, but when they come to the bottom, they cross back over to finish the hey on their own side.

Sellenger's Round (The Beginning of the World)

SOURCES: John Playford, *The Dancing Master* (London: John Playford, 1675), 1; Kate van Winkle Keller and Genevieve Shimer, *The Playford*

Figure 8.15 Sellenger's Round.

Ball (Chicago: A Cappella Books, 1990), 96; Peggy Dixon, *Nonsuch Early Dance. Vols. III and IV: Elizabethan Dances Including Playford Country Dances* (London: privately published, 1986), 85–86.

This dance had been popular since the Elizabethan period. Playford's version of the first chorus omits the steps into the circle and back, but the music would seem to demand it. Any number of couples stand in a circle facing inward, with each man on his partner's left.

1st Verse

[A] All join hands in a circle and slip-step 8 steps clockwise and 8 steps back.

[B] (Chorus) All drop hands and do 2 single steps, advancing toward the middle of the circle, and then fall back a double to places, face partners, and then set and turn single. Repeat.

2nd Verse

[A] Partners take hands and double-step into the middle of the circle and then double-step back. Repeat.

[B] Chorus.

3rd Verse

[A] "Siding": Partners advance a double step to come right shoulder to right shoulder and then return to place with a double step. Repeat, coming left shoulder to left shoulder.

[B] Chorus.

4th Verse

[A] "Arming": All couples link right arms and turn around their partners in 8 steps, to come all the way back to place. Repeat, linking left arms.

[B] Chorus.

NOTES

1. Edward Chamberlayne, *Angliæ Notitia, or, the Present State of England* (London: J. Martyn, 1669), 85–87.

2. For races, tag, and Prison Bars, see these games in Francis Willughby, *Francis Willughby's Book of Games: A Seventeenth-Century Treatise on Sports, Games, and Pastimes*, ed. David Cram, Jeffrey L. Forgeng, and Dorothy Johnston (Aldershot: Ashgate Press, 2003). Throughout this chapter, further information on games is to be sought in this text, except where noted otherwise.

3. Samuel Pepys, *The Diary of Samuel Pepys*, ed. Robert Latham and William Matthews (Berkeley and Los Angeles: University of California Press, 1983), 3.272; John Evelyn, *The Diary of John Evelyn*, ed. E.S. de Beer (London, New York, and Toronto: Oxford University Press, 1959), 448–49.

4. On early cricket, see David Underdown, *Start of Play: Cricket and Culture in Eighteenth-Century England* (London: Allen Lane, 2000), 11ff.

5. On golf, see Robert Browning, *A History of Golf: The Royal and Ancient Game* (London: A. & C. Black, 1955).

6. Underdown, *Cricket*, 10.

7. Pepys, *Diary*, 8.419.

8. Pepys, *Diary*, 1.114, 118, 119.

9. Charles Cotton, *The Compleat Gamester* [1674], in *Games and Gamesters of the Restoration* (London: Routledge, 1930), 22–23; Randle Holme, *The Academy of Armory* (London: Roxburghe Club, 1905), 69.

10. Donald Lupton, *London and the Countrey Carbonadoed* (London: N. Okes, 1632), 70–74.

11. Rules from Cotton, *Gamester*, 80–81.

12. Cf. Pepys, *Diary*, 1.5, 10.

13. Pepys, *Diary*, 1.5.

14. Henry Peacham, *The Worth of a Penny* (London: Thomas Lee, 1677), 30.

15. John Locke, *Some Thoughts Concerning Education*, ed. John W. and Jean S. Yolton (Oxford: Clarendon Press, 1989), 192–93. See also chapter 3 on the toys and games of toddlers.

16. Pepys, *Diary*, 3.300–1; cf. also 7.372. Important sources on dance include the following: Fabritio Caroso, *Nobiltà di Dame* [1600], trans. Julia Sutton (Oxford: Oxford University Press, 1986); Cunningham, James P., *Dancing in the Inns of Court* (London: Jordan and Sons, 1965); François de Lauze, *Apologie de la Danse, 1623. A Treatise of Instruction in Dancing and Deportment, Given in the Original French* (London: F. Muller, 1952); Peggy Dixon, *Nonsuch Early Dance. Vols. III and IV: Elizabethan Dances including Playford Country Dances* (London: privately published, 1986); Peggy Dixon, *Nonsuch Early Dance. Vol. V: English Country Dances 17th and 18th Century* (London: privately published, 1987); Peggy Dixon, *Nonsuch Early Dance. Vol. VI: Ballroom Dances of the 17th and 18th Century* (London: privately published, 1988); Peggy Dixon, *Nonsuch Early Dance. First Supplement: Medieval to Baroque* (London: privately published, 1989); Peter and Janelle Durham, *Dances from the Inns of Court 1570–1675* (Bellevue, WA: privately published, 1997); Kate van Winkle Keller and Genevieve Shimer, *The Playford Ball* (Chicago: A Cappella Books, 1990); John Playford, *The English Dancing Master* (London: John Playford, 1651, 1675); Melusine Wood, "Some Notes on the English Country Dance before Playford," *Journal of the English Folk Dance and Song Society* 3 (1937): 93–99.

17. On music, see Pepys, *Diary*, 1.5, 10, 19, 114, 205, 8.29, 253, 10.258ff. On music in general, see J. T. Cliffe, *The World of the Country House in Seventeenth-Century England* (New Haven and London: Yale University Press, 1999), 161. Important sources on music and song include the following: *The Bagford Ballads, Illustrating the Last Years of the Stuarts* (Hertford: Ballad Society, 1878); William Chappell, *Popular Music of the Olden Time* (London: Chappell and Co., 1859); Thomas D'Urfey, *Wit and Mirth, or Pills to Purge Melancholy* (London: J. Tonson 1719–20); J. O. Halliwell-Phillipps, ed., *The Euing Collection of English Broadside Ballads in the Library of the University of Glasgow* (Glasgow: University of Glasgow Publications, 1971); John Hilton, *Catch That Catch Can, or, A Choice Collection of Catches, Rounds & Canons for 3 or 4 Voyces* (London: John Benson and John Playford, 1652); *The Melvill Book of Roundels*, ed. Granville Bantock and H. Orsmund Anderton (London: Roxburghe Club, 1916); Marin Mersenne, *Harmonie Universelle* [1636] (Paris: Éditions du Centre National de la Récherche Scientifique, 1963); Geoffrey Day, ed., *Pepys Ballads* (Cambridge: Brewer, 1987); John Playford, *A Musical Banquet* (London: John Benson and John Playford, 1651); John Playford, *The Musical Companion* (London: J. Playford, 1673); John Playford, *The Second Book of the Pleasant Musical Companion* (London: J. Playford, 1686); Edward F. Rimbault, *The Rounds, Catches and Canons of England. A Collection of Specimens of the Sixteenth, Seventeenth and Eighteenth Centuries, Adapted to Modern Use* (New York: DaCapo Press, 1976); Thomas Ravenscroft, *Pammelia, Deuteromelia, and Melismata* [1609, 1611], Publications of the American Folklore Society Bibliographical and Special Series 12 (Philadelphia: American Folklore Society, 1961); William Chappell, ed., *The Roxburghe Ballads* (Hertford: Ballad Society, 1871–1899).

18. Cf. Pepys, *Diary*, 5.120, 332.

19. On the history of these festive entertainments, see Ronald Hutton, *The Rise and Fall of Merry England: The Ritual Year 1400–1700* (Oxford: Oxford University Press, 1994).

20. On the theaters, see Andrew Gurr, *Playgoing in Shakespeare's London* (Cambridge and New York: Cambridge University Press, 1996).

21. On hunting, Eric S. Wood, *Historical Britain* (London: Harvill Press, 1995), 121; J. T. Cliffe, *The World of the Country House in Seventeenth-Century England* (New Haven and London: Yale University Press, 1999), 156ff. On angling, see Joseph Blagrave, *The Epitome of the Art of Husbandry* (London: Benjamin Billingsley and Obadiah Blagrave, 1669), 182ff.

22. Pepys, *Diary*, 7.245–46.

23. Pepys, *Diary*, 1.57

24. Evelyn, *Diary*, 433.

25. Chamberlayne, *Angliæ Notitia*, 68. On publishing, see Margaret Spufford, *Small Books and Pleasant Histories: Popular Fiction and Its Readership in Seventeenth-Century England* (Cambridge: Cambridge University Press, 1981); Marjorie Plant, *The English Book Trade* (London: G. Allen and Unwin, 1939).

26. Lupton, *London*, 140–43.

27. Pepys, *Diary*, 1.15.

28. Pepys, *Diary*, 4.59.

29. Pepys, *Diary*, 5.235, 241.

30. Pepys, *Diary*, 6.289–90. On intellectual pursuits in general, see Cliffe, *Country House*, 163ff.; Julian Hoppit, *A Land of Liberty? England 1689–1727* (Oxford: Clarendon Press, 2000), ch. 6.

31. Pepys, *Diary,* 6.98; Evelyn, *Diary,* 795–803. See also Myra Reynolds, *The Learned Lady in England, 1650–1760* (Boston: Houghton Mifflin, 1920).

32. Robert Burton, *The Anatomy of Melancholy* (Oxford: Henry Cripps, 1621), 343 (Pt 2, Sect. 2., memb. 4).

33. James I, *The King's Majestie's Declaration to His Subjects, concerning Lawfull Sports to Be Used* (London: printed by Bonham Norton and John Bill, 1618), 5.

34. On the history of these regulations, see Robert Hardy, *Longbow* (New York: Aro, 1977).

35. James I, *The King's Majestie's Declaration to His Subjects, concerning Lawfull Sports to Be Used* (London: printed by Bonham Norton and John Bill, 1618), 2, 7–8; Hutton, *Merry England,* 154, 168ff.; Christopher Hill, *Society and Puritanism in Pre-Revolutionary England* (New York: Schocken Books, 1964), 67, 189, 193, 199, 201, 205.

36. C.H. Firth and R.S. Rait, eds., *Acts and Ordinances of the Interregnum 1642–1660* (London: His Majesty's Stationery Office, 1911), 1.81, 420, 2.385, 2.1163, 1168; Hutton, *Merry England,* DA 400 A4 1911; Firth and Rait, *Acts,* 1.81, 954, 985; Hutton, *Merry England,* 201, 206–8, 211–12. In 1654, Parliament also issued a six-month ban on horse races, although this measure was primarily in response to the threat of subversion at gatherings that naturally attracted large numbers of potential counterrevolutionaries (*Acts and Ordinances* 2.941); Hutton, *Merry England,* 212.

37. Christopher Hill, *The Century of Revolution* (Edinburgh: T. Nelson, 1961), 198, 215.

38. On Dover's games, see Christopher Whitfield, *Robert Dover and the Cotswold Games* (London: Henry Sotheran, Ltd.; Ossining, New York: William Salloch, 1962); Hutton, *Merry England,* 164.

39. Pepys, *Diary,* 6.220.

40. Rules from Willughby, *Treatise,* 178.

41. Rules from Willughby, *Treatise,* 189.

42. Rules from Willughby, *Treatise,* 206–7.

43. Rules from Willughby, *Treatise,* 212–13.

44. Rules from Willugby, *Treatise,* 123–25.

45. Rules from Willughby, *Treatise,* 215–17.

46. Rules from Cotton, *Gamester,* 80.

47. Rules from Willughby, *Treatise,* 154–55.

48. Rules from Willughby, *Treatise,* 160.

49. Rules from *The Mysteries of Love & Eloquence, Or, the Arts of Wooing and Complementing* (London: N. Brooks 1658), 2.

50. Pepys, *Diary,* 9.469.

51. And when that I the same had done,
   I made the people all to run.
   And when the people all were gone,
   I held the town myself alone.
   And when the people all were gone,
   I held the town myself alone.
   When valiant Ajax fought with Hector,
   I made them friends with a bowl of Nectar.
   When Saturn warred against the Sun,
   Then through my help the field he won.
   With Hercules I tossed the Club;

I rolled Diogenes in a Tub.
When Tamberlaine overcame the Turk,
I blew up thousands in a work.
When Caesar's pomp I overthrew,
Then many a Roman Lord I slew.
When the Ammorites besieged Rome's walls
I drove them back with fiery balls.
And when the Greeks besiegèd Troy,
I rescued off dame Helen's joy.
And when that I had won this fame,
I was honored of all men for the same.

9

CYCLES OF TIME

The seventeenth century witnessed a significant transition in the understanding of time for the ordinary Englishman. At the opening of the century, the experience of time was heavily shaped by the ritual year as inherited from the Middle Ages, expressed through a cycle of church holy days that were closely tied to the rhythms of the agricultural calendar. By the end of the century, most of the traditional festivals had lost their prominence, and the dominant pattern of time was the working week, punctuated by Sunday as a day of religious observation and leisure.[1]

The Day The course of the day was defined by the cycle of the hours, either rung by parish church bells or marked by the face of a clock—public clocks were becoming increasingly common during the century. Watches were also in use, though they were expensive and therefore accessible only to the upper classes. Time was generally reckoned no more closely than the quarter hour: timepieces did not have minute hands before the latter half of the century, and even then they were a rare and expensive feature, requiring the skills of an outstanding clockmaker.[2]

The shape of the day depended heavily on one's position in society. Those who had sufficient income from land were essentially the masters of their own affairs and could set their own schedule for such work as they needed to do (for example, managing their estates). Even those who relied on a salary were not generally subject to close supervision of their

Figure 9.1 A family at table (Hindley 1837–1874).

time—Samuel Pepys pretty much set his own hours for his civil service work at the Admiralty, and could occasionally indulge in the luxury of dawdling in bed in the morning. The majority had a living to earn and needed to rise a bit before dawn to take advantage of every minute of daylight. Candlelight was sufficient for simple morning routines such as urinating, washing one's face and hands, saying prayers, getting dressed, rekindling the fire, and perhaps grabbing a bit of food and drink. By the time daylight took over from the candles, the working man or woman needed to be ready to begin the day's work.[3]

Work would continue from dawn until late morning or midday, when most people would take a break for dinner, which was generally the main meal of the day. Dinner was an important occasion for socializing, either in a public eating establishment (especially for city-dwellers) or by visiting the homes of others. Indeed, hospitality played an important role in seventeenth-century life overall: people gave meals to friends, neighbors, and associates, affirming their social networks and establishing their respective standings in society—the ability to offer hospitality was an important means of establishing one's social prestige.

The duration of the working day depended on the season: daylight was limited during the winter, and most work had to cease when the sun went down. In the summer, there was enough daylight to do a full day's work and still have some light left at the end of the day. A typical summer schedule

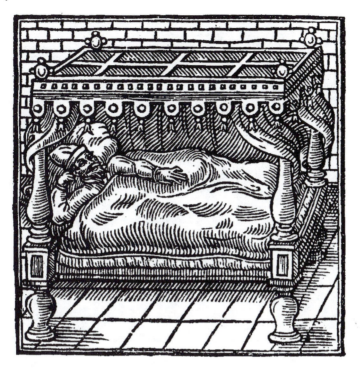

Figure 9.2 A seventeenth-century bed (Traill and Mann 1909).

was that of the laborers at the navy dockyards, who were required to work from 5:30 A.M. until 6:30 P.M., with a half-hour break for breakfast and an hour and a half for dinner.[4] Most people would take a light meal at the end of the working day, and there might be a bit of time left for socializing and entertainment before retiring to bed at about 9 or 10. Before retiring, people normally said evening prayers, extinguished lights, and covered up fires for the night—a few hot coals were left to smolder under the ashes, not enough to put the house at risk of fire, but enough to facilitate rekindling in the morning. Most people slept in their shirts, although specialized nightshirts existed for those wealthy enough to afford them.

This routine applied to working days, although some people had half-holidays on Saturday afternoons. Work was not legally permitted on Sunday: even travel was frowned upon except in cases of substantive need. On Sunday morning, people were expected to don clean linens and their best clothes to attend church services; until the Glorious Revolution, attendance was required by law under punishment of a fine, but this was never rigorously enforced, except when authorities wished to put pressure on Catholics or Protestant Nonconformists. After Sunday dinner, there were afternoon services at church, but these were even less rigorously attended. Puritan-minded Englishmen felt that the entirety of

Figure 9.3 A watchman patrols the night with partisan, lantern, bell, and dog (*Shakespeare's England* 1916).

the day should be reserved for religious observation, whether through church attendance, family prayers, or reading. Traditional practice held that church attendance in the morning was entirely sufficient and that the afternoon might be given over to leisure activities. The least religious-minded might not attend church at all, except perhaps on important holy days. Even those who attended were not always filled with religious zeal: John Evelyn noted multiple occasions when he slept through the priest's sermon.

THE YEAR

Most annual festivals were tied to the church calendar. The only truly secular holidays were Gunpowder Treason Day (November 5) and the days associated with the monarchs, chiefly their birthdays, accession days, and coronation days, as well as the special days of commemoration on January 30 and May 29, instituted after the Restoration. The actual observation of such days in honor of the monarch varied with the local political climate: they were often ignored by those who were unhappy with current royal policies. Indeed, all of the annual festivals were in a state of flux during the course of the century, as reformist and traditional-ist forces competed to impose their agendas on the calendar. Reformists generally disapproved of the traditional cycle of holy days and their associated customs, and the authorities of the Commonwealth made active efforts to suppress these holidays, replacing them with monthly days of recreation.

There were a few striking holdovers of tradition in the English year. One was the country's adherence to the ancient Julian calendar, slightly less accurate than the Gregorian calendar instituted by Pope Gregory XIII in 1582. Because the Gregorian system was associated with the papacy, it would not be accepted in England until 1752, and as a result, the date in England was 10 days behind that in Catholic Europe.[5] England also differed from most Continental countries in how it numbered the years: calendars began with January 1, but the number of the year changed on March 25; dates in the early part of the year were sometimes styled "1634/5" because of this discrepancy.

The following calendar gives some idea of the traditional annual cycle, but the details of observation varied markedly according to the time and place. Official holidays (meriting a day off from work) are indicated in **boldface.**

January

1 New Year's Day (*Feast of the Circumcision of Christ*). New Year's Day rather than Christmas was a time for the exchange of gifts: typical choices included rings, gloves, pins, apples, oranges, and nutmegs. This was also an occasion for making resolutions for the upcoming year. Samuel Pepys mentions another New Year's custom: "as soon as ever the clock struck one, I kissed my wife in the kitchen by the fireside, wishing her a merry New year, observing that I believe I was the first proper wisher of it this year, for I did it as soon as ever the clock struck one."[6]

5 *Twelfth Night.* The last night of the Christmas season, traditionally marked by revelry in which the company divided up a spiced fruitcake into which were baked a bean and a pea; the man and woman who received these became a mock king and queen to preside over the festivities.

6 Twelfth Day (*Epiphany*).

—*Plow Monday, St. Distaff Day.* The first Monday after Twelfth Day. This day marked the return to labor after the Christmas season and commemorated the work of both men and women. Among customs of the day, young women might go from house to house, looking to find whether any of them were spinning flax, in which case they would burn the material to punish the overindustrious spinstress; young plowmen would also go door-to-door gathering money and sometimes performing songs or dances.

8 *St. Lucian*

13 *St. Hilary*

18 *St. Prisca*

20 *St. Fabian*

21 *St. Agnes*

22 *St. Vincent*

25 *The Conversion of St. Paul*

30 *Fast Day for the Execution of Charles I* (from 1660)

February

2 Candlemas (*Feast of the Purification of Mary*). This day was traditionally observed by the lighting of candles in church, but the custom was becoming rare in Protestant England. This was sometimes regarded as the closing day of the Christmas season, when any remaining Christmas decorations were to be removed.

5 *St. Agatha*

14 *St. Valentine.* On this day, people chose a "valentine," who might be the first person of the opposite sex they saw that day, the first to cross their threshold, or someone chosen by lot at a gathering. The man was expected to give a present to his valentine (who might be a woman or a child), and valentines sometimes exchanged slips of paper bearing courtly mottoes—the ultimate origin of the modern valentine card.

24 St. Matthias the Apostle. Many fairs took place on this day.

Movable Feasts

Shrove Tuesday: The day before Ash Wednesday. This day was marked by various rough entertainments, including cockshies (throwing sticks at roosters), throwing or beating cats and dogs, and football; London apprentices often vented their energies by destroying playhouses and brothels. Other traditions of the day included eating pancakes and fritters.

Ash Wednesday: The Wednesday before the sixth Sunday before Easter. This day marked the beginning of Lent, traditionally a period of penitence observed by abstinence from meat; the religious dimension had declined, but the abstinence was still mandated by law, as a way to support England's fishing industry. The arrival of Lent was generally associated with the coming of springtime.

March

1 *St. David*

2 *St. Chad*

7 *St. Perpetua*

12 *St. Gregory*

18 *St. Edward*

21 *St. Benedict*

25 The Annunciation (*Lady Day in Lent*). Many fairs were held on this day, and the number of the year changed.

April

3 *St. Richard*

4 *St. Ambrose*

19 *St. Alphege*

23 *St. George.* Many fairs were held on this day. St. George was the patron saint of England, so this was observed as an important day in the national calendar; some communities held parades, typically featuring a mock dragon in commemoration of the saint's legend.

25 *St. Mark the Evangelist*

Movable Feasts

Palm Sunday. The Sunday before Easter.

Maundy Thursday: The Thursday before Easter.

Good Friday: The Friday before Easter.

Easter: The first Sunday after the first full moon on or after March 21; if the full moon was on a Sunday, Easter was the next Sunday. Easter brought an end to Lent and was therefore an occasion for feasting; it was one of the most common days in the year for attending church services. Stoolball was also a traditional Easter pastime.

Easter Monday

Easter Tuesday

Hocktide. The second Monday and Tuesday after Easter. On the Monday, the women of the parish would go about the streets to capture young men and tie them up with rope, demanding a payment for their release; on Tuesday, the men would do the same to the women. The proceeds traditionally went into the parish funds, but the custom was rapidly declining during the century.

May

1 Sts. Philip and James the Apostles (*Mayday*). Many fairs were held on this day, which traditionally marked the beginning of the summer season. This was one of the chief occasions for the summer festivities known as "maying": this might involve bringing greenery in from the countryside to decorate the community and build a ceremonial bower; folk plays, parades, and military displays; dancing around a maypole, morris dancing by men, and dancing with garlands for women; and choosing a "lord and lady of the May" to preside over the festivities. Maying could take place anywhere between Mayday and Whitsun and might coincide with a parish festival called a church ale or wake. However, such festivals were on the wane over the century, although morris dancing persisted.

3 *The Discovery of the Cross*

6 *St. John at the Lateran Gate*

19 *St. Dunstan*

26 *St. Augustine of Canterbury*

27 *St. Bede*

29 *Charles II's Birthday and entry into London at the Restoration* (observed as a festival day from 1660).

Movable Feasts

Rogation Sunday: Five weeks after Easter. On this day or Ascension Day, many parishes took young boys out to perambulate the parish boundaries, after which they would be given food or gifts; the custom helped preserve the knowledge of these boundaries.

Ascension: The Thursday after Rogation Sunday.

Pentecost (*Whitsun*): 10 days after Ascension. This was one of the most important days in the church calendar and a common time for church attendance and taking communion. It was also a prime occasion for "maying" festivals.

Whit Monday

Whit Tuesday

Trinity Sunday: One week after Pentecost; this day was another occasion for maying.

June

1 *St. Nicomede*

5 *St. Boniface*

11 *St. Barnabas the Apostle*

17 *St. Alban*

20 *The Translation of St. Edward*

24 St John the Baptist (*Midsummer*). Many towns held their fairs on this day, which was also traditionally an occasion for festivities focused on the town community. Customs included the lighting of bonfires and parades that included the town watch and mock giants. Such festivals were on the decline during the century.

July

2 *The Visitation of Mary*

3 *The Translation of St. Martin*

15 *St. Swithun*

20 *St. Margaret*

22 *St. Mary Magdalene*

25 St. James the Apostle. Many fairs were held on this day.

26 *St. Anne*

August

1 Lammas (*St. Peter ad Vincula*). Many fairs were held on this day, as well as civic festivals similar to those on Midsummer.

6 *The Transfiguration of Christ*

10 *St. Laurence.* Many fairs were held on this day.

15 *The Assumption of the Virgin.* Many fairs were held on this day.

24 St. Bartholomew the Apostle. Many fairs were held on this day, including the famous Bartholomew Fair in the west end of London.

28 *St. Augustine of Hippo*

29 *The Beheading of St. John the Baptist*

September

1 *St. Giles*

7 *St. Enurchus the Bishop*

8 The Nativity of Mary (*Lady Day in Harvest*). Many fairs were held on this day, including Lady Fair in Southwark and Sturbridge Fair in Cambridgeshire.

14 Holy Cross Day (*The Exaltation of the Cross*). Many fairs were held on this day.

17 *St. Lambert*

21 St. Matthew. Many fairs were held on this day.

26 *St. Cyprian*

29 St. Michael (*Michaelmas*). Many fairs were held on this day, which also corresponded to the beginning of the new agricultural year. At about this time, rural communities often celebrated the completion of the harvest with a "harvest home," in which the last sheaf of wheat was brought into the barn with great ceremony, and there was feasting that often featured roast goose and seedcake.

30 *St. Jerome*

October

1 *St. Remigius*

6 *St. Faith*

9 *St. Dennis*

13 *Translation of St. Edward the Confessor*

17 *St. Etheldred*

18 St. Luke the Evangelist

25 *St. Crispin*

28 *Sts. Simon and Jude the Apostles*

November

1 All Saints (*Hallowmas*)

5 Powder Treason Day (from 1606). This day commemorated the failure in 1605 of a Catholic conspiracy to blow up the king and Parliament with gunpowder. It was observed with a special church service, ringing of bells, fireworks and bonfires in the evening, and sometimes burning unpopular figures (such as the pope) in effigy. The holiday had a strongly anti-Catholic dimension and was often used for political purposes—it was one of few festivals actually permitted under the Commonwealth.

6 *St. Leonard*

11 *St. Martin of Tours* (*Martinmas*). This day was traditionally associated with the slaughtering of livestock for the winter (chiefly swine) and was often marked by feasting.

13 *St. Brice*

15 *St. Machutus*

17 *St. Hugh* (*Queen Elizabeth's Accession Day*). This day was intermittently observed during the century and had a strongly political character: Elizabeth I was seen as a champion of the Protestant cause, and celebration of her accession often expressed disapproval toward the conduct of the Stuarts.

20 *St. Edmund the King and Martyr*

22 *St. Cecily*

23 *St. Clement*

25 *St. Catherine*

30 *St. Andrew the Apostle*

Movable Feasts

Advent: Begins on the nearest Sunday to St. Andrew's Day.

December

6 *St. Nicholas*

8 *The Conception of Mary*

13 *St. Lucy*

21 *St. Thomas the Apostle*

24 *Christmas Eve.* Then as now, Christmas was one of the most important holidays in the calendar. The "Twelve Days" of Christmas began with Christmas Eve and continued until January 6; the full Christmas season began with Advent and continued until Candlemas. This was an important time for almsgiving and hospitality and for visiting with friends, neighbors, and relatives. Houses and churches were decorated with greenery, chiefly rosemary, bay, holly, ivy, and mistletoe (the Christmas tree came to England much later). Also typical of Christmas was the Yule log, a large log burned progressively through the season; a small piece would be saved at Candlemas to kindle the log next year. At Christmas time, households served the best food they could afford, with particular emphasis on sweets: favorite fare of the season included the finest white bread, nuts, turkey, beef, brawn and souse (pickled pork), mince pies, plum pudding, cakes, and spiced ale served with apples in it. Christmas revels often included folk plays known as "mumming," caroling, and playing indoor games such as cards, blindman's buff, and hot cockles. A distinctive Christmas custom was wassailing, in which revelers would sing and pass around a wooden "wassail bowl" decorated with ribbons and rosemary and filled with spiced ale; wassailing was especially done by women, who would travel door-to-door on New Year's Eve singing in exchange for food, drink, or money. As with other church holy days unsanctioned by Scripture, the parliamentary authorities of the Commonwealth tried to suppress the observation of Christmas, but they met with predictably stiff resistance.

25 Christmas (*The Nativity of Christ*). This was one of the most common days in the year for attending church services and for receiving Communion.

26 St. Stephen the Martyr. This was a day for distributing money to apprentices, servants, tradesmen, and children; the money would often be collected in small clay banks known as "boxes."

27 *St. John the Evangelist*

28 *The Holy Innocents (Childermas)*

31 *St. Silvester*

NOTES

1. Useful sources on time include the following: John Aubrey, "Remaines of Gentilisme and Judaisme," in *Three Prose Works: Miscellanies, Remaines of Gentilisme and Judaisme, Observations,* ed. John Buchanan-Brown (Carbondale: Southern Illinois University Press, 1972), 134ff.; *The Book of Common Prayer* (London: Church of England, various editions); *The City and Countrey Chapman's Almanack* (London: Company of Stationers, various editions); John Evelyn, *The Diary of John Evelyn,* ed. E. S. de Beer (London, New York, and Toronto: Oxford University Press, 1959); Robert Herrick, *Hesperides* (London: John Williams and Francis Eglesfield, 1648), 309ff.; Ronald Hutton, *The Rise and Fall of Merry England: The Ritual Year 1400–1700* (Oxford: Oxford University Press, 1994); Jack Daw [pseudo.], *Vox Graculi, or Jack Dawes Prognostication* (London: Nathaniel Butter, 1623); Samuel Pepys, *The Diary of Samuel Pepys,* ed. Robert Latham and William Matthews, 10 vols. (Berkeley and Los Angeles: University of California Press, 1983); Matthew Stevenson, *The Twelve Moneths, or A Pleasant and Profitable Discourse of Every Action, Whether of Labour or Recreation, Proper to Each Particular Moneth* (London: Thomas Jenner, 1661).

2. On timekeeping, see Lawrence Wright, *Clockwork Man: The Story of Time, Its Origins, Its Uses, Its Tyranny* (New York: Horizon Press, 1969).

3. Cf. Paul Seaver, *Wallington's World: A Puritan Artisan in Seventeenth-Century London* (Stanford: Stanford University Press, 1985), 113.

4. Pepys, *Diary,* 10.94.

5. Cf. Edward Chamberlayne, *Angliæ Notitia, or, the Present State of England* (London: J. Martyn, 1669), 95.

6. Pepys, *Diary,* 5.359.

10

THE EARLY
MODERN WORLD

Across the facets of society we have seen so far, the Stuart age was a time
of significant transitions between a medieval and a modern world. In
many respects, Englishmen in 1600 were living in a society still shaped
by the inherited culture of the Middle Ages, but by 1700, that society had
become recognizably modern in numerous meaningful ways. The political tumult of the middle part of the century played an important role in
accelerating and consolidating these transformations, breaking down old
structures and starting to create new ones in their place. The architects of
the Restoration, in trying to restore key elements of the old order, were
in many ways only able to restore its façade: underneath, changes had
taken place that were irreversible and that would gain momentum over
the following centuries. In this final chapter, we look at similar processes
at work at a broad level in people's experience of their world—both in
the material sense of travel, communication, and trade and in the more
abstract domain of how people understood the world they inhabited and
their own place in it.

TRAVEL

For the majority, life played out largely within the limited sphere
of the village or urban neighborhood. Nonetheless, travel and long-
distance communication touched everybody's lives to some degree.

Village-dwellers frequented local markets on a weekly basis and regional fairs over the course of a year. Rural laborers took to the road to find work, many of them leaving the countryside permanently in search of employment in the cities, whether London or one of the growing provincial centers. The well-to-do divided their time between London and their country residences; they traveled within England for both business and pleasure, and many expanded their horizons by touring the Continent at some point in their lives. Traders, sailors, and emigrants ventured even further, as English mercantile interests in Asia and colonial settlements in the New World grew dramatically over the course of the century.[1]

The degree of travel is all the more remarkable given the obstacles that hindered it. Most people traveled by foot, covering about 2 to 3 miles in an hour and perhaps 20 miles in a day. A rider could do rather better, typically covering 30 to 40 miles in a day, though a rider in a hurry could do twice that and could go over a 100 miles a day if he had access to fresh horses on the way. Wheeled vehicles were slower: a large eight-horse wagon, carrying upward of 6,000 pounds in goods and passengers, could cover 10 to 15 miles in a day; a passenger coach could cover 25 to 30 miles, or more if fresh horses were available en route.[2] Other modes of land transport included pack animals (horses, donkeys, and mules) for goods and horse litters and sedan chairs for people.

Figure 10.1 A private coach with attendants (Hindley 1837–1874).

Rates of travel could be significantly affected by weather conditions. Roads were unpaved, and only the ancient Roman roads had solid foundations, so rain would quickly turn the surfaces to mud. Equally significant was the danger of robbery. Between towns and villages there were long stretches of lonely roads, and firearms had proven very effective in the hands of the highwayman.[3] John Evelyn recorded an incident that took place in 1652 on his way home to London from Tunbridge Wells—his narrative rings true in general, even if there may be some embellishment of the details of what must have been an intense personal experience:

At a place called the Procession Oak, started out two cutthroats, and striking with their long staves at the horse, taking hold of the reins, threw me down, and immediately took my sword, and hauled me into a deep thicket, some quarter of a mile from the high-way, where they might securely rob me, as they soon did; what they got of money was not considerable, but they took two rings, the one an emerald with diamonds, an onyx, and a pair of buckles set with rubies and diamonds which were of value; and after all, barbarously bound my hands behind me, and my feet, having before pulled off my boots; and then set me up against an oak, with most bloody threatenings to cut my throat if I offered to cry out or make any noise. . . . I told them, if they had not basely surprised me, they should not have made so easy a prize, and that it should teach me hereafter never to ride near a hedge; since had I been in the mid way, they durst not have adventured on me; at which they cocked their pistols, and told me they had long guns too, and were 14 companions, which were all lies. I begged for my onyx and told them it being engraven with my arms, would betray them, but nothing prevailed. My horse's bridle they slipped, and searched the saddle which they likewise pulled off, but let the horse alone to graze, and then turning again bridled him, and tied him to a tree, yet so as he might graze, and so left me bound. The reason they took not my horse was, I suppose, because he was marked, and cropped on both ears, and well known on that road. . . . Being left in this manner, grievously was I tormented with the flies, the ants, and the sun, so as I sweated intolerably, nor little was my anxiety how I should get loose in that solitary place . . . till after near two hours attempting, I got my hands to turn palm to palm, whereas before they were tied back to back, and then I stuck a great while ere I could slip the cord over my wrist to my thumb, which at last I did, and then being quite loose soon unbound my feet. . . . So I rode to Colonel Blount's, a great justiciary of the times, who sent out hue and cry immediately, and . . . the next morning . . . I went from Deptford to London, got 500 tickets printed and dispersed, by an officer of Goldsmiths' Hall, describing what I had lost, and within two days after had tidings of all I lost, except my sword, which was a silver hilt, and some other trifles.[4]

Even the travelers who reached their destinations might still face uncertainties at the end of the road. Local officials were wary of incoming strangers, not the least because indigent immigrants could become a burden on parish coffers. By law, travelers were supposed to carry travel passes, issued by a person of standing in their place of origin, to certify the legitimacy of their journey. Travelers of uncertain social standing who lacked documentation, and those who did not appear to have the means to support themselves, might be deemed vagrants and sent packing. As in so many aspects of seventeenth-century life, it helped to belong to the privileged classes or at least to be able to convince others that one did.

Lodgings for the well-to-do were available at inns, at least in the larger towns. Ordinary travelers, especially in rural areas, might find a bed in a tavern or alehouse. Sometimes lodgings might simply be arranged in a private home. The very poor traveler often had to seek shelter as best he might, sleeping under a country hedgerow or other makeshift shelter. In general, travelers' accommodations were less private than people expect today: guests might be expected to share beds with each other, and depending on the facilities, even privileged travelers like Samuel Pepys and his wife Elizabeth sometimes found themselves sleeping in the hallway of their hosts.[5]

Fynes Moryson's *Itinerary* offers a vivid glimpse at the experience of staying at an English inn:

As soon as a passenger comes to an inn, the servants run to him, and one takes his horse and walks him till he be cold, then rubs him, and gives him meat [food], yet I must say that they are not much to be trusted in this last point, without the eye of the master or his servant to oversee them. Another servant gives the passenger his private chamber, and kindles his fire, the third pulls off his boots and makes them clean. Then the host or hostess visits him, and if he will eat with the host, or at a common table with others, his meal will cost him six pence, or in some places but four pence (yet this course is less honorable, and not used by gentlemen); but if he will eat in his chamber, he commands what meat he will. . . . It is the custom and no way disgraceful to set up part of supper for his breakfast. In the evening or in the morning after breakfast (for the common sort use not to dine, but ride from breakfast to supper time, yet coming early to the inn for better resting of their horses), he shall have a reckoning in writing.[6]

Seventeenth-century England saw some significant developments in the national infrastructure for travel and communication. At the opening of the century, there already existed a network of communications posts for government use. Each post was overseen by a postmaster, in many cases a local innkeeper whose inn served as the post. The postmaster kept horses ready so that individuals on government business could ride from one post to the next, changing horses at each post for the next stage of the journey. This system was also used for the rapid dissemination of messages in the hands of government couriers traveling from post to post, and private citizens could also hire the horses, for an extra fee. Over the course of the seventeenth century, this system was expanded to cover new routes and to allow private citizens to have letters carried by the government couriers. The cost to send a letter depended on the number of sheets and distance it was to be carried; it could be sent express for an extra charge. A single sheet could be carried 80 miles for 2d.; an express letter could travel 120 miles in a day.[7]

Figure 10.2 A postman (Traill and Mann 1909).

Aside from this emerging public system, travelers could also hire private horses or coaches, much as cars are rented today. The typical rate for a horse was a bit over 1s. a day, plus fodder, which would generally cost as much again; a coach would cost 10–20s. plus fodder.[8] Already by 1600, travelers could secure a place on a stage wagon for a long-distance journey. These vehicles were essentially large freight wagons, drawn by about eight horses and having a cloth awning to reduce the passengers' discomfort from heat, cold, and dust. They could carry up to 20 to 30 people as well as freight and letters, and regular wagons plied the roads between London and many of England's market towns. This mode of transportation was relatively slow and uncomfortable and was generally avoided by those who could afford an alternative.[9] During the century, scheduled stage coach service made its first appearance, offering swifter and more comfortable carriage for the traveler; at a rate of 2–3d. a mile, a coach could carry a traveler as far as 50 miles in a day's journey.[10] But even this form of travel had its inconveniences, as described by one detractor in 1673:

What advantage is it to man's health to be called out of their beds into the coaches an hour before day in the morning, to be hurried in them from place to place, till one hour, two, or three within night; insomuch that, after sitting all day in the summertime stifled with heat, and choked with the dust, or the wintertime, starving and freezing with cold, or choked with filthy fogs, they are often brought into their inns by torch-light, when it is too late to sit up to get a supper; and next morning they are forced into the coach so early, that they can get no breakfast? What addition is this to men's health or business, to ride all day with strangers, oftentimes sick, ancient, diseased persons, young children crying, to whose humours they are obliged to be subject?[11]

Depending on the itinerary, travel by water might be an option, or even a necessity. England's rivers afforded a smoother ride than travel by coach or horse and were especially economical for carrying goods in bulk.[12] The inland waterways were dotted with craft carrying goods and people, from small rowboats to large barges. Journeys beyond Britain required a trip overseas. The journey across the English Channel to France took about four to five hours and cost around 5s. for passage; the voyage across the Atlantic to the New World colonies was normally expected to last about a month. The traveler also had to expect incidental expenses: those going to the Continent were required to obtain a passport and to swear an oath of allegiance before departing, and travelers likewise required permission from the local authorities when entering a foreign country.[13]

As well as the risks from the weather, piracy was an ever-present danger, and even if the journey went well, the conditions of sea travel were far from pleasant. In warm weather, life below decks was hot, stuffy, and malodorous, and in cold weather, the risk of fire meant that there was minimal heat to counteract the constant damp of the sea. Yet in spite of these conditions, significant numbers of English people traveled by sea, and for some of them such voyages were a recurring experience. The achievement represented by seventeenth-century seafarers is that much more impressive when one considers the ships that were used: a typical large oceangoing

Figure 10.3 Wenceslaus Hollar's sketch of ships and barges at anchor near the Tower of London (Hind 1922).

craft of the day was a square-rigger with three masts, only about 100 feet in length and 25 in beam; and many transoceanic voyages were made in ships considerably smaller.[14]

Even those who never traveled had increasing oppor- **The Shrinking** tunities to expand their world. Literacy was increasing **World** dramatically, and a growing body of printed books on geography and travel was bringing the experiences of world travelers home to England. News sheets appeared during the early part of the century, initially as a means to keep abreast of developments on the Continent during the Thirty Years' War. Throughout the century, maps were a highly fashionable form of interior decoration. For the edu-cated at least, it was becoming increasingly common to understand the world through the bird's-eye view of the cartographer, rather than the ground-level orientation of personal experience that had been the norm throughout human history.

Some indication of the increasing penetration of the global world into English daily life can be found in the pages of John Evelyn's diary. At various times, Evelyn had opportunities to see a lemur from Madagascar, an alligator from the West Indies, and a rhinoceros from India; in 1682 he met ambassadors from Russia, Morocco, India, and Java; in the same year, he expressed admiration for the interior decoration of a neighbor whose house was well supplied with painted screens from China as well as decorations from India.[15] At a more mundane level, such household commodities as tea, coffee, and cotton were beginning to be imported from Asia in quantity. By 1700, England had clearly entered a genuinely global environment, and for the educated, horizons were expanding even beyond Earth itself. By 1600, heliocentric cosmology (in which the sun stands in the middle of the universe) had displaced the older geocentric view (which placed Earth at the center); the Greenwich Royal Observatory was founded by Charles II in 1675 to study the skies, to improve maritime navigation, and to establish a precise system of longitude; and even pri-vate individuals like Samuel Pepys were purchasing telescopes to view the planets, moons, and stars.

STUART WORLD VIEWS

In the domain of personal belief, the seventeenth century saw an increas-ing penetration of rationalism into ordinary life. Traditional folkloric be-liefs inherited from the Middle Ages were in decline: as the antiquarian John Aubrey put it, "Before printing, old wives' tales were ingenious; and since printing came in fashion, till a little before the Civil Wars, the ordi-nary sort of people were not taught to read. Nowadays books are common, and most of the poor people understand letters; and the many good books, and variety of turns of affairs, have put all the old fables out of doors;

and the divine art of printing and gunpowder have frighted away Robin Goodfellow and the fairies."[16]

Aubrey somewhat exaggerates the rationalism of his contemporaries: as in other aspects of Stuart culture, there was considerable variation, influenced by such factors as geography and social class. Many people retained traditional beliefs in supernatural beings such as ghosts and fairies. Accusations of witchcraft continued to be brought before English courts during the first half of the century, and there was a substantial increase in such accusations during the tumult of the late 1640s, although they were considerably rarer after the Restoration—the last execution for witchcraft would take place in 1712, and legislation against witchcraft would be repealed in 1736. Folk charms and folk customs remained a part of English culture, and not only for uneducated country folk: Pepys's wife Elizabeth in 1669 went out early on a May morning to gather May-dew, which was believed to make women more beautiful, and Pepys himself wore a hare's foot as a remedy against indigestion.[17]

In fact, the modern distinction between science and magic can confuse our understanding of the seventeenth century. Many areas of belief that

Figure 10.4 Consulting an astrologer (*Shakespeare's England* 1916).

today might be classed as nonscientific remained a part of contemporary scientific thinking during the seventeenth century. The theory of "humors" inherited from ancient Greece still dominated contemporary medicine, and many intellectuals saw alchemy and divination as viable subjects for scientific study: Sir Isaac Newton was deeply involved in both alchemy and the interpretation of biblical prophecy.

As in many respects, the perspectives of Samuel Pepys can offer a useful touchstone as to the attitude of an educated but not exceptional intellect of the day. In 1663 he noted a rumor that the devil had been appearing in Wiltshire "who beats a drum up and down; there is books of it, and they say very true. But my Lord [the earl of Sandwich] observes that though he doth answer to any tune that you will play to him upon another drum, yet one tune he tried to play, and could not; which makes him suspect the whole, and I think it is a good argument."[18]

Perhaps even more important than the decline of supernatural beliefs was a growing faith in science and technology. The naturalist John Ray in 1690 expressed gratitude to have been born into such an age:

It is an age of noble discovery: the weight and elasticity of air, the telescope and microscope, the ceaseless circulation of the blood through veins and arteries ... and too many others too numerous to mention. The secrets of Nature have been unsealed and explored; a new Physiology has been introduced. It is an age of daily progress in all the sciences.[19]

Scientific advancement was seen not only as an abstract goal in itself, but also as a means of furthering humanity's practical capabilities and improving people's day-to-day lives. Sir Francis Bacon, Attorney-General and Lord Chancellor under James I, articulated a vision of a future shaped by science and technology: "The true and lawful goal of the sciences is none other than this: that human life be endowed with new discoveries and power."[20] Bacon's vision of the power of science and technology informed much of England's intellectual activity for the rest of the century and helped set the stage for the country's Industrial Revolution during the 1700s: already by the latter half of the 1600s, English technologists were developing early versions of the steam engine.

As people's beliefs about the external world changed, so too did their understanding of themselves. Through-   **Individualism**
out history, personal identities had been defined chiefly
by external factors: family relations, social hierarchy, religious community, tradition. These forces remained powerful in Stuart England, but they were visibly losing their monopoly as the century progressed. Already in the Middle Ages, Christianity had suggested a new importance for the individual: as a religion of personal salvation, it emphasized the Christian's inner spiritual state, although for most medieval people this inner state was still largely overshadowed by the external structures of church ritual

and organization. The Protestant Reformation had shifted emphasis away from the church and toward the individual, starting a process that undermined traditional religious authorities in favor of the individual's own spiritual journey. Protestantism's emphasis on Scripture also encouraged the faithful to become literate, furthering a spirit of independent inquiry and critical thought. By the 1600s, vigorous governmental intervention was needed in order to maintain even outward conformity to the national church, and with the disruption of the Civil Wars and Interregnum, spiritual seekers such as Gerrard Winstanley were openly challenging the traditions of inherited religion:

Whosoever worships God by hearsay, as others tells them, knows not what God is from light within himself; or that thinks God is in the heavens above the skies, and so prays to that God which he imagines to be there and everywhere ... this man worships his own imagination, which is the Devil.[21]

A growing role for the individual in spiritual matters was mirrored by comparable trends in political thought. The reformists who struggled against traditional "Catholic" church practices under James I and Charles I were also leaders in the struggle to assert the liberties of Parliament and the parliamentarian classes. These opponents of royal autocracy generally saw themselves as conservatives, protecting the traditional rights of the propertied classes and upholding the principle of religious conformity, yet their resistance to royal authority in church and state opened the door to concepts of individual rights that transcended the traditional social hierarchy.

Such forces exploded into the political arena during the upheavals of the 1640s and 1650s. Radical religious and political thinking was vigorously suppressed after the Restoration, but individualism was by this time too deeply embedded into English culture to be rooted out. By the end of the century, the Church of England had lost its monopoly on the religious life of the nation, and influential Whig thinkers such as John Locke were espousing views of social organization that championed the individual against the power of the state.[22]

Traditional forms of religious conformity and centralized political authority were ultimately impossible to sustain in a culture where individualism was becoming a part of people's day-to-day sense of themselves. This individualistic trend in people's daily lives is nowhere more evident than in the genres of the diary and autobiography, rare in England before 1600, but abundant in the Stuart age. In the writings of such men and women as Samuel Pepys, John Evelyn, Richard Baxter, Nehemiah Wallington, and Elizabeth Freke, we can see a growing emphasis on the authors' personal feelings and experiences.[23] Both the genre and the content of these diaries point toward modernity. Wallington's autobiography documents the trials of seventeenth-century teenage angst, marked by a profound sense of personal worthlessness and punctuated by intense suicidal urges.[24] Elizabeth Freke expressed open resentment toward a husband whom she married for love, yet who ultimately proved neglectful and exploitative—her responses to a disappointing marriage easily resonate today. The diary of Samuel Pepys, whom we can get to know better than any other person in the century, presents a personality whose strengths and weaknesses are instantly recognizable to the modern reader: conventionally religious, preoccupied with financial self-betterment, and probably well intentioned overall, yet weak in the face of temptation. The complacent, materialistic tone of his final entry for 1664 offers a keynote for the spirit of his age:

At the office all the morning, and after dinner there again, dispatched first my letters, and then to my accounts, not of the month but of the whole year also, and was at it till past twelve at night, it being bitter cold; but yet I was well satisfied with my work, and above all to find myself—by the great blessing of God—worth £1349, by which, as I have spent very largely, so I have laid up above £500 this year above what I was worth this day twelvemonth. The Lord make me for ever thankful to his holy name for it! Thence home to eat a little and so to bed. Soon as ever the clock struck one, I kissed my wife in the kitchen by the fireside, wishing her a merry new year, observing that I believe I was the first proper wisher of it this year, for I did it as soon as ever the clock struck one.

So ends the old year, I bless God, with great joy to me, not only from my having made so good a year of profit, as having spent £420 and laid up £540 and upwards; but I bless God I never have been in so good plight as to my health in so very cold weather as this is, nor indeed in any hot weather, these ten years, as I am at this day, and have been these four or five months. But I am at a great loss to know whether it be my hare's foot, or taking every morning of a pill of turpentine, or my having left off the wearing of a gown. My family is: my wife, in good health, and happy with her; her woman Mercer, a pretty, modest, quiet maid; her chambermaid Bess; her cookmaid Jane; the little girl Susan; and my boy, which I have had about half a year, Tom Edwards, which I took from the King's Chapel; and a pretty and loving quiet family I have as any man in England. My credit in the world and my office grows daily, and I am in good esteem with everybody, I think.[25]

NOTES

1. On geographic mobility, see Julian Hoppit, *A Land of Liberty? England 1689–1727* (Oxford: Clarendon Press, 2000), 67; Peter Clark and David C. Souden, eds., *Migration and Society in Early Modern England* (Totowa, NJ: Barnes & Noble Books, 1988); David Cressy, *Coming Over: Migration and Communication between England and New England in the Seventeenth Century* (Cambridge: Cambridge University Press, 1987).

2. Parkes, *Travel,* 62, 78, 80, 84–85. Norbert Ohler, *The Medieval Traveller,* trans. Caroline Hillier (Woodbridge: Boydell, 1989), is full of detail on the practicalities of medieval travel, many of which remain relevant for this period; see p. 101 and passim.

3. On highwaymen, see Parkes, *Travel,* 152ff.

4. John Evelyn, *The Diary of John Evelyn,* ed. E. S. de Beer (London, New York, and Toronto: Oxford University Press, 1959), 321–23. See also A. F. Scott, *Every One a Witness: The Stuart Age* (New York: Crowell, 1975), 211–12.

5. Samuel Pepys, *The Diary of Samuel Pepys,* ed. Robert Latham and William Matthews (Berkeley and Los Angeles: University of California Press, 1983), 10.337.

6. Moryson, *Itinerary,* 3.151; see also 3.61. For other sources on inns and other travel lodgings, see A. Everitt, "The English Urban Inn 1560–1760," in A. Everitt, ed., *Perspectives in English Urban History* (London: Macmillan, 1973), 91–137; Peter, Clark, *The English Alehouse. A Social History 1200–1830* (London and New York: Longman, 1983); R. F. Bretherton, "Country Inns and Alehouses," in *Englishmen at Rest and Play: Some Phases of English Leisure 1558–1714* (Oxford: Clarendon Press, 1931), 145–202.

7. Parkes, *Travel,* 52ff.; Pepys, *Diary,* 10.343; Moryson, *Itinerary,* 3.61; Scott, *Stuart Age,* 202–3; Edward Chamberlayne, *The Second Part of The Present State of England* (London: J. Martyn, 1671), 240.

8. Parkes, *Travel,* 58–59, 78; Moryson, *Itinerary,* 3.61–62.

9. Parkes, *Travel,* 79ff.; Moryson, *Itinerary,* 3.62.

10. Parkes, *Travel,* 84–85; Scott, *Stuart Age,* 202–4; Chamberlayne, *Second Part,* 241.

11. Parkes, *Travel,* 92–93.

12. Parkes, *Travel,* 96ff.; Hoppit, *Liberty,* 329.

13. Parkes, *Travel,* 112–13, 122; Evelyn, *Diary,* 18.

14. On ships of the period, see William A. Baker, *Colonial Vessels: Some Seventeenth-Century Sailing Craft* (Barre, MA: Barre Publishing, 1962).

15. Evelyn, *Diary,* 379, 778, 779, 718, 726.

16. Aubrey, "Remaines of Gentilisme and Judaisme," in *Three Prose Works,* 290.

17. Pepys, *Diary,* 8.240.

18. Pepys, *Diary,* 4.186; see also 5.361, 6.177–78, 8.240, 10.388–90. On science and superstition see also Hoppit, *England,* ch. 6; Keith Thomas, *Religion and the Decline of Magic* (New York: Scribners, 1971).

19. Cited Hoppit, *Land of Liberty,* 188.

20. Cited Barry Coward, *The Stuart Age: A History of England 1603–1714* (London and New York: Longman, 1980), 91.

21. *The Works of Gerrard Winstanley,* ed. G. H. Sabine (New York: Russell and Russell, 1965), 107.

22. On these trends, see Christopher Hill, *The World Turned Upside-Down: Radical Ideas during the English Revolution* (Harmondsworth: Pelican, 1975).

23. On the increasing development of individualism, see M. Mascuch, *Origins of the Individualist Self: Autobiography and Self-Identity in England, 1591–1791* (Cambridge: Cambridge University Press, 1997).

24. Paul Seaver, *Wallington's World: A Puritan Artisan in Seventeenth-Century London* (Stanford: Stanford University Press, 1985), 15–16, 22–23, 26.

25. Pepys, *Diary,* 5.359–60.

GLOSSARY

alderman—A member of a city council.

ale—An early form of beer made without hops.

Anglican—A modern term for an adherent of the Church of England.

apprentice—A young person learning a craft or trade.

archdeacon—A church officer assigned to assist the bishop in administering his bishopric, having especial authority for church courts.

assizes—Courts held twice a year in every county by judges from the royal courts in London on circuit through the counties.

bailiff—An official responsible for law enforcement.

balloon—A sport of Italian origins, similar to volleyball.

Baptist—An adherent of a Protestant sect outside of the Church of England, believing in rebaptism of its members as adults.

barm—Leaven.

bearbaiting—A blood-sport in which dogs are pitted against a bear.

bolster—A long pillow running across the top of a bed.

broadside—A single printed sheet, often a ballad, sold for a penny.

buttery—A room used for storage of drinks and food.

cage—A human-sized cage used as a punishment.

capon—A castrated male chicken, raised for its meat.

charnel house—A building used for the storage of bones removed from old graves.

cheat bread—A bread made from wheat of medium fineness.

churching—A ceremony for women in the Church of England, marking the woman's return to church after childbirth.

churchwarden—A parish executive officer, chosen from the leading parishioners and responsible for parish administration.

citizen—An inhabitant of a town having the full rights and privileges of the town; also, a citizen of a country.

civil law—The legal tradition based on ancient Roman practices.

close—In the city, a dead-end street; in the country, an enclosed plot of ground, usually used as pasture.

clothier—An entrepreneur engaged in the production of cloth.

clout—A diaper (literally, "cloth," "rag").

coats—The skirts of a woman's outfit; also, a child's gown.

codling—A kind of apple.

coffin—A pie crust.

coif—A linen cap worn by women.

college—A communal residence, often for the elderly poor.

common law—Law based on tradition and legal precedent.

commoner—Anyone not of the gentlemanly class; a person obliged to work for a living.

Commonwealth—The period between the execution of Charles I in 1649 and the Restoration of Charles II in 1660 (sometimes distinguished from the Protectorate of the Cromwells, 1653–1659).

communion—The religious ceremony in which the communicants receive wine, bread, or both as representing the blood and body of Christ.

company—An alternate name for a **guild**.

confirmation—The religious ceremony by which a young person is fully admitted as a member of the church.

Congregationalist—see **Independent**.

constable—A local officer chosen periodically from among local residents and responsible for law and order.

coppice—A cultivated stand of trees, systematically harvested for firewood while leaving the base of the trees intact to provide future harvests.

corn—Grain (usually meaning "wheat").

cottager—The smallest sort of landholding commoner, holding insufficient land to support a family without doing additional paid labor.

county—One of the 52 royal administrative regions in England and Wales; also called a shire.

Covenanters—Scottish opponents of Charles I's religious policies in Scotland.

cucking stool—see **ducking stool**.

daub—A combination of clay, sand, dung, and straw, used in making walls.

diocese—A bishopric; the area under the ecclesiastical jurisdiction of a bishop.

Dissenter—In the period of the Restoration, a Protestant who adhered to a congregation outside of the Church of England.

distaff—A long staff used in spinning flax fibers into linen thread.

doublet—A short fitted jacket.

dowry—Money or property brought by a woman into her marriage according to the terms of the marriage contract.

drawers—Underwear.

drawing and quartering—The severest form of execution, in which the victim was hanged and disemboweled and, after death, cut into four pieces.

ducking stool—A wooden punishment apparatus, used to duck the victim in water. Also called a **cucking stool**.

enclosure—The process of surrounding farm lands with a hedge, cutting off the communal access traditionally accorded to the residents of the manor.

episcopacy—The hierarchy of bishops in the government of the church.

equity—The administration of justice based on "common-sense" notions of fairness.

esquire—A substantial gentleman, especially one who has a knight among his ancestors. Also **squire**.

excommunication—A sanction issued by the church courts, separating the individual from participation in the Church of England.

falling band—A detachable collar.

fallow field—A field out of use for a season to allow it to recover for future crops.

farthingale—An underskirt made to flare by means of hoops.

forestalling—To buy up goods from vendors prior to their arrival at an open market.

freeholding—The most privileged form of commoner-level landholding, in which the land is held in perpetuity, generally for insignificant rent; effectively equivalent to outright ownership.

Free School—An endowed school that did not charge tuition.

furlong—A discrete parcel of agricultural land in the village fields, commonly about an acre in size.

garter—A strip of leather or fabric used to hold up one's stockings.

gentleman—A man of the class traditionally holding sufficient lands not to be required to work for a living; any man of a gentlemanly family.

glebe—The manorial landholding belonging to the parish church.

Glorious Revolution—The replacement of James II by William and Mary in 1688–1689.

goodman/goodwife/goody—Terms of address for a householder of commoner status.

gorse—A species of evergreen shrub.

grammar school—A secondary school for boys of about 8 to 15, teaching Latin grammar and literature.

groom porter—A royal official in charge of games at court.

guild—An organization regulating the practice of a craft or trade in a particular town. "Guild" is the usual modern term; the most common seventeenth-century term was "company."

guild master—A governing officer in a guild.

headland—A strip of land at the end of a plowed field, often used for turning the plow.

hedgerow—A tall and thick hedge, carefully cultivated over a period of years to serve as a fence around a plot of agricultural land.

holding—A parcel or quantity of land rented to a holder in accordance with the traditions associated with that holding. Also called a **landholding** or **tenancy**.

horn—The material from the horns of cattle, often sliced thin for its translucent properties or heated and shaped for household implements.

humors—The four component substances of the human body (blood, choler, phlegm, and bile) according to ancient Greek physiology.

husbandman—A small but self-sufficient landholding commoner.

Independent—An adherent of a Protestant sect outside of the Church of England, believing in the right of the congregation to govern itself, and therefore also known by the end of the century as **Congregationalists**.

Interregnum—The period between the execution of Charles I in 1649 and the Restoration of Charles II in 1660.

joint stool—A stool made with mortice-and-tenon joints, superior to a "boarded" stool made without joints.

journeyman—A craftsman or tradesman who has completed apprenticeship but does not possess a business of his own, instead working as an employee for others.

justice of the peace—A gentleman empowered by the crown to administer minor legal matters in a locality and to work with other justices of the peace in administering law at the county level.

kimnel—A wooden trough.

landholding—see **holding**.

Lent—The period from Ash Wednesday until Easter, during which people were supposed to abstain from eating meat and poultry.

Leveller—An adherent of the political movement active in the late 1640s and 1650s, advocating abolition of the social hierarchy.

limewash—A mixture of water and lime (calcium oxide), used to provide a hard white coating for walls.

link—A torch.

Long Parliament—The parliament summoned by Charles I in 1640, which continued (with some interruptions and reorganizations) until 1660.

magistrate—Any governmental officer having power for administering the law, especially a justice of the peace.

manchet—A small roll of bread made from fine flour.

manor—The smallest unit of "gentlemanly" feudal landholding, typically from a few hundred acres in size to a few thousand.

marl—A naturally occurring type of calcium-rich clay, used as a fertilizer.

master—A craftsman or tradesman who has his own shop; also, a schoolmaster, a teacher.

mechanic—A tradesman or craftsman.

messuage—The plot of land on which a villager's home lies.

New Model Army—The reformed army fielded by Parliament as of 1645.

Nonconformist—see **Dissenter**.

ordinary—An eating and drinking establishment, generally serving a fixed meal.

outservant—A servant not resident in his or her household of employment.

overseer of the poor—A parish official responsible for implementation of the national **poor laws**.

parlor—The main public room of an ordinary home, serving for dining and social activities.

petticoat—A skirt.

pickadill—One of a row of decorative tabs on the edge of a garment.

Pie-Powder court—A court held at a fair, administering prompt justice for those temporarily present at the fair (named from the French *pieds poudreux*, "dusty feet").

pillory—A wooden punishment device that immobilized a standing person's head and hands.

pipkin—A small pot.

poor laws—Statutes passed by Parliament beginning in the 1560s, mandating parish support for poor people who were unable to support themselves and ordering punishment or workhouse labor for those unemployed who were believed capable of work.

poor rate—A tax mandated by the **poor laws** for support of the parish poor.

Presbyterianism—A system of church government by a council of clergymen.

prerogative court—A law court under the direct authority of the monarch.

privy—A toilet.

Privy Council—The committee of royal officers with primary responsibility for advising the monarch and carrying out royal policies.

Protectorate—The government of Oliver Cromwell and his son Richard, 1653–1659.

Puritan—In the first half of the century, a term used by opponents to describe those who sought further reform in the Church of England.

Purposes—A word game.

Quaker—An adherent of the Religious Society of Friends, a Nonconformist Protestant sect which began to take shape in the late 1640s.

quarter sessions—Criminal courts held by county justices of the peace four times a year at the county seat.

Questions—A word game.

raker—An urban waste collector.

rate—A tax imposed on substantial householders.

rectory—The rights associated with the office of a parish priest, including the right to appoint the priest, the right to collect parish tithes, and the property associated with the **glebe**.

Reformation—England's break with the Catholic Church, which began in the 1530s.

Restoration—The return of the monarchy to power in 1660.

roll—A padded roll of fabric worn about a woman's hips.

saint's day—A holy day traditionally commemorating a particular saint.

salad—In the 1600s, a general term for any vegetable dish.

samphire—A maritime plant used in pickling.

sanctuary—The medieval custom by which people on church grounds could not be arrested by secular authorities.

seam—Animal fat.

Separatist—In the first half of the century, a term used by opponents for members of Protestant sects outside of the Church of England. After the Restoration, typically called **Dissenters** or **Nonconformists**.

serf—In the Middle Ages, an unfree peasant tied to the manor and owing labor service to the manor lord.

sexton—A parish employee responsible for physical work on the church grounds.

shift—A woman's shirt.

squire—see **esquire**.

stocks—A wooden restraining device that enclosed the feet.

steelyard—A balance-device for weighing.

subsidy—A grant of taxation conferred on the monarch by Parliament, paid for by substantial householders.

tenancy—see **holding**.

tenement—A holding of land or other real estate.

tenure—The terms under which a tenement is held.

tithes—An annual tax, theoretically representing a tenth of an individual's income, originally created in the Middle Ages to support the church, though in reality often collected by a secular beneficiary.

Tories—The political party that opposed exclusion of James II from succession to the throne; also generally associated with conservative and royalist principles.

tow—The waste fibers left over from making linen thread.

trained bands—The militia.

usher—A master's assistant at a school, often delegated to teach the younger boys.

usury—Traditionally, any lending out of money on interest, but by the 1600s, defined by law as limited to those who charge excessive interest.

verjuice—The juice extracted from crabapples, sour in flavor and used in cooking.

vestry—A council of parish laymen in charge of parish administration.

vicar—A priest appointed to an "impropriated" living (i.e., a position as parish priest where the tithes are collected by a third party, who uses part of the money to employ the vicar).

watch—Armed local officials responsible for local law enforcement and for patrolling the streets at night.

Whigs—The political party that advocated exclusion of James II from succession to the throne; also generally associated with liberal and reformist causes.

Whitsun—The Sunday seven weeks after Easter (Pentecost), traditionally an occasion for summer festivals.

winnowing—The process of separating cracked grain husks from the seed.

workhouse—An institution created by the **poor laws**, in which the unemployed but able-bodied poor were housed and put to labor.

yardland—A landholding sufficient to support a household in moderate comfort, varying by locality, but typically around 30 acres.

yeoman—The upper rank of landholding commoners having freehold land.

FURTHER READING

The notes for the various chapters and subheadings include introductory bibliographies for the individual topics covered in this volume. For general bibliographies on England in the period, see G. Davies and M. F. Keeler, eds., *Bibliography of British History: Stuart Period, 1603–1714* (Oxford: Oxford University Press, 1970), and J.S. Morrill, *Seventeenth-Century Britain, 1603–1714* (Folkestone: Dawson, 1980).

The *Oxford English Dictionary* is often a good starting place for researching individual topics, as each entry includes a selection of quotations from primary sources. Another important resource is the full corpus of seventeenth-century English books as reproduced in both microfilm and digital format. For a catalogue of these works, see Donald Wing, *A Short-Title Catalogue of Books Printed in England, Scotland, Ireland, Wales and British America and of English Books Printed in Other Countries 1641–1700*, rev. John J. Morrison, Carolyn Nelson, and Matthew Seccombe (New York: Modern Language Association, 1994). For an index to this collection, see *Early English Books 1641–1700: A Cumulative List to Units 1–60 of the Microfilm Collection*, 9 vols. (Ann Arbor: UMI, 1990). The pre-1641 texts lack an index but are catalogued in A.W. Pollard and G.R. Redgrave, *A Short-Title Catalogue of Books Printed in England, Scotland, and Ireland and English Books Printed Abroad 1475–1640* (2nd ed. rev. W.A. Jackson, F.S. Ferguson, and Katherine F. Pantzer. London: The Bibliographical Society, 1986). These books are all available in pdf format through the Early English Books Online database, accessible at large research libraries.

For an excellent narrative introduction to late seventeenth-century England, covering a range of topics including political history, economics, and culture, see Julian Hoppit, *A Land of Liberty? England 1689–1727.* The remainder of the century regrettably has not yet been covered in the New Oxford History of England series, but is covered in the older Oxford History of England: Godfrey Davies, *The Early Stuarts 1603–1660,* and Sir George Clark, *The Later Stuarts 1660–1714.* A valuable, if somewhat old, introduction to the broader Tudor and Stuart period is Roger Lockyer, *Tudor and Stuart Britain 1471–1714* (London: Longman, 1964).

Among primary sources of the period, several stand out as particularly valuable starting points for the study of daily life. Comenius's *Orbis Sensualium Pictus* (available in multiple editions and reprints) is an extremely useful orientation point for a wide range of topics, including worldview, society, and material culture. Randle Holme's *Academy of Armory,* ostensibly a treatise on heraldry, is in fact a remarkable encyclopedia covering a wide range of topics relating to society, material culture, and daily life. Holme assembled his information over several decades, publishing the bulk in 1688, but the final portion was not published until 1905; the entirety has recently been reedited from manuscript in CD-ROM format. Samuel Pepys's diary provides a uniquely broad-ranging and detailed view of daily life, and the final volume of the Latham and Matthews edition includes copious background notes on the period. Other diaries of the period are less extensive, but can offer alternative experiences and perspectives to those of Pepys: a selection is included in the bibliography, including Ralph Houlbrooke's valuable compendium *English Family Life, 1576–1716: An Anthology from Diaries* (Oxford and New York: Basil Blackwell, 1988). Also useful as starting points are the general surveys of English society written at the time, among them Edward Chamberlayne's *Angliæ Notitia* (London: J. Martyn, 1669; 2nd part 1671), and Guy Miege, *The New State of England* (London: R. Clavel, H. Mortlock, and J. Robinson, 1699).

Two vivid modern interpretations of daily life, although they deal with the colonial setting, are Kate Waters's *Sarah Morton's Day: A Day in the Life of a Pilgrim Girl* (New York: Scholastic, 1989) and *Samuel Eaton's Day: A Day in the Life of a Pilgrim Boy* (New York: Scholastic, 1993). Geared toward younger readers, they are nonetheless interesting and enjoyable at any level and are richly illustrated with photographs taken at the Plimoth Plantation living history site of Plymouth, Massachusetts, which itself ranks as one of the world's leading resources in the study of seventeenth-century England.

SELECTED
BIBLIOGRAPHY

GENERAL

Aubrey, John. *Three Prose Works: Miscellanies, Remaines of Gentilisme and Judaisme, Observations,* ed. John Buchanan-Brown. Carbondale: Southern Illinois University Press, 1972.

Andrews, John F., ed. *William Shakespeare: His World, His Works, His Influence. Vol. 1: His World.* New York: Scribner, 1985.

Ashley, Laura. *England in the Seventeenth Century.* Pelican History of England 4. London: Pelican Books, 1968.

Ashley, Maurice. *Life in Stuart England.* London: Batsford, 1964.

Chamberlayne, Edward. *Angliæ Notitia, or, the Present State of England.* London: J. Martyn, 1669.

———. *The Second Part of The Present State of England.* London: J. Martyn, 1671.

Clark, Sir George. *The Later Stuarts 1660–1714.* 2nd ed. The Oxford History of England. Oxford: Clarendon Press, 1956.

Cliffe, J. T. *The World of the Country House in Seventeenth-Century England.* New Haven and London: Yale University Press, 1999.

Comenius, Johannes Amos. *Orbis Sensualium Pictus,* trans. Charles Hoole. London: J. Kirton, 1659.

Coward, Barry. *A Companion to Stuart Britain.* Oxford: Blackwell, 2003.

———. *The Stuart Age: A History of England 1603–1714.* London and New York: Longman, 1980.

Davies, Godfrey. *The Early Stuarts 1603–1660.* 2nd ed. The Oxford History of England. Oxford: Clarendon Press, 1959.

Garret, George. "Daily Life in City, Town, and Country." In Andrews, *Shakespeare,* 215–32.

Gough, Richard. *The History of Myddle*, ed. David Hey. Harmondsworth: Penguin, 1981.

Holme, Randle. *The Academy of Armory*. Chester: R. Holme, 1688; fasc. ed. Menston: Scolar Press, 1972.

———. *The Academy of Armory*. London: Roxburghe Club, 1905.

———. *Living and Working in Seventeenth-Century England: An Encyclopedia of Drawings and Descriptions from Randle Holme's Original Manuscripts for the Academy of Armory (1688)* [CD-ROM], ed. N. W. Alcock and Nancy Cox. London: British Library, 2001.

Hoppit, Julian. *A Land of Liberty? England 1689–1727*. Oxford: Clarendon Press, 2000.

Houston, R. A. *The Population History of Britain and Ireland, 1500–1750*. Basingstoke: Macmillan Education, 1992.

Knobel, E. B. et al. "The Sciences." In *Shakespeare's England*, 1.444–515.

Laslett, Peter. *The World We Have Lost*. London: Methuen, 1971.

Lupton, Donald. *London and the Country Carbonadoed*. London: N. Okes, 1632.

Markham, Gervase. *The English Huswife* [1615], ed. Michael R. Best. Kingston and Montréal: McGill-Queen's University Press, 1986.

Mather, William. *The Young Man's Companion*. 5th ed. London: S. Clarke, 1699.

McMurtry, Jo, *Understanding Shakespeare's England. A Companion for the American Reader*. Hamden, CT: Archon, 1989.

Miege, Guy. *The New State of England under our Present Monarch King William III*. London: R. Clavel, H. Mortlock, and J. Robinson, 1699.

Moryson, Fynes. *An Itinerary*. London: John Beale, 1617; reprinted Amsterdam and New York: Da Capo Press, Theatrum Orbis Terrarum, 1971.

———. *Shakespeare's Europe*, ed. Charles Hughes. London: Sherratt and Hughes, 1903.

Murrell, John. *A Daily Exercise for Ladies and Gentlewomen* [1617], ed. Susan J. Evans. Albany, NY: Falconwood Press, 1990.

———. *A Delightful Daily Exercise for Ladies and Gentlewomen* [1621], ed. Susan J. Evans. Albany, NY: Falconwood Press.

Ogg, David. *England in the Reign of Charles II*. 2 vols. Oxford: Clarendon Press, 1934.

———. *England in the Reigns of James II and William III*. Oxford: Clarendon Press, 1955.

Parkes, Joan. *Travel in England in the Seventeenth Century*. London: Oxford University Press, 1925.

Peacham, Henry, Jr. *The Compleat Gentleman* [1622], ed. G. S. Gordon, Tudor and Stuart Library, 1906.

Rogers, James E. Thorold. *A History of Agriculture and Prices in England*. Oxford: Clarendon Press, 1882.

Schofield, John, ed. *The London Surveys of Ralph Treswell*. London: London Topographical Society, 1987.

Scott, A. F. *Every One a Witness: The Stuart Age*. New York: Crowell, 1975.

Seaver, Paul. *Wallington's World: A Puritan Artisan in Seventeenth-Century London*. Stanford: Stanford University Press, 1985.

Shakespeare's England. An Account of the Life and Manners of His Age. 2 vols. Oxford: Clarendon Press, 1916.

Shesgreen, Sean, *The Criers and Hawkers of London* (Stanford: Stanford University Press, 1990).

Smith, Lacey Baldwin. "'Style Is the Man': Manners, Dress, Decorum." In Andrews, *Shakespeare*, 201–14.

Spurr, John. *England in the 1670s: "This Masquerading Age."* Oxford: Blackwell, 2000.

Taylor, John. *The Carrier's Cosmographie.* London: A. G., 1637.

The City and Countrey Chapman's Alamanack for the Year of Our Lord 1685. London: Company of Stationers, 1684.

Thirsk, Joan. *The Agrarian History of England and Wales 1500–1750.* Vols. 4–5. Cambridge: Cambridge University Press, 1967, 1984, 1985.

Thornton, Peter. *Seventeenth-Century Interior Decoration in England, France and Holland.* New Haven: Yale University Press, 1978.

Trevelyan, G. M. *England Under the Stuarts.* Oxford: Routledge, 2002.

———. *Illustrated English Social History.* Harmondsworth: Penguin, 1942.

Wedgwood, C. V. *The King's Peace.* New York: Macmillan, 1955.

———. *The King's War, 1641–1647.* New York: Macmillan, 1959.

Wood, Eric S. *Historical Britain.* London: Harvill Press, 1995.

Woolley, Hannah. *The Compleat Servant-Maid.* London: T. Passinger, 1683.

Worden, Blair. *Stuart England.* Oxford: Phaidon, 1986.

Wrightson, Keith. *Earthly Necessities: Economic Lives in Early Modern Britain.* New Haven: Yale University Press, 2000.

———. *English Society, 1580–1680.* New Brunswick, NJ: Rutgers University Press, 1982.

Wrigley, E. A., R. S. Davies, J. E. Oeppen, and R. S. Schofield. *English Population History from Family Reconstitution, 1580–1837.* Cambridge: Cambridge University Press, 1997.

Wrigley, E. A., and R. S. Schofield. *The Population History of England 1541–1871.* Cambridge, MA: Harvard University Press, 1981.

Wroughton, John. *Longman Companion to the Stuart Age, 1603–1714.* London: Longman, 1997.

SOCIETY

Chamberlayne, Edward. *Angliæ Notitia, or, the Present State of England.* London: J. Martyn, 1669.

Hoppit, Julian. *A Land of Liberty? England 1689–1727.* Oxford: Clarendon Press, 2000.

Houston, R. A. *The Population History of Britain and Ireland, 1500–1750.* Cambridge: Cambridge University Press, 1995.

Laslett, Peter. *The World We Have Lost.* London: Methuen, 1971.

Mather, William. *The Young Man's Companion.* 5th ed. London: S. Clarke, 1699.

Miege, Guy. *The New State of England under our Present Monarch King William III.* London: R. Clavel, H. Mortlock, and J. Robinson, 1699.

Wrightson, Keith. *Earthly Necessities: Economic Lives in Early Modern Britain.* New Haven: Yale University Press, 2000.

———. *English Society 1580–1680.* New Brunswick, NJ: Rutgers University Press, 1982.

WOMEN

Amussen, Susan. *An Ordered Society: Gender and Class in Early Modern England.* Oxford and New York: Blackwell, 1988.

Clark, Alice. *Working Life of Women in the Seventeenth Century.* London: Cass, 1919.

E., T. *The Lawes Resolutions of Womens' Rights: or, the Lawes Provision for Women.* London: assigns of John More, 1632.

Eccles, Audrey. *Obstetrics and Gynaecology in Tudor and Stuart England.* Kent, OH: Kent State University Press, 1982.

Fraser, Antonia. *The Weaker Vessel.* New York: Knopf, 1984.

Miege, Guy. *The New State of England under our Present Monarch King William III.* London: R. Clavel, H. Mortlock, and J. Robinson, 1699. 2.164ff.

Woolley, Hannah. *The Compleat Servant Maid.* London: T. Passinger, 1683.

———. *The Gentlewoman's Companion, or a Guide to the Female Sex.* London: Dorman Newman, 1673.

MEMOIRS AND DIARIES

Clifford, Lady Anne. *The Diaries of Lady Anne Clifford,* ed. D.J.H. Clifford. Stroud: Alan Sutton, 1990.

Evelyn, John. *The Diary of John Evelyn,* ed. E. S. de Beer. London, New York, and Toronto: Oxford University Press, 1959.

Fanshawe, Ann, Lady [née Ann Harrison]. *The Memoirs of Ann Lady Fanshawe.* London and New York: John Lane, 1907.

Freke, Elizabeth. *The Remembrances of Elizabeth Freke 1671–1714,* ed. Raymond A. Anselment. Camden 5th Series 18. London: Cambridge University Press for the Royal Historical Society, 2001.

Houlbrooke, Ralph A., ed. *English Family Life, 1576–1716: An Anthology from Diaries.* Oxford and New York: Basil Blackwell, 1988.

Pepys, Samuel. *The Diary of Samuel Pepys,* ed. Robert Latham and William Matthews. 10 vols. Berkeley and Los Angeles: University of California Press, 1983.

HOUSEHOLDS AND THE LIFE CYCLE

Abbott, Mary. *Life Cycles in England 1560–1720: Cradle to Grave.* London and New York: Routledge, 1996.

Adair, R. *Courtship, Illegitimacy, and Marriage in England, 1500–1850.* Manchester: Manchester University Press, 1996.

Amussen, Susan. *An Ordered Society: Gender and Class in Early Modern England.* Oxford and New York: Blackwell, 1988.

Clarkson, L. A. *Death, Disease, and Famine in Pre-Industrial England.* New York: St. Martins' Press, 1975.

Cooke, A. J. *Making a Match: Courtship in Shakespeare and His Society.* Princeton: Princeton University Press, 1991.

Cressy, David. *Birth, Marriage, and Death: Ritual, Religion, and the Life-Cycle in Tudor and Stuart England.* Oxford: Oxford University Press, 1997.

Evendon, Doreen. *The Midwives of Seventeenth-Century London.* Cambridge: Cambridge University Press, 2000.

Gouge, William. *Of Domesticall Duties.* London: William Bladen, 1622.

Grafton, Anthony, "Education and Apprenticeship." In John F. Andrews, ed., *William Shakespeare: His World, His Works, His Influence. Vol. 1: His World.* New York: Scribner, 1985. 55–66.

Houlbrooke, Ralph A. *Death, Religion and the Family in England, 1480–1750.* Oxford: Oxford University Press, 1998.

———. *The English Family, 1450–1700.* London and New York: Longman, 1984.

———, ed. *English Family Life, 1576–1716: An Anthology from Diaries.* Oxford and New York: Basil Blackwell, 1988.

Kussmaul, Ann. *Servants in Husbandry in Early Modern England.* Cambridge: Cambridge University Press, 1981.

Locke, John. *Some Thoughts Concerning Education,* ed. John W. Yolton and Jean S. Yolton. Oxford: Clarendon Press, 1989.

Quaife, G. R., *Wanton Wenches and Wayward Wives: Peasants and Illicit Sex in Early Seventeenth Century England.* New Brunswick, NJ: Rutgers University Press, 1979.

Stone, Lawrence. *The Family, Sex, and Marriage in England 1500–1800.* New York: Harper and Row, 1977.

Whately, William. *A Bride-Bush, or a Direction for Married Persons, Plainely Describing the Duties Common to Both, and Peculiar to Each of Them.* London: Thomas Man, 1619.

Woolley, Hannah. *The Gentlewoman's Companion, or a Guide to the Female Sex.* London: Dorman Newman, 1673.

Wrightson, Keith. *English Society 1580–1680.* New Brunswick, NJ: Rutgers University Press, 1982.

MATERIAL CULTURE

Ayres, James. *Domestic Interiors: The British Tradition 1500–1850.* New Haven: Yale University Press, 2003.

Cotgrave, Randle. *A Dictionarie of the French and English Tongues.* London: A. Islip, 1611.

Evans-Thomas, Owen. *Domestic Utensils of Wood, 16th to 19th Century.* London: Owen Evan-Thomas, 1932.

Hall, Hubert, and Frieda Nicholas, eds. *Select Tracts and Table Books of English Weights and Measures.* Camden Miscellany 15. London: Camden Society, 1929.

Holme, Randle. *Living and Working in Seventeenth-Century England: An Encyclopedia of Drawings and Descriptions from Randle Holme's Original Manuscripts for the Academy of Armory (1688)* [CD-ROM], ed. N. W. Alcock and Nancy Cox. London: British Library, 2001.

Hornsby, Peter R. G., Rosemary Weinstein, and Ronald F. Homer. *Pewter: A Celebration of the Craft 1200–1700.* London: Museum of London, 1989.

Jekyll, Gertrude. *Old English Household Life. Some Account of Cottage Objects and Country Folk.* London: Batsford, 1925.

Lindsay, J. Seymour. *Iron and Brass Implements of the English House.* London and Boston: Medici Society, 1927.

MacGregor, Arthur. *Bone, Antler, Ivory, and Horn: The Technology of Skeletal Materials Since the Roman Period.* London: Croom Helm, 1985.

MacQuoid, Percy. "The Home." In *Shakespeare's England. An Account of the Life and Manners of His Age.* Oxford: Clarendon Press, 1916. 2.119–52.

Michaelis, Ronald F. *A Short History of the Worshipful Company of Pewterers, and a Catalogue of Pewterware in Its Possession.* London: published by the authority of the Court of Assistants, 1968.

Miege, Guy. *The New State of England under our Present Monarch King William III.* London: R. Clavel, H. Mortlock, and J. Robinson, 1699. 2.14ff.

Moxon, Joseph. *Mechanick Exercises, or the Doctrine of Handy-Works, Applied to the Arts of Smithing, Joinery, Carpentry, Turning, Bricklayery.* 3rd ed. London: Daniel Midwinter and Thomas Leigh, 1703; fasc. ed. Morristown, New Jersey: Astragal Press, 1989.

Pelling, Margaret. "Medicine and Sanitation." In John F. Andrews, ed., *William Shakespeare: His World, His Works, His Influence. Vol. 1: His World.* New York: Scribner, 1985. 75–84.

The Pewter Society. *Pewter: A Handbook of Selected Tudor and Stuart Pieces.* London: the Pewter Society in association with the Museum of London, 1983.

Rogers, James E. Thorold, *A History of Agriculture and Prices in England* (1882).

Singer, Charles Joseph, ed. *A History of Technology.* 5 vols. Oxford: Clarendon Press, 1954–1978.

Spufford, Margaret. *The Great Reclothing of Rural England.* London: Hambledon Press, 1984.

Waterer, John W. *Leather Craftsmanship.* London: Bell, 1968.

Woolley, Hannah. *The Compleat Servant-Maid.* London: Thomas Passenger, 1691.

———. *A Supplement to the Queen-Like Closet, or a Little of Everything.* London: Richard Lowndes, 1674.

Wood, Eric S. *Historical Britain.* London: Harvill Press, 1995.

Wrightson, Keith. *Earthly Necessities: Economic Lives in Early Modern Britain.* New Haven: Yale University Press, 2000.

Yarwood, Doreen. *The English Home.* London: Batsford, 1979.

CLOTHING AND ACCESSORIES

Arnold, Janet. "Elizabethan and Jacobean Smocks and Shirts." *Waffen- und Kostümkunde* 19 (1977): 89–110.

———. *Patterns of Fashion: The Cut and Construction of Clothes for Men and Women c. 1560–1620.* New York: Drama Books, 1985.

———. "Three Examples of Late Sixteenth and Early Seventeenth Century Neckwear." *Waffen- und Kostümkunde* 15 (1973): 109–24.

Boucher, François. *20,000 Years of Fashion.* New York: H. N. Abrams, 1965.

Buckland, Kirstie. "The Monmouth Cap." *Costume* 13 (1979): 23–37.

Cunnington, C. Willett, and Phillis Cunnington. *Handbook of English Costume in the Seventeenth Century.* Boston: Plays Inc., 1970.

Cunnington, Phyllis, and Anne Buck. *Children's Costume in England.* London: Black, 1965.

Davenport, Millia. *The Book of Costume.* New York: Crown, 1948.

Ginsburg, Madeline, and Averil Hart. *Four Hundred Years of Fashion—The Victoria and Albert Museum.* London: Collins, 1984.

Holme, Randle. *Living and Working in Seventeenth-Century England: An Encyclopedia of Drawings and Descriptions from Randle Holme's Original Manuscripts for the*

Academy of Armory (1688) [CD-ROM], ed. N. W. Alcock and Nancy Cox. London: British Library, 2001. Bk. 3, ch. 1, 2, 5.

Hunnisett, Jean. *Period Costume for Stage and Screen.* Los Angeles: Players Press, 1991.

Köhler, Carl. *A History of Costume,* trans. Alexander K. Dallas. New York: Dover, 1963.

Leloir, M. *Histoire du Costume Vol. 8: 1610–1643.* Paris: Ernst, 1933.

Linthicum, M. Channing. *Costume in the Drama of Shakespeare and His Contemporaries.* Oxford: Clarendon Press, 1936.

MacQuoid, Percy. "Costume." In *Shakespeare's England. An Account of the Life and Manners of his Age.* 2 vols. Oxford: Clarendon Press, 1916. 2.91–118.

Nevinson, John L. *Catalogue of English Domestic Embroidery of the Sixteenth and Seventeenth Centuries.* London: His Majesty's Stationery Office, 1938.

Poppy, Pat. *Englishwoman's Dress 1640–1655.* N.p.: privately published, 1993.

Rothstein, Natalie, et al. *Four Hundred Years of Fashion.* London: Victoria and Albert Museum, 1984.

Rutt, Richard. *A History of Hand Knitting.* Loveland, CO: Interweave Press, 1987.

Spufford, Margaret. *The Great Reclothing of Rural England.* London: Hambledon Press, 1984.

Tilke, Max. *Costume Patterns and Designs.* New York: F. A. Praeger, 1957.

Waugh, Norah. *The Cut of Men's Clothes 1600–1900.* London: Faber and Faber, 1964.

———. *The Cut of Women's Clothes 1600–1930.* New York: Theater Arts, 1968.

Weavers' Guild of Boston. *Seventeenth-Century Knitting Patterns as Adapted for Plimoth Plantation.* Boston: n. p., 1990.

COUNTRY LIFE

Best, Henry. *The Farm and Memorandum Books of Henry Best of Elmswell, 1642,* ed. Donald Woodward. Records of Social and Economic History New Series 8. London: Oxford University Press for the British Academy, 1984.

Blagrave, Joseph. *The Epitome of the Art of Husbandry.* London: Benjamin Billingsley and Obadiah Blagrave, 1669.

Blith, Walter. *The English Improver Improved, or the Survey of Husbandry Surveyed.* London: J. Wright, 1653.

Hartley, Dorothy. *Lost Country Life.* New York: Pantheon, 1979.

Hartlib, Samuel. *The Compleat Husband-man.* London: Edward Brewster, 1659.

Holme, Randle. *Living and Working in Seventeenth-Century England: An Encyclopedia of Drawings and Descriptions from Randle Holme's Original Manuscripts for the Academy of Armory (1688)* [CD-ROM], ed. N. W. Alcock and Nancy Cox. London: British Library, 2001. Bk. 3, ch. 3, 5, 7–9, and passim.

Hoppit, Julian. *A Land of Liberty? England 1689–1727.* Oxford: Clarendon Press, 2000. Ch. 11.

Jekyll, Gertrude. *Old English Household Life. Some Account of Cottage Objects and Country Folk.* London: Batsford, 1925.

Laslett, Peter. *The World We Have Lost.* New York, Scribner, 1966.

Markham, Gervase. *Country Contentments. Or, the Husbandmans Recreations.* London: John Harison, 1633.

———. *The English Husbandman.* London: John Brown, 1613.

———. *Markham's Farewell to Husbandry.* London: Roger Jackson, 1620.

Orwin, C. S., and C. S Orwin. *The Open Fields*. 3rd ed. Oxford: Clarendon Press, 1967.

Prothero, R. E. "Agriculture and Gardening." In *Shakespeare's England. An Account of the Life and Manners of His Age*. 2 vols. Oxford: Clarendon Press, 1916. 1.346–80.

Spufford, Margaret. *Contrasting Communities*. Cambridge: Cambridge University Press, 1974.

Thirsk, Joan. *The Agrarian History of England and Wales 1500–1750*. Vols. 4–5. Cambridge: Cambridge University Press, 1967, 1984, 1985.

———. *Chapters from the Agrarian History of England and Wales 1500–1750* (Cambridge: Cambridge University Press, 1990). Vol. 1. Economic Change: Wages, Profits and Rents. Vol. 5: The Buildings of the Countryside.

Tusser, Thomas. *Five Hundred Points of Good Husbandry*, ed. Geoffrey Grigson. Oxford: Oxford University Press, 1984.

Wood, Eric S. *Historical Britain*. London: Harvill Press, 1995.

Worlidge, John. *Mr. Worlidge's Two Treatises; the First, of Improvement of Husbandry . . . : the Second, a Treatise of Cyder and of the Cyder-Mill and a New Sort of Press*. London: M. Wotton, 1694.

Wrightson, Keith. *Earthly Necessities: Economic Lives in Early Modern Britain*. New Haven: Yale University Press, 2000.

CITY LIFE

Barry, Jonathan. *The Tudor and Stuart Town: A Reader in English Urban History 1530–1688*. London and New York: Longman, 1990.

Beier, A. L., and Roger Finlay. *London 1500–1700: The Making of the Metropolis*. London and New York: Longman, 1986.

Brett-James, Norman G. *The Growth of Stuart London*. London: George Allen and Unwin, 1935.

Clark, Peter. *The Transformation of English Provincial Towns, 1600–1800*. London: Hutchinson, 1984.

De Laune, Thomas. *Angliae Metropolis, or, the Present State of London*. London: John Harris and Thomas Hawkins, 1690.

Earle, Peter. *The Making of the English Middle Class: Business, Society, and Family Life in London, 1660–1730*. Berkeley: University of California Press, 1989.

Finlay, Roger. *Population and Metropolis: The Demography of London 1580–1750*. Cambridge and New York: Cambridge University Press, 1981.

Hoppit, Julian. *A Land of Liberty? England 1689–1727*. Oxford: Clarendon Press, 2000. Ch. 13.

Howel, James. *Londinopolis: An Historical Discourse or Perlustration of the City of London*. London: Henry Twiford, George Sawbridge, Thomas Dring, and John Place, 1657.

Laslett, Peter. *The World We Have Lost*. New York, Scribner, 1966.

Treswell, Ralph. *The London Surveys of Ralph Treswell*, ed. John Schofield, London Topographical Society Publication No. 135. London: London Topographical Society, 1987.

Wood, Eric S. *Historical Britain*. London: Harvill Press, 1995.

Wrightson, Keith. *Earthly Necessities: Economic Lives in Early Modern Britain*. New Haven: Yale University Press, 2000.

FOOD

A Book of Fruits and Flowers [1656], ed. Susan J. Evans. Albany: Falconwood Press, 1991.

Clinton, Douglas, and Mary Liquorice, eds. *Mrs. Cromwell's Cookery Book: The Court and Kitchen of Elizabeth Wife of Oliver Cromwell*. Peterborough: Cambridgeshire Libraries Publications Committee, 1983.

Cooper, Joseph. *The Art of Cookery* [1654]. London: Prospect Books, 1986.

Culpeper, Nicholas. *Culpeper's Complete Herbal* [1652]. London and New York: W. Foulsham, 1950.

Digby, Kenelm, Sir. *The Closet of Sir Kenelme Digby, Knight, Opened*. London: printed for H. Brome, 1677.

Driver, Christopher. *Pepys at Table. Seventeenth-Century Recipes for the Modern Cook*. Berkeley: University of California Press, 1984.

Evelyn, John. *Acetaria: A Discourse of Sallets* [1699]. Brooklyn: Women's Auxiliary, Brooklyn Botanic Garden, 1937.

Grey, Elizabeth, countess of Kent. *A True Gentlewoman's Delight, Wherein Is Contained All Manner of Cookery*. London: W. J., 1653.

Hess, Karen. *Martha Washington's Booke of Cookery*. New York: Columbia University Press, 1981.

Isitt, Verity. *Take a Buttock of Beefe*. Southampton: Ashford Press, 1987.

Marcoux, Paula. *Recipes from Plimoth Plantation's J. Barnes Bake Shop: Recipes Adapted from 17th-Century Originals*. Plymouth, MA: Plimoth Plantation, n.d.

Markham, Gervase. *The English Housewife* [1615], ed. Michael R. Best. Kingston and Montreal: McGill-Queen's University Press, 1986.

McSween, Turloch. *Seventeenth Century Vegetable Uses*. Bristol: Stuart Press, 1992.

Miege, Guy. *The New State of England under Our Present Monarch King William III.* London: R. Clavel, H. Mortlock, and J. Robinson, 1699. 2.16ff.

Murrell, John. *A Daily Exercise for Ladies and Gentlewomen* [1617], ed. Susan J. Evans. Albany: Falconwood Press, 1990.

———. *A Delightful Daily Exercise for Ladies and Gentlewomen* [1621], ed. Susan J. Evans. Albany: Falconwood Press, 1990.

———. *Murrels Two Bookes of Cookerie and Carving*. 5th ed. London: printed for John Marriot, 1641.

Peachey, Stuart. *The Book of Bread 1580–1660*. Bristol: Stuart Press, 1996.

———. *The Book of Cheese 1580–1660*. Bristol: Stuart Press, 1993.

———. *Civil War and Salt Fish: Military and Civilian Diet in the Seventeenth Century*. Leigh-on-Sea: Partizan Press, 1988.

———. *Cooking Techniques and Equipment 1580–1660*. 2 vols. Bristol: Stuart Press, 1994.

———. *The Tipler's Guide to Drink and Drinking in the Early 17th Century*. Bristol: Stuart Press, 1992.

Ruthven, Lord. *The Ladies Cabinet* [1655], ed. Susan J. Evans. Albany: Falconwood Press, 1990.

Salmon, William. *The Family Dictionary, or Household Companion*. London: H. Rhodes, 1696.

Tryon, Thomas. *A New Art of Brewing Beer, Ale, and Other Sorts of Liquors*. London: printed for Thomas Salisbury, 1690.

The Widowes Treasure. London: printed for Robert Bird, 1639.

Willan, Anne. *Great Cooks and Their Recipes from Taillevent to Escoffier.* Boston, Toronto, and London: Bulfinch, 1992.

Woolley, Hannah. *The Compleat Servant Maid.* London: T. Passinger, 1683.

———. *The Queen-Like Closet, or a Rich Cabinet Stored with All Manner of Rare Receipts.* 3rd ed. London: Richard Lowndes, 1675.

ENTERTAINMENTS

Cotton, Charles. *The Compleat Gamester* [1674]. In *Games and Gamesters of the Restoration.* London: Routledge, 1930. 1–114.

Holme, Randle. *Living and Working in Seventeenth-Century England: An Encyclopedia of Drawings and Descriptions from Randle Holme's Original Manuscripts for The Academy of Armory (1688)* [CD-ROM], ed. N. W. Alcock and Nancy Cox. London: British Library, 2001. Bk. 3, ch. 5, 16.

Hoppit, Julian. *A Land of Liberty? England 1689–1727.* Oxford: Clarendon Press, 2000. Ch. 11.

Hutton, Ronald. *The Rise and Fall of Merry England: The Ritual Year 1400–1700.* Oxford: Oxford University Press, 1994.

Vale, Marcia. *The Gentleman's Recreations: Accomplishments and Pastimes of the English Gentleman, 1580–1630.* Cambridge: D. S. Brewer; Totowa, NJ: Rowman and Littlefield, 1977.

Willughby, Francis. *Francis Willughby's Book of Games: A Seventeenth-Century Treatise on Sports, Games, and Pastimes,* ed. David Cram, Jeffrey L. Forgeng, and Dorothy Johnston. Aldershot: Ashgate Press, 2003.

TRAVEL

Holme, Randle. *Living and Working in Seventeenth-Century England: An Encyclopedia of Drawings and Descriptions from Randle Holme's Original Manuscripts for The Academy of Armory (1688)* [CD-ROM], ed. N. W. Alcock and Nancy Cox. London: British Library, 2001. Bk. 3, ch. 3, 8, 9, and passim.

Hughes, Charles. "Land Travel." In *Shakespeare's England. An Account of the Life and Manners of His Age.* 2 vols. Oxford: Clarendon Press, 1916. 1.198–223.

Miege, Guy. *The New State of England under Our Present Monarch King William III.* London: R. Clavel, H. Mortlock, and J. Robinson, 1699.

Moryson, Fynes. *An Itinerary.* London: John Beale, 1617; reprinted Amsterdam and New York: Da Capo Press, Theatrum Orbis Terrarum, 1971.

Ogilby, John. *Itinerarium Angliae; or, a Book of Roads, Wherein Are Contain'd the Principal Roadways of England and Wales.* London: Author, 1675.

Parkes, Joan. *Travel in England in the Seventeenth Century.* London: Oxford University Press, 1925.

Quinn, David. "Travel by Sea and Land." In John F. Andrews, ed., *William Shakespeare: His World, His Works, His Influence. Vol. 1: His World.* New York: Scribner, 1985. 195–200.

RECORDINGS

The Baltimore Consort. *A Trip to Kilburn: Playford Tunes and Their Ballads.* Dorian, 1996.

———. *Watkins Ale. Music of the English Renaissance.* Dorian, 1991.

The Baltimore Consort and the Merry Companions. *The Art of the Bawdy Song.* Dorian, 1992.

The Broadside Band. *English Country Dances from Playford's Dancing Master 1651–1703.* Saydisc, 1991.

———. *John Playford's Popular Tunes.* Amon Ra, 1987.

———. *Songs and Dances from Shakespeare.* Saydisc, 1995.

Circa 1500 and Redbyrd. *"New Fashions." Cries and Ballads of London.* CRD Records, 1992.

The City Waites. *"How the World Wags." Social Music for a 17th Century Englishman.* Hyperion, 1999.

———. *Low and Lusty Ballads from the Elizabethan Underworld.* Soundalive, 1992.

The Consort of Musicke. *There Were Three Ravens.* Virgin Classics, 1991.

Deller Consort. *Shakespeare Songs and Consort Music.* Harmonia Mundi, 1967.

The Dufay Collective. *Johnny, Cock Thy Beaver: Popular Music-Making in Seventeenth-Century England.* Chandos, 1996.

His Majestie's Clerkes. *Goostly Psalmes. Anglo-American Psalmody 1550–1800.* Harmonia Mundi, 1996.

Jouissance. *Dances from the Inns of Court: London 1570–1675.* Privately produced, 1997.

The King's Noise. *The King's Delight: Seventeenth-Century Ballads for Voice and Violin Band.* Harmonia Mundi, 1994.

New York Ensemble for Early Music. *So Quick, So Hot, So Mad.* MusicMasters Classics, 1981.

The New York Renaissance Band. *Country Capers. Music from John Playford's The English Dancing Master.* Arabesque, 1984.

Penny Merriment. *English Songs from the Time of the Pilgrims.* Plimoth Plantation, 1986.

Pro Cantione Antiqua. *Purcell in the Ale House: English Part Songs.* Das Alte Werk, 1995.

St. George's Canzona. *Music for Roundheads and Cavaliers.* ASV, 1994.

Vic Gammon et al. *The Tale of Ale.* Free Reed Records, 1976.

The York Waites. *The Punk's Delight: Popular Musick of the Seventeenth Century Played by a Band of Waites.* Huntsup, 1992.

OTHER MEDIA

Cromwell. Chico, CA: Tamarelle International Films, 1970.

The Crucible. Beverly Hills: Twentieth Century Fox Home Entertainment, 1996.

Cyrano de Bergerac. Culver City, CA: MGM/UA Home Video, 1990.

Girl with a Pearl Earring. Santa Monica: Artisan Home Entertainment, 2004.

Orlando. London: Fox Video, 1992.

Restoration. Burbank: Buena Vista Home Video, 1995.

The Three Musketeers. New York: Wellspring, 1973; *The Four Musketeers.* New York: Wellspring, 1973.

Tudor and Stuart London: Court and Commons, 1500–1666. Princeton: Films for the Humanities and Sciences, 1976.

Winstanley. New York: Milestone Film and Video, 1975.

ILUSTRATION SOURCES

Besant, Sir Walter. *London in the Time of the Tudors.* London: Adam and Charles Black, 1904.

Brooke, George C. *English Coins from the Seventh Century to the Present Day.* London: Methuen, 1932.

Clark, Andrew, ed. *The Shirburn Ballads 1585–1616.* Oxford: Clarendon Press, 1907.

Clinch, George. *English Costume.* Chicago and London: Methuen, 1910.

Comenius, Johannes. *The Orbis Pictus of John Amos Comenius.* Syracuse: Bardeen, 1887.

Cotton, Charles. *The Compleat Gamester* [1674]. In *Games and Gamesters of the Restoration.* London: Routledge, 1930.

Furnivall, F. J. *Harrison's Description of England in Shakspere's Youth.* London: Trübner, 1877.

———. *Phillip Stubbes' Anatomy of Abuses.* London: Trübner, 1879.

Godfrey, Elizabeth. *Home Life under the Stuarts.* New York: Dutton, 1903.

Hartley, Dorothy, and Margaret M. Elliot. *Life and Work of the People of England. A Pictorial Record from Contemporary Sources. The Seventeenth Century.* London: B. T. Batsford, 1928.

Hatcher, Orie Latham. *A Book for Shakespeare Plays and Pageants.* New York: E. P. Dutton, 1916.

Hind, Arthur. *Wenceslaus Hollar and His Views of London and Windsor in the Seventeenth Century.* London: John Lane, 1922.

Hindley, Charles, ed. *The Roxburghe Ballads.* London: Reeves and Turner, 1837–1874.

Jackson, Mason. *The Pictorial Press: Its Origin and Progress.* London: Hurst and Blackett, 1885.

Shakespeare's England. An Account of the Life and Manners of his Age. 2 vols. Oxford: at the Clarendon Press, 1916.

Traill, H. D., and J. S. Mann. *Social England.* London: Cassell; New York: Putnam's, 1909.

Unwin, George. *Industrial Organization in the Sixteenth and Seventeenth Centuries.* Oxford: Clarendon Press, 1904.

INDEX

Page numbers in *italics* indicate illustrations.

ABOUT THE AUTHOR

JEFFREY FORGENG is Paul S. Morgan Curator at Higgins Armory Museum in Worcester, Massachusetts.